D0908314

Brutal Need

Brutal Need

Lawyers and the

Welfare Rights Movement,

1960–1973

Martha F. Davis

Yale University Press   New Haven and London

Published with assistance from the foundation established in memory of Philip Hamilton McMillan of the Class of 1894, Yale College.

Designed by James J. Johnson.
Set in Trump Roman type by The Composing Room of Michigan, Inc., Grand Rapids, Michigan.

Printed in the United States of America by BookCrafters, Inc., Chelsea, Michigan.

Library of Congress Cataloging-in-Publication Data

Davis, Martha F., 1957–
    Brutal need : lawyers and the welfare rights movement, 1960–1973 / Martha F. Davis.
        p.   cm.
    Includes bibliographical references and index.
    ISBN 0-300-05378-9

    1. Public welfare—Law and legislation— United States—History. I. Title.
KF3720.D38   1993
344.73′0316—dc20
[347.30416]   93-1313

A catalogue record for this book is available from the British Library.
The paper in this book meets the guidelines for permanence and durability of the Committee on Production Guidelines for Book Longevity of the Council on Library Resources.

10 9 8 7 6 5 4 3 2 1

To my parents, Marian and Robert

Contents

Acknowledgments

Many people have provided their support and encouragement during my work on this book. My greatest thanks go to Gabriel Gorenstein and Daniel Wakin, who read early drafts of the manuscript and whose comments and sustained interest helped me immeasurably. Thanks also to Eric Arnesen and Brian Balogh, who provided helpful comments and bibliographic suggestions.

Henry Freedman and Wayne Hawley were unfailingly generous with their time and ideas, not to mention their historical records. My thanks, as well, to all of the individuals who granted me interviews, particularly Michael Sparer, Tanya Sparer, Lee Albert, and George Brager, each of whom made special efforts to assist me.

My former employer, Cleary, Gottlieb, Steen & Hamilton, generously granted me a year-long leave of absence to work on this project and continued to support it once I returned. During that year the Bunting Institute provided precious space and time and a supportive environment. I am grateful to Harvard Law School's Mark DeWolfe Howe Fund for Civil Rights and Civil Liberties, which awarded me a grant toward completion of my archival research. Thanks also to my current employer, the NOW Legal Defense and Education Fund, for allowing me the flexibility to finish this project.

My editors, John S. Covell and Heidi Myers, have provided good cheer, good sense, and a continuity of interest and understanding in this book since its early stages. At crucial points in the writing process, Judy Resnick, Lance Liebman, Sylvia Law, George Grumbach, Richard Ziegler, Gwen O'Sullivan, Chris Henderson, and Wanyong Austin also gave me encouragement, for which I thank them. Sally Goldfarb and Jennifer Tabakin provided technical expertise during the final stages of the project. Finally, Mimi Abramovitz and Guida West, both of whom I met as a result of writing this book, were constant sources of inspiration through their writings on welfare rights, their tireless activism, and their friendship.

Brutal Need

Introduction

The 1960s was a decade of innovation and expansion in government programs providing services to the poor. It began with President Kennedy's
efforts to fund, on a small scale, creative programs addressing poverty and
juvenile delinquency. From the 1964 declaration of the War on Poverty
through the 1968 election, President Johnson oversaw the implementation of an array of federal programs for Medicare and Medicaid, housing
assistance, job training, and public education.[1]

The 1960s was also a time of increased interest in individual rights as
an organizing principle for a diverse society. The civil rights movement,
then in full flower, was joined later in the decade by the women's rights
movement, the welfare rights movement, and the gay rights movement.
Activists, perhaps naively and certainly optimistically, viewed the federal
courts as the ultimate protectors of individual rights and, under the appropriate circumstances, arbiters of social change. Courts' willingness to act
in these capacities was in ample evidence, from judicial desegregation of
public schools to restructuring of prisons.

There is no dearth of scholarly and popular writing dissecting the social
programs and social movements of the 1960s and early 1970s, including
the welfare rights movement.[2] Specific developments in welfare during the
1960s have also been examined at length elsewhere, as has the role of
lawyers in the civil rights movement both before and during the period.[3]
These studies provide a backdrop for this account of the part that a new
breed of lawyer-activist—the poverty lawyer—played in the welfare rights
movement. By using lawyers' recollections and contemporary records I
explore the origins of poverty law and the perspectives of welfare rights
lawyers on their roles in the movement.

A combination of factors contributed to the poverty law explosion of
the 1960s. Michael Harrington's book *The Other America*, the Ford Foundation's "gray areas" program to fund community projects in the inner
city, the civil rights movement, and the War on Poverty all encouraged
hundreds of young lawyers who were committed to representing the poor.

Even the popular explanation for poverty's tenacity suggested that law
would be an effective tool for eliminating need in America. Harrington, as
well as scholars like Lloyd Ohlin and Richard Cloward, stressed that pov-

erty was the structural by-product of contemporary society rather than evidence of personal or moral weakness.[4] The civil rights movement provided activist poverty lawyers with a ready model for using litigation to change legal and social structures that marginalized a segment of society. The lawyers added to this model an emphasis on neighborhood-based legal services and social work borrowed from the settlement house movement of the Progressive Era, as well as grass-roots organizing techniques drawn from organized labor. The poverty law of the 1960s was a radical departure from the earlier idea that legal aid to the poor would encourage newcomers to assimilate into American society and allow lawyers to shore up their legal monopoly by controlling access to legal institutions.

In many ways the litigation strategy developed by welfare rights lawyers was more ambitious than its prototype, the NAACP Legal Defense and Educational Fund's campaign to desegregate public schools. Welfare rights lawyers envisioned a constitutional "right to live" that would require the federal government to guarantee a minimum standard of living to all citizens. They also intended to bring welfare administration, generally left to the discretion of the states, within the legal confines of the federal constitution and to extend the strict scrutiny given racial classifications to classifications based on wealth. Though the lawyers were only partially successful, the legal precedents that resulted from their collaboration with the welfare rights movement are tremendously significant in terms of defining fundamental rights and refining the relationship between individuals and government.

Importantly, individual poor people also benefited from the welfare rights litigation strategy and from the general increase in poverty lawyers. The litigation strategy was grounded in real problems faced by welfare recipients: arbitrary benefit terminations, residency laws, violations of privacy, inadequate benefits. When lawyers won cases that raised these issues, their clients won reinstatement, more humane administrative practices, and increased public assistance grants.

The initial courtroom successes of the welfare rights movement also increased political pressure for more dramatic restructuring of the welfare system. Indeed, by the late 1960s there was serious interest in reforming and expanding federal cash assistance programs for the poor—an area that had been essentially untouched by the war on poverty. President Nixon's Family Assistance Plan would have provided a federally guaranteed income of $1,600 for a family of four; other proposals before Congress were substantially more generous.

In part because of political miscalculations by supporters of welfare reform who sought higher guaranteed benefits, none of the proposals became law. By the early 1970s, with courts increasingly rejecting welfare recipients' arguments and the public rhetoric shifting against them, the welfare rights movement was effectively over.

Lawyers continue to practice poverty law in significant numbers and to pursue litigation strategies for their clients through federally funded legal services, legal aid programs, and community-based organizations. Their work builds on that of an earlier generation of lawyers, some of whom were interviewed for this book. For lawyers today, the questions of how to effectively collaborate with social movements and how to successfully advocate broad reforms to benefit their clients remain constant considerations. The historical picture offered here is intended to provide both inspiration and perspective to those engaged in this work.

The chapters are in roughly chronological order, and each chapter begins with a quote, often an excerpt from a document relevant to the chapter that follows. In selecting these quotes, I have tried to favor recipient activists and other women in the movement. Typical of the time, though the welfare rights movement was led by "welfare mothers," few women were acknowledged as leaders in litigation efforts.

In the first chapter I discuss the development, structure, and rationale of the welfare system in the United States through 1960.

In the second chapter I describe the development of legal aid for the poor and the law reform efforts mounted by settlement house activists from the late nineteenth century through the 1960s. I also examine how changes in legal doctrine—in particular, legal realism and the rise of constitutional equal protection theories—affected both the welfare system and the practice of poverty law.

Ed Sparer is widely acknowledged as the father of welfare law and, in 1960s parlance, a guru for new poverty lawyers.[5] In Chapter 3 I describe Sparer's early career, including his efforts to depart from the Legal Aid model in shaping the Mobilization for Youth Legal Unit in New York City and federally funded legal services. Sparer's blueprint for a welfare rights litigation strategy was extremely influential in clarifying and defining legal issues in the new field of poverty law.

I describe the emerging social movement of welfare recipients in the 1960s in Chapter 4, and I explore early organizing strategies and collaboration between poverty lawyers and recipients, including the National Welfare Rights Organization, led by George Wiley.

King v. Smith, which raised the "substitute father" issue identified in Sparer's litigation strategy, was the first welfare case ever heard by the U.S. Supreme Court. Under substitute father rules, a welfare mother found to be cohabiting with a man would be cut off from welfare on the assumption that the man was responsible for supporting the recipient's children. *King v. Smith* emerged from welfare rights lawyers' so-called Southern strategy, designed to focus reform efforts in the South, where welfare practices allegedly were most egregious. In Chapter 5 I examine the Southern strategy and lawyers' decisions in developing and litigating the issues in *King v. Smith*.

I extend the discussion of the welfare rights litigation strategy in Chapter 6, focusing on the relations between the recipient movement and welfare rights lawyers, as well as the strategic issues involved in litigating the second welfare case before the Supreme Court, *Shapiro v. Thompson*, which challenged residency laws that deny welfare benefits to recent arrivals in a state.

The work of Yale University law professor and author Charles Reich is surveyed in Chapter 7. I relate his theories on the meaning of the due process clause to the litigation of *Goldberg v. Kelly*, which claimed that welfare benefits were constitutionally protected "property." In *Goldberg* welfare recipients asserted that their benefits should not be terminated without a hearing.

Goldberg v. Kelly, a seminal case both in terms of the welfare rights movement and due process clause jurisprudence, was decided by the Supreme Court in 1970. The decision was notable not only for its rejection of the notion that welfare is "mere charity," but also for its recognition that poor people's "brutal need" in the face of termination from the welfare rolls weighs in favor of constitutional safeguards. In Chapter 8 I review the oral argument before the Supreme Court, as well as the Supreme Court's decision making process, through draft opinions and interviews.

Chapter 9 marks the beginning of the end of this period of welfare rights activism. Welfare rights attorneys filed a number of cases designed to culminate in a direct challenge to the adequacy of welfare benefits. But after the Supreme Court decision in *Dandridge v. Williams*, a rejection of recipients' arguments that the equal protection clause barred the creation of maximum grants per family, the welfare rights litigation strategy was largely abandoned.

After *Dandridge* lawyers and welfare recipient activists cast about for a plan of action to frame legislative and litigation efforts. However, as I describe in Chapter 10, no plan was forthcoming. With the defeat of guaranteed income proposals pending in Congress and George Wiley's death in 1973, the welfare rights movement drew to a close. In the final chapter I examine the welfare rights movement as the first sustained collaboration between organized welfare recipients and poverty lawyers, review the movement's successes and failures, and discuss alternative organizing strategies.

Chapter 1

Welfare and "The Man"

The truth is that [Aid to Families with Dependent Children] is like a supersexist marriage. You trade in *a* man for *the* man. But you can't divorce him if he treats you bad. He can divorce you, of course, cut you off anytime he wants. But in that case *he* keeps the kids, not you. *The* Man runs everything. In ordinary marriage, sex is supposed to be for you and your husband. On AFDC you're not supposed to have any sex at all. . . . You may even have to agree to get your tubes tied so you can never have more children just to avoid being cut off welfare. *The* man, the welfare system, controls your money. He tells you what to buy and what not to buy, where to buy it, and how much things cost. If things—rent, for instance— really cost more than he says they do, it's just too bad for you.

—Johnnie Tillmon, first chair of the National Welfare Rights Organization, 1972

The story of welfare in the early to mid twentieth century is one of gradually increasing control by federal and state governments. For 300 years prior to the New Deal the federal government had eschewed direct responsibility for care of America's poor. During most of that time poor relief was the province of such private agencies as churches or social clubs that offered assistance to the "deserving" poor (children, widows, trainable immigrants) with minimal state support or regulation. But during the two prosperous decades leading up to the Great Depression, Progressive party activists ushered significant welfare reforms through many state legislatures, including "mother's pensions" for widows with children and "general assistance" for other so-called unemployables.

States adopted 400 new public welfare laws between 1917 and 1920 alone, creating a relatively modern and rational welfare system from the patchwork of philanthropic and local initiatives of the nineteenth century. But government spending remained low, and centralization of the welfare administration within each state, though a professed goal, was not the reality. In New Hampshire, for instance, poor relief was separately administered by 700 officials in 245 county, city, and town units; in Ohio public relief was in the hands of 1,535 local governments as late as 1934.[1]

As newcomers to the social welfare field, local and state governments were unprepared for the massive administrative and financial stresses that accompanied the onset of the Great Depression.[2] Expenses soared; a survey of eighty-one major cities indicated that the combined amount of public and private relief went from about $42 million in 1929 to $70 million in 1930 to $171 million in 1931. Even for people lucky enough to get on the relief rolls, the amounts were minuscule: in Detroit, $3.60 a week for two adults; in Baltimore, 80 cents a week in commodities; in New York City, $2.97 a week.[3] President Hoover seemed paralyzed by the crisis and refused to consider federal aid. "You cannot extend the mastery of government over the daily lives of the people without at the same time making it the master of their souls and thoughts," he asserted.[4]

President Roosevelt was prepared to act, however. Within a few months of taking office in 1933, Roosevelt and his New Deal staff—"boys with their hair ablaze," as one New Dealer described them—moved in to alleviate the burden on state governments. In May Congress appropriated $500 million for direct relief, and the president established the Federal Emergency Relief Administration (FERA) to administer the funds, most of which were distributed as cash doles. Within the year, Roosevelt authorized the Civil Works Administration (CWA) and the Civilian Conservation Corps (CCC) to provide work relief. Altogether these agencies extended funds to 28 million people in 1934, or 22.2 percent of the population.[5]

Despite the success of the federal government's foray into social welfare, Roosevelt, echoing Hoover, wanted to keep relief from becoming "a habit with the country." According to Roosevelt, "Continued dependence upon relief induces a spiritual and moral disintegration fundamentally destructive to the national fiber. To dole out relief in this way is to administer a narcotic, a subtle destroyer of the human spirit."[6] Acting on these convictions, Roosevelt eliminated the CWA in 1934 and FERA in 1935.[7] Although other New Deal relief agencies hobbled along for a few more years, they were in essence superseded by the Social Security Act of 1935.

That act reflected Roosevelt's view that the federal government should take steps to prevent poverty through social security and leave direct relief, if any were still necessary, to the states. With the enactment of social security, the president's aides said, "the residual relief problem will have diminished to a point where it will be possible to return primary responsibility for the care of people who cannot work to the state and local governments."[8] This rationale for limiting federal responsibility dovetailed with a practical limitation on Roosevelt's welfare legislation: the possibility—borne out by the Supreme Court's earlier decisions striking down New Deal legislation—that the Supreme Court would find that any act giving the federal government sweeping powers over public relief was an unconstitutional imposition on states' rights to administer welfare.[9]

The carefully crafted Social Security Act did not overstep the bounds set by the Supreme Court.[10] Responsibility for general assistance, traditionally extended to such "unemployables" as drunks, vagrants, and the unskilled poor, was returned to the states and localities. Work relief, provided by the Works Progress Administration and other New Deal programs, remained under the auspices of the federal government. Social insurance, or social security, became an exclusive federal responsibility. Public assistance for the blind, the aged, and dependent children, traditionally a concern of states—which provided, for example, pensions that allowed single mothers (presumptively widows) to stay home with their young children—was to be administered through a federal and state partnership.[11] Under these programs, federal matching funds would be available as long as state welfare plans conformed to federal guidelines.

The importance of the Social Security Act resided not so much in its particulars but in its broad outline: the act shifted responsibility for some public welfare programs from the states to the federal government and, because of statutorily mandated federal participation, the act provided welfare with a degree of permanence and, ultimately, a measure of legal entitlement that local and private programs had lacked for three centuries.

The act also rested, however, on a tragic demographic miscalculation: despite Roosevelt's predictions, federally funded social security was not sufficient to lift people from poverty. Instead, the number of those qualified for public assistance programs rose steadily. The Aid to Families with Dependent Children program, for example, hardly caused a ripple in Congress when it was enacted; based on the states' experiences with mother's pensions, Roosevelt's social security experts calculated that only 300,000 female-headed families would need economic assistance at any one time. AFDC nevertheless grew from 372,000 families in 1940 to 803,000 in 1960. During the same period, program costs rose from $133 million to $994 million. The composition of the AFDC caseload also changed. By 1961 families headed by widows constituted only 7.7 percent of the AFDC rolls, compared with 43 percent in 1937. The majority of AFDC recipients were separated, divorced, or unmarried women; the numbers of African-American women on AFDC were disproportionately high.[12] AFDC recipients were a vulnerable population with little political support who depended on a costly program.

As AFDC grew, many states attempted to reduce the number of recipients by limiting the program to "fit mothers" with "suitable homes"—restrictions that gave welfare administrators free rein to judge the moral character of their clients and withhold benefits if the clients were deemed undeserving. In the 1950s many states stepped up their enforcement of these and other regulations designed to purge the welfare rolls of undesirables.[13] Though the federal government periodically reviewed state implementation of the AFDC program, the political reality was that state plans were routinely approved; the conformity between written plans and actual practice was rarely examined at all.[14] By dividing responsibility for welfare between the federal and state governments, the Social Security Act of 1935 created, as Michael Katz has observed, "a unique, unsatisfactory, semi-welfare state" that allowed both the states and the federal government to abdicate leadership and responsibility for administering welfare programs fairly.[15]

By 1960 the distinction between the deserving and undeserving poor within the AFDC program had become stark indeed. Merely to receive and remain on public benefits recipients were forced to comply with baroque reporting requirements intended to weed out those who were too disorganized or dysfunctional to obtain public support and therefore unlikely to use it as a springboard to permanent employment. In states with a large agricultural base, a mother's benefits might be suspended during harvest season to force her to seek work in the fields, despite substandard wages and abhorrent working conditions. In some states, efforts to deny public assistance to children of unwed mothers took on enormous proportions; in 1960 the Louisiana state legislature attempted to cut off benefits to 23,000 children.[16] Across the country, single mothers who were suspected of cohabiting with a man could expect midnight raids of their homes by welfare caseworkers who were looking for a reason to curtail benefits.[17] As yet no lawyer for the poor had stepped forward to challenge these practices.

Chapter 2

Poor Law and Poverty Lawyers

Discourage litigation. Persuade your neighbor to compromise whenever you can. Point out to them how the nominal winner is often the real loser—in fees, expenses, and waste of time. As a peacemaker the lawyer has a superior opportunity of being a good man.

—Abraham Lincoln, from placard distributed to the New York City Legal Aid Society's offices in 1907

Until the 1960s practicing poverty law meant little more than giving routine legal advice to poor people. A handful of lawyers—most notably the 400 or so employed by Legal Aid societies across the country—had specialized in representing the poor since the late nineteenth century, but no cohesive body of poverty law had been developed by the litigants or the courts. Except in a few academic circles, labor law, family law, administrative law, and constitutional law were not recognized as having unique impacts on poor people. Instead, legal theorists held to the laissez-faire notion that the law was class-blind.[1]

Poverty law changed dramatically in the 1960s. Between 1963, when federal grants were first made available to experimental offices in New Haven, Connecticut, and New York City, and 1971, when the federally funded legal services program was in full swing, the number of lawyers for poor people rose by 650 percent to more than 2,500.[2] In 1959 Legal Aid Society lawyers took only 6 percent of their cases to court while the rest of their clients made do with advice or assistance with out-of-court negotiations; by 1971 federally funded legal services lawyers took 17 percent of their client's cases to court.[3] Until 1965 no course on poverty law had ever been taught at a law school; by 1967 poverty law courses were offered at thirty-six law schools. Despite eighty-nine years of representing the poor, Legal Aid lawyers had never appealed a case to the U.S. Supreme Court; but from 1965 to 1974 the new poverty lawyers appealed 164 cases to the Court on behalf of their clients. Seven percent of all Supreme Court opinions written during those years were decisions in poverty law cases.[4]

From the nineteenth century through the 1960s a succession of organizations—the Legal Aid Society, settlement houses, Mobilization for Youth, and the Center on Social Welfare Policy and Law—used New York City as a base for efforts to address the problems of poverty through litigation and law reform.

The Legal Aid Society exercised a virtual monopoly over the representation of poor people in New York from its creation in 1876 until 1964, when the Mobilization for Youth (MFY) Legal Unit was chartered. Originally called Der Deutsche-Rechtsschutz-Verein, the society was founded by Edward Salomon, former governor of Wisconsin, to "render legal aid and assistance, gratuitously, to those of German birth, who may appear worthy thereof, but who from poverty are unable to procure it."[5] Only after Salomon's retirement in 1889 was the society's charter amended to allow it to render free legal assistance to all.[6]

By that time the wave of German immigration had subsided; the newest influx of immigrants to New York was made up of Russian and Eastern European Jews.[7] According to Arthur Von Briesen, president of the New York Legal Aid Society from 1890 to 1915, the society had a mission to introduce these immigrants to democracy. "Once a poor jobless fellow-being learns that in this country he will have his rights ensured and enforced," Von Briesen asserted, "be he ever so poor, he will promptly join the ranks of those who are the most ardent supporters of our institutions."[8]

Von Briesen's tenure at the society was marked by dogged fund-raising and steady expansion as he worked to achieve this goal. The society had been funded almost exclusively through the contributions of German immigrants and staffed primarily by volunteers when Von Briesen assumed control. Its annual budget was about $3,000.[9] Von Briesen moved to establish a stable and sizable budget through membership drives and law firm contributions, refusing financial support from New York City itself.[10] In addition, Legal Aid Society clients were required to pay a retaining fee of up to twenty-five cents, if possible, and attorneys were authorized to collect a 10 percent commission on all sums recovered in excess of five dollars.[11] In 1904 alone the society collected $5,483, about one-quarter of its budget, in this way. By 1906 the New York Legal Aid Society's budget had risen to $28,553, by far the largest of any Legal Aid society in the country.[12]

Von Briesen's tenacity translated into expanded services for New York's poor. In 1900, for example, the Legal Aid Society expeditiously handled 14,365 cases—almost triple the caseload in 1898—recovering $96,704.45 for its clients at an average overhead of less than a dollar a case. This rise in activity was attributable, in part, to Von Briesen's innovative decision to dilute the resources of Legal Aid's main office in the heart of downtown Manhattan to establish branch offices in New York's most impoverished neighborhoods.[13]

One satellite office was the East Side Branch, established in 1899 at the University Settlement House at 185 Eldridge on the Lower East Side.[14] At the time the Lower East Side was the most densely populated neighborhood in the world, housing more than 1,000 people per acre. Most of the neighborhood's inhabitants lived in dumbbell tenements, five- or six- story structures build around dark, narrow air shafts with few windows.[15] Because of the overcrowding, filth, and crime bred by the tenements, the death rate on the Lower East Side was double that of any other part of the city.[16]

The national origin of Legal Aid's clients at the East Side Branch during the first two and a half months of 1899 reflected the neighborhood's character: sixty-six clients were Russian; thirty-seven, German; twenty-eight, Austrian; fourteen, Polish; eight, American; six, Rumanian; two, Irish; one, Scottish; one, Italian; one, Turkish; and one, Hungarian. Less than a third were U.S. citizens; 115 of the clients were men, and 50 were women.[17]

As recent arrivals learning the mores of the United States, many of these clients required only basic advice regarding contracts, real estate transactions, or family troubles. According to the attorney in charge of the office, "Common sense is a greater requisite than the law." A few additional cases sought "redress for misfortunes common to us all, and with which the law has little to do."[18]

The great majority of the cases handled by the East Side Branch, however, involved unpaid wages, a common denominator of the sweatshop employment that prevailed on the Lower East Side. A typical wage case, according to a Legal Aid attorney, arose when

> the 'greener' just over from Poland, Russia, or Roumania looks about for a chance to earn a living. He sees in one of the Yiddish papers an attractive advertisement to teach beginners machine operating or cigarette and cigar making. He applies at the shop and is told that he must learn for four weeks and then he will be employed steadily, with pay. To this end he gives the fee of from $5 to $15, which generally takes the last cent he owns. . . . At the end of that time the apprentice is very apt to be discharged at once, or else told that he is not fit to earn money and must keep working for nothing if he wishes to stay. Whether the man leaves in disgust or is discharged, the result is the same: the master has the money and the apprentice is in a

desperate situation. . . . We have complaints of this sort every week, and there is little that can be done in the majority of them.[19]

The Legal Aid Society's policy was to settle most of these wage cases; only six were brought to trial in 1899. Of the six, four were initially settled to the lawyer's satisfaction, but the client, "through obstinacy or ill-temper," insisted on taking the case to trial.[20] According to Legal Aid staff attorney Samuel Goldberg, "It is undoubtedly true that our clients are naturally litigious." Staff attorney Arthur G. H. Lester agreed that "the spirit of compromise does not exist with them."[21]

Despite their clients' obstinacy, the Legal Aid Society enforced a "general policy of reasonable compromise," whatever the client's wishes.[22] Placards distributed to each of the Legal Aid Society's offices in 1907 admonished lawyers to settle cases if at all possible.[23] Legal Aid lawyers reasoned that an early settlement was preferable to waiting for a trial: "The clients lived from hand to mouth and needed their money without delay. The local courts were frightfully congested."[24] Both to maximize their own time and to speedily obtain at least some recompense for their clients, Legal Aid lawyers focused on settling cases.

The dire conditions on the Lower East Side also attracted more than a dozen fledgling settlement houses that were, like the Legal Aid Society, devoted to reforming the poor by exposing them to middle-class values—a sort of American chivalry for recent immigrants.

Influenced by the philosophy of Felix Adler, founder of the Ethical Culture Society, and moved by Jacob Riis's 1890 book *How the Other Half Lives,* an account of ghetto life on the Lower East Side, settlement house residents believed that they could reform the conditions that created New York's ghettos by living and working among the poor.[25] These aspirations were inextricably linked to the development and institutionalization of social work. Not only did the social work profession emerge from the settlement house movement, but the profession's early focus on social justice and reform was a direct result of settlement house goals and ideology.[26]

The University Settlement on the Lower East Side—home of the Legal Aid Society's East Side Branch—was the first settlement house in the United States, founded in 1886. Its purpose was to bring "men of education into closer relations with the laboring classes of the city, for mutual instruction and benefit," by establishing "'settlements' in the tenement-house districts, where college men interested in the workers may live, and mingle with their poor neighbors, on terms of perfect equality."[27]

The settlement house idea caught on quickly, particularly among young women in cities like Philadelphia, Chicago, and New York, which were inundated with tens of thousands of impoverished immigrants. Settlement houses offered this first generation of college-educated women independence from their families and a respectable, challenging career other than teaching or nursing.[28] At least one of New York's settlement houses, College Settlement (affiliated with Smith College), was operated exclusively by women. Several others, such as the famous Hull House in Chicago headed by Jane Addams and the Henry Street Settlement House in New York directed by Lillian Wald, were founded by women.

The University Settlement was the only settlement house in New York that provided *direct* legal services to its clients (through the Legal Aid Society), but as settlement house residents moved into the arena of Progressive politics, law reform became a significant part of their work. Reflecting Progressives' emphasis on scientific management as an alternative to the cronyism prevalent in city and state governments, settlement houses published reams of sociological data gathered from their clients, then used this data to promote Progressive policies. New York's Lower East Side was their laboratory. Between 1897 and 1909 the Henry Street Settlement investigated dispossessed tenants, the licensing of midwives, child labor, and working conditions for women. In 1900 the University Settlement conducted an early survey of the criminal courts. The College Settlement mounted a comprehensive survey of unemployment. Settlement residents lobbied to get nurses in the public schools and helped organize the Women's Trade Union League and the National Association for the Advancement of Colored People. Beginning in 1902 a coalition of settlement leaders led the fight to enact national child labor laws, an effort that culminated in 1912 when Congress passed a bill establishing the Children's Bureau in the Department of Labor.

Ironically, Legal Aid lawyers—serving the same poor constituency as settlement houses—contributed little to the settlements' law reform work, which was handled by settlement house leaders in consultation with elite private attorneys.[29] Lillian Wald of the Henry Street Settlement House, for example, relied on the prominent corporate lawyer Louis Marshall of Guggenheim, Untermeyer & Marshall for advice concerning her efforts in support of laws regulating night work for women.[30] Florence Kelley, a fixture at the Henry Street Settlement House, enlisted the able representation of Louis D. Brandeis in 1908 when the issue of regulating women's work was presented to the U.S. Supreme Court in *Muller v. Oregon*.[31]

In part, Legal Aid chose to stay on the sidelines in order to maintain an image of professional objectivity. But Legal Aid's absence from the great law reform debates of the day also reflected the meager political clout wielded by the society. Von Briesen had envisioned Legal Aid as a "stepping stone to success" for young lawyers, much like a physician's internship, but in reality Legal Aid attracted women and Jews, who were excluded from most law firms.[32] As a result, these lawyers were marginalized even in the area with which they were most familiar—poverty law.

Legal Aid's apolitical stance did, however, help save it from the financial insecurity of the settlement house movement. Funding for settlement houses came almost exclusively from individuals, and as the movement came of age, many patrons withdrew support because of the residents' participation in Progressive politics, advocacy of women's suffrage, support of labor unions, and outspoken pacifism.[33] By the 1920s the type of activist social work pioneered by settlement houses was no longer fundable.[34] Social workers increasingly stressed individual casework and psychology rather than the social context and community of their clients.[35] Settlement houses were forced to change their focus or disband.

In contrast, Legal Aid societies had a pool of well-heeled potential supporters in the legal profession. Bar associations were initially uneasy about Legal Aid societies, as many attorneys viewed Legal Aid as a potential competitor for scarce clients. But the societies tailored their programs to allay this fear. New York's Legal Aid Society turned away personal injury cases that, because of potential damage awards, might seem attractive to the private bar. As Von Briesen reassured his colleagues, "The attorneys of The Aid Society never take charge of cases which lawyers in actual practice would be ready to undertake."[36]

It was, however, the great influx of immigrants from southern and eastern Europe between 1905 and 1914 that finally convinced bar leaders that supporting Legal Aid was in their own best interests. As immigration increased, so did the "lawlessness and disorder"[37] of the ghettos and the potential for social unrest unless clients were shown that "their rights could and would be enforced by the mechanisms of the existing capitalistic order."[38] With increased financial support of elite lawyers, the number of Legal Aid societies nationwide jumped from five to forty-one between 1905 and 1920. In 1921, after decades on the sidelines of the poverty debate, the legal profession's most powerful organization, the American Bar Association, appointed a standing committee on legal aid. Two years later, the National Association of Legal Aid Organizations was formed.[39]

The architect of the alliance between Legal Aid societies and the organized bar was Reginald Heber Smith, a young partner at the Boston law firm Hale & Dorr and general counsel to Boston's two-person Legal Aid Society. In 1917 the Carnegie Foundation hired Smith to undertake a nationwide survey of the delivery of legal services to the poor.[40] In *Justice and the Poor*, his 1919 report to the foundation, Smith candidly concluded that "the administration of American justice is not impartial, the rich and the poor do not stand on an equality before the law, [and] the traditional method of providing justice has operated to close the doors of the courts to the poor, and has caused a gross denial of justice in all parts of the country to millions of persons."[41] According to Smith, merely providing Legal Aid lawyers to advise the poor would not solve the problem. He advocated that Legal Aid societies use their expertise to lobby for broad legal reforms.[42]

Published at a time when the country was struggling to absorb millions of recent arrivals, Smith's report might easily have led to a broad reexamination of the legal system—the restrictive educational requirements for practicing law and the bar's monopoly over judicial appointments and courtroom representation, as well as other privileges that attend the profession. Instead, Smith's conclusion that America's institutions were fraught with class injustice was diluted—apparently with Smith's acquiescence—by bar leaders interested in using the survey to strengthen the bar's exclusive access to legal institutions.

In his foreword to *Justice and the Poor*, for example, Elihu Root, Sr.—former Secretary of State, Secretary of War, and U.S. senator from New York—wrote that Smith's report was addressed to "the multitude of Americans who are interested in the Americanization of the millions of foreigners who have immigrated to this country, and who fail to understand or who misunderstand American institutions."[43] Through the efforts of Root and other bar leaders, Americanization rather than class injustice became the central focus when the American Bar Association considered Smith's report. The organized bar endorsed this goal by providing financial and administrative support to Legal Aid societies. Instead of tying up the courts with the myriad problems of poor people or putting private attorneys in the uncomfortable position of turning away clients who could not afford assistance, Legal Aid societies would both socialize the poor and efficiently dispose of their cases, extending rough justice to people who otherwise had no hope for justice at all.[44]

The support of the organized bar, though nominal in some areas of the country, continued to stimulate the growth of the Legal Aid movement:

thirty new Legal Aid organizations were started in the 1920s, and the number of cases handled by Legal Aid societies nearly doubled, rising from 96,034 in 1920 to 171,961 in 1929. But with the onset of the Depression, the interests of many in the legal profession shifted again. Established clients of small firms cut back on the luxury of legal advice. Individuals who might have once hired attorneys instead joined the lines at Legal Aid societies. From 1929 to 1932 the nationwide Legal Aid caseload almost doubled again, from 171,000 to more than 307,000 cases. At the same time, financial support for Legal Aid declined. For example, only 229 of 17,000 lawyers practicing in New York City made contributions to the Legal Aid Society in 1934.[45]

Small law firms and sole practitioners specializing in representing individuals languished during the Depression. But law firms handling corporate work—the province of lawyers from the most prestigious schools and elite backgrounds—kept busy with bankruptcies and corporate reorganizations and, as one attorney stated, were "very little affected" by the economy.[46] The widening gap between individuals of low or moderate income who needed legal assistance and those corporations and wealthy individuals who could actually afford assistance again exposed lawyers and legal institutions to charges of class bias.

This time, no less a personage than Supreme Court Justice Harlan F. Stone led the attack on his profession. In a widely publicized address at the University of Michigan Law School in 1934 Stone asserted that lawyers' primary allegiance now went to corporations rather than to communities.[47] This development had transformed "the learned profession of an earlier day [into] the obsequious servant of business, and tainted it with the morals and manners of the market place in its most anti-social manifestations."[48]

Law professors rallied around Stone. Fueled by the public antagonism against big business during the Depression years, they published a series of devastating critiques of large law firms and their powerful place in the legal profession. The most influential of these critical theories, "legal realism," argued that law, far from being a collection of formal, objective rules, was a product of politics and morality.[49] Legal realists argued that the orthodoxy that judges decided cases on objective rules was a "wishful" rationalization; they maintained that because a judge's decision was, in essence, a political response to the facts presented, lawyers could use law as an instrument of social change through their presentation of the facts and selection of litigation tactics.[50] According to Karl Llewellyn of Columbia Law

School, legal realism represented "a new and timely voicing of the function of law: to serve society. Society as a whole, not merely the White-collars and the Haves. . . . Let this be written large, for senior partners in law-factories to ponder on: Law does not exist for corporation executives alone."[51]

Legal realism and its attendant cynicism about the supposed classless nature of the law was particularly popular among liberal lawyers who moved between university law schools and New Deal agencies during the Roosevelt administration.[52] The president's willingness to initiate bold new federal programs coincided with lawyers' own ideas that federal intervention was justified, as a legal matter, by the social policy needs of the country. The realists' readiness to use law for social change, combined with the extreme exigencies of the Depression, contributed to the significant reworking and partial federalization of welfare laws in the Social Security Act of 1935.[53]

Incredibly, the dramatic changes in welfare law and policy did not, by and large, pierce the consciousness of Legal Aid lawyers representing the poor in the 1930s and 1940s. For instance, soon after World War I Legal Aid organizations adopted a standard classification scheme for civil cases to facilitate statistical studies. Yet as late as 1951 these classifications did not include public assistance among the types of cases routinely handled by Legal Aid societies.[54]

Though legal realists continued to harangue the legal profession for its failure to serve the poor, only those at the political fringes of the profession took the occasion to reassess the existing model for delivery of legal aid. In response to realists' criticism, the leftist National Lawyers Guild in 1938 initiated a small-scale experiment to provide legal services to the poor and to members of the middle class. With the blessings of Llewellyn and Reginald Heber Smith, guilds in Chicago and Philadelphia set up neighborhood offices to provide low-cost legal services. The experiments were a modest success; by 1949 the Philadelphia office was serving 4,200 clients annually and operating at a profit. Yet similar offices were not opened elsewhere, perhaps because of the organized bar's resistance to competition.[55]

Lawyers for the NAACP Legal Defense and Educational Fund also incorporated the realists' philosophy into their legal strategy for the desegregation of public schools. Realism not only influenced their view of litigation's potential to effect change, it also expanded the scope of their factual arguments against segregation. As envisioned by the Legal Defense Fund lawyers, the constitutional argument for desegregation under the equal protection clause was inseparable from the sociological evidence that separate schools were inevitably unequal—a direct reflection of the realists' argument that all law, even constitutional law, was at bottom social policy.[56]

These innovations at the margins of the profession had little effect on either the bar associations or the Legal Aid societies. The organized bar's support for poverty law continued to stagnate until 1950, when Great Britain instituted its Legal Aid and Advice Scheme, which mandated that every member of the legal profession be available to provide legal aid to the poor, to be reimbursed by the government.[57] A vocal minority of the profession, led by members of the National Lawyers Guild, took up the call for a similar program in the United States. According to the guild's estimates, two-thirds of the American population was unable to afford legal services. It was time for a radical reworking of Legal Aid.[58]

Terrified lest a plan modeled on the British scheme be adopted in the United States—setting a precedent for restricting the bar's self-regulation—state and local bar associations stepped into the breach to demonstrate the continued viability of American Legal Aid societies. By the end of the 1950s Legal Aid lawyers reported "a breakthrough. Whereas in 1949 . . . 43% of the large cities were without offices, the percentage . . . was reduced to 21% by the end of 1959."[59]

While shoring up support for privately funded legal aid, the American Bar Association launched a counteroffensive against the guild and others who might support the "socialization" of law. The association's Special Committee to Study Communist Tactics, Strategy, and Objectives concluded that the time had come to "drive such lawyers from the profession" and to exclude those found guilty of "embracing and practicing" communism or Marxism-Leninism.[60] Many state bar associations adopted loyalty oaths as a prerequisite to practice. Even Reginald Heber Smith warned in 1951 that "it is a fundamental tenet of Marxian Communism that law is a class weapon used by the rich to oppress the poor through the simple device of making justice too expensive."[61] Comprehensive legal services to the poor, the organized bar asserted, was un-American.

Throughout the 1950s the organized bar was largely successful in forestalling federally sponsored legal services for the poor. At the same time, however, a West Coast academician was laboring to develop a legal theory that would redefine the rights of poor people and lead to dramatic changes in the practice of poverty law, whether by traditional legal aid organizations or by government lawyers.

Jacobus tenBroek, blinded in a bow and arrow accident at age seven, earned two law degrees from Berkeley's Boalt Hall and one from Harvard before his appointment to the speech and political science faculties at University of California at Berkeley. A founder of the National Federation for the Blind, tenBroek was dedicated to integrating the blind into sighted society. To demonstrate his commitment, he insisted on moving about the Berkeley campus without a guide.[62]

TenBroek's academic interest—poverty—was also a personal crusade. He began to lay the intellectual foundations of welfare law in the late 1940s, more than a decade before it was recognized as a field of legal practice and scholarship.[63]

At that time the meaning of the equal protection clause of the Constitution was in flux. In 1944, in *Korematsu v. United States*—which challenged the restrictions on the movement of Japanese Americans in the United States during World War II—the Supreme Court suggested that the equal protection clause might allow federal courts to scrutinize and strike down state laws that used racial classifications.[64] According to Justice Hugo L. Black's opinion, "All legal restrictions which curtail the civil rights of a single racial group are immediately suspect."[65] This proposition was confirmed and explained in 1954 in the Supreme Court's decision in *Brown v. Board of Education.*[66] But tenBroek argued in 1949 that poor people, as well as racial groups, should be considered a class requiring special judicial attention and that state laws resulting in unequal treatment of the poor should be struck down by the courts.[67] He believed that "the mere state of being without funds [should be] a neutral fact" under the law.[68]

In 1955 tenBroek detailed a compelling example of the unequal treatment of the poor. Many states had enacted onerous residency requirements that denied welfare benefits to individuals who had not resided in the state for a specified length of time, in some cases several years. As a result, welfare recipients could not move to another state to be with family and friends or to search for a job without forgoing their meager benefits. These laws, tenBroek argued, "operate as an impairment of the [constitutional] right to free movement" of U.S. citizens.[69] TenBroek's logic was beyond question, but no court had yet agreed with his interpretation of the law.

TenBroek's magnum opus, a three-part article published in 1965 in the

Stanford Law Review, reformulated his arguments around the idea that welfare laws create dual systems of family law in the United States, one for the indigent and one for everyone else.[70] Under the welfare regime, for example, residency laws restricted recipients' movements, and regulations required that women receiving AFDC keep men out of their homes, even if the men were simply boyfriends who had no obligation to support children of a prior relationship. Relying on the *Brown* opinion and the intimations in *Gideon v. Wainwright*—which ruled that states must provide trial counsel for indigents in criminal proceedings—tenBroek argued that poverty commanded the special solicitude of the courts.[71] He called again for the application of the equal protection clause to strike down laws that used public assistance to impose special standards of behavior on poor people.[72]

By the close of the 1950s these emerging legal theories were beginning to challenge the fundamental assumptions of the welfare system. Legal Aid societies, however, by and large failed to respond to these changes. Despite the bar's concerted resistance to federal involvement in the provision of legal services, Legal Aid and the private bar seemed unable to meet the legal needs of the poor.

Chapter 3

The Welfare Law Guru

The government's obligation to establish legal recourse for the poor in their dealings with governmental agencies is today merely in the argument stage. It is an
obligation, however, which should be assumed, particularly in the war against
poverty: partly because the poor themselves need representation; partly because
the law is best developed with representation; partly because the war against
poverty needs that 'civilian perspective . . . of dissent, of critical scrutiny, of advocacy and of impatience' which lawyers for the poor can bring to it.

—Edward V. Sparer, quoting Edgar S. Cahn and Jean C. Cahn, 1964

Edward V. Sparer was concerned with issues of class and of economic
redistribution at a time when most progressive lawyers were focused on
establishing racial equality.[1] Sparer was a few years older than most of his
law school classmates, who had come of age in the 1950s, once the United
States was entrenched in the cold war against Eastern Europe and after
Brown v. Board of Education had heralded a new age of racial equality.
Sparer's adult life had begun in the 1940s, when the promise of socialism
hinted at by the New Deal had not yet been abandoned and before the labor
movement became yet another special interest group in the Democratic
Party's fold. Lawyers of Sparer's ilk were more common a decade or two
before—they were active in organizing unions and litigating workers'
rights. But by the 1960s litigation addressing economic rights was out of
vogue.

Sparer traced his political birth to the summer of 1947 when, at age
eighteen and finished with his first year at City College in New York, he
traveled south to organize textile workers for third-party presidential can-
didate Henry A. Wallace, FDR's commerce secretary during the New Deal.
According to Sparer, "I returned some months later, shaken to my core,
radicalized, as were many others a generation later in the civil rights and
antipoverty movements. What so shook me were my encounters with
textile workers who were paralyzed with fear; with gaunt twenty-five-year-
old mothers in the textile communities who looked as if they were forty
years old; with one-time militant labor organizers who—literally—had
had their life essence beaten out of them by thugs; with black poverty

which surpassed my imagination." Eyes opened, Sparer resolved to devote his life to eliminating "poverty, discrimination, fear and violence and the absence of the freedom of speech."[2]

The following school year City College was torn by charges that certain faculty members and administrators were anti-Semitic and racist. As vice-president of the student council Sparer could pressure the administration to take action against these individuals. Under his leadership a coalition of liberals, socialists, communists, apolitical students, and a few faculty members planned a course of action.[3]

First, several hundred students participated in a sit-down strike led by Sparer and two other students. "For nine hours," the *New York Times* reported, "the group sat, sang, talked, adopted resolutions and joined a guitar player in songfests."[4] When the City College administration ignored the demonstrators, the students called a full-blown general student strike. According to Sparer, it was "the first such strike on a major American campus since the 1930s."[5]

The results were mixed at best. On the first day of the strike, April 11, 1949, more than half of the 7,230 students of the college stayed away from classes and joined the picket lines.[6] By the second day, only 40 percent of the students honored the strike. Interest continued to wane on the next day and the next. After five days, the strike was broken. The strike committee acknowledged defeat and students returned to classes.

Embittered by the college administration's utter failure to respond to student demands, Sparer and his fiancée, Tanya Schechter, also a City College student, joined the Communist party and dropped out of school, suspending, for the time being, their uneasiness about the party's stance on free speech.[7] A few months later they married and, on the instructions of the party, moved to Schenectady, New York. Their task was to consolidate the party's presence at the General Electric plant in Schenectady by joining the United Electrical Workers Union that represented GE employees.

The Sparers arrived in Schenectady by train with two large suitcases—one filled with clothes and one with party literature. Fearing that they might be followed, they walked separately from the train station. Tanya, small and slender, went first, struggling with two heavy bags. Ed, a heavyset man about six feet tall, followed far behind, his hands free. They had decided that he was the more politically important of the pair and should be free to run or deny his party affiliation if they were caught.[8]

The Sparers' initial attempts to penetrate the work force were unsuccessful. But in 1953, after a two-year hiatus while Ed served in the army—first as a teacher and then as a lifeguard in Panama—Ed was hired by GE as a "chipper" on the turbine assembly line. He used an air hammer to gouge metal from rough forms that moved past him on a conveyor. Sparer was frightened of the flying metal at first. After some months of practice, however, he grew proud of his skill with the hammer and was not pleased when GE transferred him to the washroom cleaning crew to curtail his organizing activities.[9]

Throughout their time in Schenectady the Sparers were haunted by the specter of Senator Joseph McCarthy and the Un-American Activities Committee of the U.S. House of Representatives. The national mood of anticommunism could not be shrugged off. "Few of us in those days spoke freely, even inside our own homes, without covering our telephones with blankets and checking for other signs of electronic invasion," Ed Sparer later wrote. "It was not unknown for Communist factory workers, when their affiliation was discovered, to be thrown bodily out of the factory window."[10] To avoid disruption of the party's activities if they were discovered and arrested, the Sparers were in touch with only three other couples in the party.[11] In Ed Sparer's mind, however, the risks and isolation were more than outweighed by the solidarity he felt with fellow Communists. "The Party was my community," he wrote, "and it determined where I lived and what I did."[12]

The Sparers' apprenticeship in the party ended abruptly in March 1956 when Ed Sparer picked up a copy of the *New York Times* and read the text of Nikita Khrushchev's speech to the 20th Congress of the Communist Party of the Soviet Union, which detailed Stalin's slaughter of tens of thousands of capitalists and Communists alike in the late 1930s and early 1940s.[13] The Sparers were devastated. "When my doubts about the Communist Party first started," Ed Sparer recalled, "they were followed by a rush of more doubts—till finally, in but a month's time, years of fond belief were no more."[14]

Ed and Tanya Sparer resigned from the party and returned to New York City. For years Ed's friends and family had told him that he should be a lawyer, given his interest in politics and his skill at public speaking. In the fall of 1956 Ed Sparer enrolled in Brooklyn Law School, the only one in the city that would accept him without an undergraduate degree.[15]

Sparer applied himself to his law studies with a certain desperation. He knew that his career choices would always be limited by his Communist background, but he hoped that if he excelled he would at least be able to get a job. By dint of hard work, sometimes to the detriment of his personal life—which now included three young children—Sparer graduated first in his law school class, won the moot court competition, and served as editor-in-chief of the *Brooklyn Law Review*.[16]

But Sparer's past was not so easily eclipsed. When the Brooklyn Law School dean invited the star student to serve as his research assistant, Sparer wrote him an anguished letter of apology: "The crux of the situation is this—for several years, terminating only a couple of months prior to my law school application, I held membership in the Communist Party. . . . I plain don't know what to say except forgive me please if I have hurt or embarrassed this school in any way."[17]

The dean took Sparer's admission seriously and quietly asked Sparer to step aside as the law school graduation speaker, an honor reserved for the top student, in favor of someone who would project a better image of the school.[18]

As graduation approached, Sparer began looking for jobs with labor unions, and he applied for a position as an associate attorney with the International Ladies Garment Workers' Union (ILGWU), a progressive, socialist-led union that had pioneered union-sponsored cooperative housing, health programs, and worker education.[19]

The general counsel of the ILGWU, Morris Glushien, interviewed Sparer on April 7, 1959. Two weeks later, Glushien called Professor Sol Klein at Brooklyn Law School for a reference. "He told me that Sparer is extremely hard working," Glushien recorded in his notes of the conversation. "He writes well. His oral performance in Moot Court was exceedingly good. . . . He gets along well with people, was liked by his fellow students, and is a sincere person."[20] Glushien offered Sparer the job and Sparer accepted, joining the ILGWU's four-person legal team in their cramped quarters at 1700 Broadway in New York.[21]

Sparer passed the New York State bar examination that summer. But in 1959, despite a mild reprimand from the U.S. Supreme Court, the local bar associations that controlled membership in the legal profession were still intent on policing their ranks for Communist sympathizers. Before he could finally gain admission to the bar Sparer had to be approved by the New York state Committee on Character and Fitness, a group of bar leaders who were certain to ask whether Sparer had ever been a member of the Communist party. If Sparer admitted his affiliation, his application would likely be denied because he lacked "good character." And if he refused to answer it was virtually certain that he would be rejected, because bar associations were adamant that, whatever the First Amendment implications, they had the right to inquire into applicants' political backgrounds.

Sparer asked for Glushien's help and Glushien arranged a meeting between Sparer and the venerable president of the ILGWU, David Dubinsky, a Socialist with impeccable anticommunist credentials. Thirty years before, he had assumed leadership in the ILGWU by driving out the Communists who were in control of the union, and he was a founding member of the staunchly anticommunist Liberal party.[22]

Dubinsky, convinced of Sparer's sincere rejection of Communism, agreed to write a letter on Sparer's behalf to the Committee on Character and Fitness—a letter that carried a great deal of weight. Sparer then went before the committee and, though he admitted his Communist past, was approved as a member of the bar.[23]

Sparer's caseload at the ILGWU included everything from defending a striking worker arrested for picketing the home of a scab to calculating workers' disability benefits to advising union locals on their rights to organize. He not only conducted a number of trials and hearings, but also wrote how-to articles on arbitration and labor law for union members.[24] After three years at the ILGWU, however, Sparer grew restless and began looking for a new position.

Sparer had always been interested in teaching, but he feared that his applications would be rejected because his alma mater did not have a strong academic reputation. So in 1962 Sparer took a job that he hoped would lead directly to a teaching position. Monrad Paulsen, a professor at Columbia Law School, was embarking on a study of New York's juvenile courts and their treatment of lower-class youth. He hired Sparer as his assistant.[25]

For the next year Sparer observed court proceedings, interviewed judges, clerks and juvenile offenders, and drafted recommendations for juvenile court reform. He finished the report but Paulsen refused to release it, perhaps because of political pressure. Sparer was furious and disappointed but unable to change Paulsen's mind.[26]

Smarting from having worked for a year with nothing to show for it, Sparer decided to put off teaching until his children were older and he began casting about for his next job. The same year, 1963, Paulsen was appointed to the faculty board responsible for overseeing the creation of a new legal office, the Mobilization for Youth (MFY) Legal Unit. Designed by social workers, MFY represented one of the most comprehensive assaults on poverty ever mounted in the United States. With Paulsen's support,

Sparer was hired as the new Legal Unit's director, and through the unit welfare law theory was finally put into practice.[27]

MFY was conceived on May 13, 1957, at a meeting of the Board of Directors of the Henry Street Settlement House. Henry Street Settlement, founded in 1893 as the first independent public nursing service in the nation, was still grappling with the social problems of the Lower East Side community six decades later. While many settlement houses had long ago closed or shifted their focus to psychological casework, the Henry Street Settlement clung to its original mandate of social reform.[28]

The board meeting began with presentations by social workers involved in a delinquency prevention project. When they finished, a prosperous businessman attending the meeting, Jacob M. Kaplan, asked half-rhetorically, "What would it take, how much would it cost," to really deal with delinquency?[29] By the end of the meeting, the board members agreed that to attack the mammoth problem of juvenile delinquency, they must saturate the Lower East Side with traditional social services—recreation, camping, home visits, day care, and the like. Kaplan offered a grant from his own Kaplan Foundation to pay for the planning of the project.[30]

The ambitious "action" plan developed by the Henry Street staff over the next few months called for a budget of $6 million over six years.[31] The plan's components, however, did not reflect any rethinking of turn-of-the-century settlement house theories of social assimilation. Saturating the community was exactly what settlement houses had been doing for decades, but on a less-expensive scale.

No one was interested in funding such a project. The National Institute for Mental Health (NIMH) suggested that the settlement enlist social science professionals to develop a more innovative research design. Still hoping to get the project off the drawing board, the Henry Street Board turned to two experts on delinquency affiliated with the Columbia School of Social Work: Lloyd Ohlin and Richard Cloward.

Ohlin was director of the Columbia School of Social Work, and Cloward was an assistant professor. Together they were writing a book, *Delinquency and Opportunity*, which spelled out their "opportunity theory."[32] In contrast with the prevailing academic view that delinquency could be remedied through psychiatric casework, Cloward and Ohlin argued that the social organization of ghetto communities created delinquency. Young people on the Lower East Side sought status in gangs or through drugs, they asserted, because they had no opportunities for legitimate behavior. Opportunity theory held that juvenile delinquency could be effectively attacked by providing young people with *"genuine* opportunities to behave differently," giving them "a stake in conformity."[33]

Ohlin and Cloward accepted the Mobilization for Youth project. Based on their research design—a 617-page "Proposal for Prevention and Control of Delinquency by Expanding Opportunities"—in May 1962 President Kennedy awarded MFY a $2.1 million grant from the President's Committee on Juvenile Delinquency.[34] An additional $11 million was garnered from NIMH, the Ford Foundation, New York City, and the Columbia School of Social Work. MFY opened its doors in September 1962.

Within a few months the Lower East Side was indeed saturated with MFY's staff of more than 350 family aides, gang workers, vocational guidance counselors, community organizers, recreation leaders, teachers, and clergymen. But Cloward and Ohlin's plan involved more than mere saturation; they were intent on altering the social structure of the community. According to Charles Grosser, deputy director of MFY, the staff spent 80 to 90 percent of its time "organizing the unaffiliated—the lower fifth of the economic ladder . . . who will overturn the status quo."[35]

The initial proposal for MFY made no mention of a legal unit. But the importance of legal services was apparent as early as December 1961: many of MFY's clients needed legal advice that their social workers were not equipped to give.[36] At the Ford Foundation's recommendation, MFY approached the New York-based Vera Foundation, an institute devoted to social justice research, and asked it to develop a proposal for an MFY legal arm.[37]

The tentative outline that MFY gave the Vera Foundation was modest: "In order to provide economically deprived clients with the means to cope with the myriad problems which impinge on their lives, Mobilization for Youth hopes to provide through the Neighborhood Service Center, preventative legal services to its clients. In this connection, we are concerned not with actual legal services to be provided in litigation proceedings but rather to make available advice and information which will enable people to know their rights under the law and to assert those rights where appropriate."[38] MFY proposed using law students and training "indigenous members of the community" to provide this legal advice; any litigation would be referred to the Legal Aid Society.[39]

Completed in May 1963, the Vera Foundation's report elaborated on the initial MFY outline, with the additional suggestions that MFY hire one or two staff attorneys to supervise the advice-giving and that litigation be handled by a pool of fifty volunteer lawyers drawn from New York City's political clubs. "Pool members would be oriented to the social mandate of MFY," the Vera Foundation wrote. "In this way it is hoped that the pool's services would be in harmony with MFY's objectives and philosophy."[40] In addition to advice and referral, the Vera Foundation recommended that the legal unit provide legal orientation for nonlawyers and social change through research and lobbying. Guided by these recommendations, MFY established a legal unit with a supervisory committee composed of Columbia Law School faculty. Ed Sparer began working in the autumn of 1963 to develop activities for the unit.

Without waiting for the ink to dry on his contract, Sparer let it be known that his vision of the MFY Legal Unit differed sharply from the Vera Foundation's proposals. In November 1963 he sent a report to the supervisory committee recommending that the Vera Foundation's report be abandoned. Sparer argued that instead of piecemeal direct legal services in the Legal Aid tradition, most of the MFY Legal Unit's resources should be channeled into targeted study and direct litigation designed to change the institutional structure that created and sustained poverty.[41]

The MFY staff members quickly adopted Sparer's view. In a memorandum dated January 20, 1964, George Brager, MFY's program director, spelled out their agreement that "the major objective of the Legal Unit is to affect social policy and administrative practices rather than to supply legal help to clients in an unplanful way." There was, the staff members concluded, no ethical barrier to the sort of strategic litigation that Sparer had proposed: "There is nothing in the perspective of the Legal Unit which presumes that cases will be accepted indiscriminately as a result of [the] legal aid function. I know of no ethical stance which does not permit an individual lawyer or organization to choose its clients."[42]

It was more difficult to persuade the Legal Unit's supervisory committee to abandon the model proposed by the Vera Foundation. After several drafts circulated to his colleagues on staff, Sparer sent a second, eloquent memorandum to the supervisory committee in which he argued for a deliberate "change in perspective" concerning the MFY Legal Unit.[43]

Other "small" legal units, wrote Sparer, had very effectively used litigation for social change: "The NAACP Legal Defense Fund for years operated as a law office of about the same size as our own. Only recently has it begun to expand. Yet because it drew on the right kinds of cases, and related itself to a social movement concerned with the same goals, its effect on national issues has been profound. The ACLU for years has operated with a paid legal staff which has alternated in size between one and two lawyers. Of course, it has drawn the same kind of response from volunteer lawyers and the public generally on civil liberties matters that we hope to create on 'poor man's law' matters."[44] The MFY Legal Unit's potential was strengthened, Sparer added, because "we work closely with a unique organization [MFY] which employs more than 200 social workers and 'indigenous' program personnel . . . in the same community. Through these people, we are able to cull cases of the greatest importance to the community as a whole."[45]

Sparer dismissed the Vera Foundation's emphasis on study and research, asserting instead that "our *lawyers* role within the community and our relationship to clients are the instruments by which the study-research function of the Legal Unit is realized. If such should cease, our sources of information and bases for perception will dry. Our role will become sterile. A single law-trained researcher, with an office at Columbia, could then accomplish as much."[46] Sparer's vivid memory of his fruitless year preparing Paulsen's unpublished juvenile courts report no doubt fueled his opposition to the Vera Foundation's recommendation that poverty lawyers spend their time preparing studies of their clients' problems.

After several months of debate, the supervisory committee was finally convinced by Sparer's view. The aggressive, affirmative use of "law as an instrument of social change," patterned after the methods of the NAACP and the American Civil Liberties Union, became the MFY Legal Unit's credo. Sparer only half echoed the statements of Arthur Von Briesen and Reginald Heber Smith when he wrote in November 1965 that "ultimately, it is hoped that the poor will come to look upon the law as a tool which they can use on their own behalf to vindicate their rights and their interests—in the same way that law is used by other segments of the population."[47] Like his Legal Aid predecessors, Sparer saw law as a means to redress inequality. But in contrast with those who used it as an agent of democratization, Sparer viewed the law as a means to empower the poor, a tool capable of forcing structural changes in a system that punished the poor for their poverty.

As part of his effort to empower clients, Sparer was committed to broadening the range of advocates. Convinced that social workers could play an important role in expanding clients' rights, Sparer set about training MFY staff members and settlement house workers regarding the legal issues facing their clients.[48] According to Sparer, social workers "are in regular contact with thousands of the most desperately impoverished . . . [who are] not prone to seek out lawyers on their own initiative. Yet they are often the most exploited, the most seriously disadvantaged and the most in need of legal help and legal education in the community."[49]

Even more ambitiously, Sparer envisioned welfare recipients acting as their own advocates in administrative hearings, and he arranged legal clinics at neighborhood centers and settlement houses—including University Settlement, where Legal Aid had operated an office sixty years before—to educate members of the community about their legal problems and options.[50]

In its first full year of operation, the Legal Unit's four attorneys handled a range of poverty law matters: 350 housing cases, 60 workers' compensation matters, 50 consumer credit cases, and 200 criminal cases.[51] In addition, Sparer made plans to establish students' right to counsel in school suspensions, to develop a model brief for use in consumer fraud cases in the neighborhood, and to form an action plan attacking problems in the provision of public benefits to clients. The MFY Legal Unit's work was characterized by activism and aggressive advocacy. As one attorney explained, MFY lawyers believed that their client was more important than their professionalism; they would violate court etiquette and the bounds of professional good taste by, for example, interrupting opposing counsel or following a judge into chambers to argue a case if it might mean a better result for their client.[52]

The Legal Unit's first year, however, also brought a crisis that pitted Sparer against MFY as a whole, alienated one of the Legal Unit's major funders, and very nearly resulted in the Legal Unit's demise.

MFY received funds from the city of New York. At the same time, the MFY Legal Unit regularly sued the city's welfare department on its poor clients' behalf. As these suits proliferated, the city balked at funding further litigation against itself and demanded an investigation of the Legal Unit's activities. In response—and in hopes of placating the city—MFY's Committee on Direct Operations prepared to undertake a review of the Legal Unit's case handling procedures.

To MFY's surprise, the Legal Unit refused to submit to the review, arguing that supervision and censure by nonlawyers would violate the confidential relationship between MFY lawyers and their clients. Sparer believed that the issue of the Legal Unit's independence was inseparable from the ongoing internal debate concerning the Legal Unit's litigation priorities; "if litigation on any . . . politically sensitive subject areas is contemplated," he wrote, independence from MFY is "a necessity."[53] According to

Sparer, "There is no significant area of direct lawyer-client work in which we can properly engage without creating potential conflict situations with city agencies. . . . It would not be unreasonable to suggest that the City—which has the controlling voice on MFY's Board—would not permit us to enter into such situations."[54]

The controversy was ultimately submitted to a state court judge, who upheld the Legal Unit's independence.[55] The city was free to curtail its funding to MFY, but if it chose to provide funds, it could not use its financial influence to exercise control over MFY's lawyers.

Not unpredictably, this confrontation resulted in a cutback of city funding for MFY. But the timing was perfect, at least for the Legal Unit. By declaring its independence from MFY, the Legal Unit largely avoided involvement in a virulent anticommunist attack on its parent organization by city and state politicians. Though the attack was abandoned when it was revealed that only two of the 400 MFY employees had Communist affiliations, it presaged the demise of the weakened, tainted MFY.[56] Meanwhile, the federal government was on the verge of creating its first poverty law program, one that would provide the MFY Legal Unit with a new and perhaps more secure source of financial support.

With the initiation of the War on Poverty in 1964, President Lyndon Johnson had established the Office of Economic Opportunity to administer the neighborhood-based Community Action Program. CAP was designed to provide financial support for community-based antipoverty efforts by funding existing programs and stimulating new ones. Under one of the most controversial provisions of the new law, each CAP-funded effort was to be "developed, conducted, and administered with maximum feasible participation of residents in the areas and members of the groups served."[57]

A proposed legal component of CAP was initially rejected. But through skillful lobbying, by Edgar Cahn and Jean Camper Cahn in particular—two young, politically connected lawyers who urged that legal services would give voice to a "civilian perspective" on the War on Poverty—federally funded legal services were incorporated into the program in 1965.[58]

Sparer's commitments at MFY precluded his involvement in the day-to-day lobbying to create federal legal services. He did, however, significantly influence the shape of federally funded poverty law centers. In 1964 MFY and the Washington, D.C., Neighborhood Legal Services Project (NLSP) were the only non-Legal Aid poverty law offices in the country. A third poverty law office, opened in New Haven, Connecticut, in 1963, lasted only seven weeks, largely because of the public outcry when it took on a controversial criminal case.[59] (Unlike MFY, the New Haven office had failed to establish independence from its parent social service organization.) All three of these programs were initially funded by the Ford Foundation, and each espoused a legal services philosophy quite different from the traditional model of providing the poor with no more than "access to justice."

The New Haven experiment had adopted a casework approach and envisioned sociolegal teams that would address the "whole person" by resolving the "social, economic and psychological factors" that resulted in their clients' poverty.[60] In contrast, Sparer was convinced that litigation for social change should be the MFY Legal Unit's highest priority. He concentrated, to the extent possible, on "strategic legal actions that would create new legal rights for the poor" while maintaining "a direct relationship with the community" as a "genuine neighborhood law office."[61] NLSP began operations in 1964 with a sociolegal approach similar to the one employed in New Haven, but it moved toward a practice that, like MFY's, mixed routine representation with strategic litigation.[62]

But Jean and Edgar Cahn favored a model developed along the lines adopted by the National Lawyers Guild in the 1930s. That model promoted participation of the poor in their own representation through neighborhood offices and traditional lawyer-client relationships. New Haven's sociolegal approach, the Cahns believed, would interpose nonlawyers, like social workers and psychologists, between attorneys and their clients. And the strategic impact litigation of MFY, according to the Cahns, was largely driven by lawyers' personal desire to bring "important" litigation rather than by true responsiveness to clients' needs.

Reversing decades of opposition to federal funding of legal services, the ABA publicly supported the Cahns' proposal. The lesson of the American Medical Association's unsuccessful opposition to Medicare had not been lost on bar association leaders; they recognized the political danger of waging a prolonged, losing battle over federal funding of legal services and opted for a behind-the-scenes role in shaping the program.[63] So long as representation was strictly limited to the poor and was explicitly based on the established bar's ethical standards of representation, bar leaders reasoned that federal funding would do no harm to the profession and would augment the limited, privately funded efforts of the nation's 256 legal aid offices.[64]

Within a few months of the ABA endorsement, the federal legal services program was implemented as a part of CAP, and from January 1, 1966, through January 30, 1967, three hundred legal service organizations received grants totaling $42 million.[65] Despite the theoretical debates over how poverty law should be practiced, the activities of these offices varied greatly. And, because the federal government funded them through block grant programs, they were largely beyond government control. Established programs, like MFY or Legal Aid offices, simply continued providing legal services as they always had.[66] Legal Aid societies, in particular, were not forced to abandon their opposition to law reform to qualify for federal funds.[67] On the other hand, many new legal offices set up by community action agencies were staffed by young lawyers who shared Sparer's vision of combining routine services with strategic litigation and were eager to bring the next *Brown v. Board of Education* for poor people.

Though Sparer had contemplated combining day-to-day advocacy with strategic litigation at MFY, he soon realized that neighborhood legal offices were not really equipped to do the kind of strategic work that he envisioned—a fact confirmed by Christopher Edley of the Ford Foundation on a visit to the MFY Legal Unit in early 1965. According to Edley's report, MFY was inundated with clients, not all of whose problems could be resolved through impact litigation. The press of these cases left little time for developing a comprehensive litigation strategy along the lines of the NAACP's antisegregation campaign. Edley concluded that the MFY Legal Unit "has only partially fulfilled the role of becoming legal champion of the poor—a role which it criticizes Legal Aid for not filling."[68] Unless its goals are clarified and narrowed, Edley wrote, "the risk is that through confusion and after a good start MFY's legal program may accomplish nothing of moment."[69]

Responding to these practical limitations, Sparer revised his model for delivery of legal services to the poor. He did not, however, refocus the MFY Legal Unit or make a renewed attempt to integrate strategic litigation with day-to-day representation. Instead, Sparer envisioned a two-tiered model in which routine services would be provided by neighborhood lawyers and social workers, and strategic litigation would be generated and supervised by specialists working as partners with the community-based offices. Implementing this idea, Sparer left MFY in late 1965 to set up a "backup center" with major funding from the Stern Family Fund and the Ford Foundation.[70] At the new center, called the Center on Social Welfare Policy and Law, a staff of nine lawyers would coordinate strategic welfare litigation nationwide. Because Sparer's practice of suing government agencies on his clients' behalf was so controversial, the Columbia Law School turned down Sparer's requests to house the program. Instead, the Center was located at the Columbia School of Social Work, reflecting Sparer's ties to Richard Cloward—who arranged for the space—as well as his commitment to integrate the activities of lawyers and social workers serving the poor.

Sparer passed the directorship of MFY's Legal Unit to Harold Rothwax, a former Legal Aid criminal defense attorney who fervently agreed with the Cahns' neighborhood-centered, case-by-case approach to legal services. According to Rothwax, "Law reform cannot substitute for the caseload. The caseload is power."[71] Sparer's emphasis on test cases was, Rothwax believed, misplaced: "For one thing the client doesn't understand [the test case approach] and those who understand don't care. . . . But even when you win a test case I think it is meaningless to win a principle and then not vindicate it with lawyers. . . . There are countless laws on the books today that are beautiful in their symmetry and their justice and morality and fairness that don't mean a thing because there are no lawyers to vindicate them."[72]

Sparer agreed that routine legal services available at the community level were important. But he also believed that lawyers for the poor, like lawyers for corporations, were called on to do more than simply respond to their clients' routine requests. "Businessmen, individually and in their corporate capacities, use lawyers in a multitude of ways to advance their immediate and long-range interests," he observed. "Lawyers are prime tacticians and strategists for advancing economic goals of corporations. Lawyers are lobbyists and propagandists. Lawyers are negotiators and advocates in the truest and broadest sense of the term, and not merely when suit has been brought against the corporation. . . . The new legal aid lawyer's role should be defined by the broadest reaches of advocacy, just as is the role of the corporation lawyer and the labor lawyer and the real estate board lawyer. Central to the new legal aid lawyer's role is the task of helping to articulate and promote the hopes, the dreams, and the real possibility for the impoverished to make the social changes that *they* feel are needed through whatever lawful methods are available."[73]

At the Center on Social Welfare Policy and Law Sparer focused on developing a welfare litigation agenda for the burgeoning poverty law movement—a strategy to bring the confusing half-federal, half-state system created by the Social Security Act of 1935 under the thumb of federal law. If Sparer's litigation campaign was successful, states could still administer welfare programs, but they would have to do so in a manner consistent with the federal Constitution and federal law. Relying heavily on Jacobus tenBroek's writings of the past decade, Sparer concluded that the requirements of federal statutory and constitutional law were broad indeed.

In an article published in the *UCLA Law Review* in 1965 Sparer drew on the work of influential social welfare analyst Elizabeth Wickenden, Yale Law School professor Charles Reich, and tenBroek to set out a tentative bill of rights for welfare recipients that might be established through strategic litigation: "(1) the right to privacy and protection from illegal search; (2) the right to freedom of movement and choice of residence; (3) the right to choose one's own standards of morality; and (4) the right to freedom to refuse work relief without suffering penal or other improper consequences."[74]

The following year, Sparer identified specific issues that were ripe for litigation, including residency laws, "man-in-the-house" rules, midnight raids, work-relief practices, the inadequacy of the money grant, the absence of due process protections, and the lack of uniformity in welfare laws among states. The Center's staff, wrote Sparer, was prepared to extend its "maximum aid—including brief writing, research, consultation on appropriate strategy, etc.," to attorneys engaged in litigating these issues.[75]

These lists were drawn from a memorandum on the constitutional rights of assistance recipients prepared by Wickenden in 1963 and from Sparer's personal experiences as a poverty lawyer.[76] For example, Sparer's clients on welfare had been subjected to midnight welfare raids in which city investigators entered the recipient's home without a warrant. The presence of a man in the apartment would result in suspension of the client's welfare benefits on the assumption that the man was, or should be, contributing to the client's support.[77] In fact, Tanya Sparer, who briefly considered becoming a welfare caseworker, had participated in a training session in which she was instructed to visit clients' apartments and search for telltale razor blades in the bathroom, whiskers in the sink, or ashes in the ashtrays.[78]

Sparer had also handled cases involving state residency laws, which denied welfare to needy individuals until they had resided in a given state for a certain period of time—in New York, the period was one year. In one case, Sparer represented a young woman, Minnie Nixon, who had moved away from her family in North Carolina to look for work in New York, where her two sisters already resided. According to Sparer's brief in the case, soon after Nixon arrived and began work as a domestic, complications from an unexpected pregnancy required that she stop work. When she applied for public assistance, the caseworker denied her application, asserting that she did not meet the residency requirement, that her continued presence in New York was "socially invalid," and that she should return to her estranged family in rural North Carolina. In arguing Nixon's appeal of the decision, Sparer framed the issue as a constitutional quandary: "whether the power to deny public assistance on the ground of 'social invalidity' is consistent with the equal protection . . . clause" of the Constitution.[79]

The overriding goal of Sparer's strategy was to create a constitutional "right to live"—in essence, a right to welfare or a guaranteed minimum income.[80] As a legal matter, the notion of a right to live—later adopted for very different purposes by the anti-abortion movement—was radical. One of its earliest and most complete explications was in a 1955 book by A. Delafield Smith, former attorney with the Social Security Board. The significance of the New Deal and the Social Security Act had been misunderstood, Smith wrote, and lawyers and courts were at fault because they had failed to apply "basic constitutional guarantees in the field of social welfare."[81] Smith argued that the government has a responsibility to respond to its citizens' basic needs and that, once those basic needs are identified, services should be made available to individuals without regard to whether they can pay for them.[82] According to Smith, "If that most fundamental of our constitutional guarantees, that test of all justice, the equal protection of the laws, were ever actually applied to social programs, the whole field of public welfare would soon be revolutionized."[83]

Smith's views did not find a champion until Sparer and, even then, Sparer stood virtually alone in his enthusiasm. According to Herbert Wechsler, professor at Columbia Law School, the right to live concept was "not valid as an interpretation of the Constitution."[84] Anthony Amsterdam, a law professor at Stanford University, simply stated that the principle was "of not much practical use."[85]

Sparer responded to these criticisms with analogies similar to those used by Smith. "We guarantee income to farmers for not producing crops," he told the New York Times. "We guarantee subsidies to railroads and to oil companies. It seems to me only reasonable that we should guarantee the subsidy of life to those who are starving and to those without shelter or medicine—reasonable not only on humanitarian grounds, but because there is a 14th Amendment, which guarantees equal protection of the laws."[86]

As Sparer and his colleagues formulated their litigation strategy, they felt that the equal protection clause offered their best chance to expand benefits available to recipients and to establish a federal guaranteed minimum income. The equal protection clause was the basis of most litigation involving race discrimination, so judges were accustomed to seeing it used as a vehicle for social change. Though the due process clause expressly referred to the government's obligation to protect "life" in addition to "liberty, or property," its controversial history ruled out arguments that the due process clause created a right to welfare.

Prior to 1937 the U.S. Supreme Court had regularly used the due process clause to invalidate state and federal laws that imposed limits on employers' use of labor. The most famous of these cases was *Lochner v. New York*, in which the Supreme Court struck down a New York state law that prohibited employment of bakery workers for more than ten hours a day or sixty hours a week.[87] The Court's straightforward rationale was that such a statute restricts liberty—in *Lochner*, the liberty of an employer to freely contract with an employee to work more than ten hours a day. This view of the due process clause—that it barred regulatory statutes affecting "life, liberty, or property"—was known as "substantive due process."

In 1937, however, buckling under pressure from President Roosevelt, who wanted assurances that his New Deal legislation would not be struck down, the Supreme Court abandoned the view that the due process clause could be used to invalidate entire statutes. Substantive due process was discredited as judicial overreaching, and the due process clause took on a purely procedural meaning: the state could not restrict life, liberty, or property without providing adequate opportunity to challenge the restriction. After 1937 courts could use the due process clause to require the government to improve hearing procedures; they could not use it to strike down statutes wholesale. The one controversial exception occurs when, as in *Roe v. Wade*, a majority of the Supreme Court justices agree that the statute violates a fundamental right, like privacy or procreation. Of necessity, then, activist lawyers turned to the equal protection clause as their primary vehicle for attacking discriminatory laws.

The fact was, however, that constitutional provisions and their philosophical bases were not so important to Sparer and his colleagues as the goal of creating an adequate minimum standard of welfare under the Constitution. The equal protection or due process clauses were merely the expedient vehicles for presenting the stories of welfare recipients to the courts in hopes that the courts would be compelled to reassess the constitutional protections of the Bill of Rights and use them to ease the economic plight of the poor.

By 1966 Sparer's litigation strategy was disseminated nationwide in publications read by poverty lawyers, and a national network of legal services lawyers was ready to bring cases to establish the constitutional rights of welfare recipients. At the same time, Sparer had not ignored one of the most important lessons of the civil rights movement: a successful litigation strategy must be linked to a social movement.

Chapter 4

The Movement

ITEM	UNIT PRICE
Furniture, Living Room	
Couch—regular	$30.00
Table—drop-leaf	15.00
Dishes	
Place setting (1 per person)	2.00
Serving bowl	1.00
Glass	.15
Sugar bowl	.70
Cleaning Equipment	
Dust pan	.50
Broom	1.40
Dust mop	1.60
Utility pail	.95
Scrub brush	.80

—From Special Needs Grants checklist, prepared by National Welfare Rights Organization, circa 1966

By the mid-1960s the popular view that poverty was a by-product of the social organization of the slums rather than a personal, moral failure had eliminated some of the stigma associated with welfare. The civil rights and women's movements contributed to recipients' increasing willingness to demand recognition of their rights. Welfare recipients were starting to organize.

Beginning in 1963 women on AFDC around the country met, often at the neighborhood centers established by the federal Community Action Program, to talk about their experiences. Gradually these discussion groups, many of which were organized by local chapters of Students for a Democratic Society, evolved into vehicles for AFDC recipients to enter the political arena and to express their discontent. In Minnesota, for example, recipients founded the AFDC League to present legislative ideas on welfare to elected representatives. In Massachusetts, welfare recipients organized Mothers for Adequate Welfare. Similar groups were active in California, New York, and Ohio.[1] By 1965 many local groups were firmly established and, with the support of neighborhood centers, beginning to use their muscle to confront local welfare administrations.

Most of these early welfare organizations had no access to lawyers, at least until federal legal services grants were made available in 1966. New York City was the exception. Beginning in 1963 Sparer and his MFY legal staff worked closely with MFY social workers, learning how the welfare bureaucracy worked and identifying weaknesses in the system. Social workers served on the front line, listening to "endless tales of woe" from recipients, then arguing with the caseworkers on the recipients' behalf. Sparer and his staff followed up the social workers' advocacy with litigation whenever the bureaucracy failed to respond. Because the New York City welfare department wanted to avoid precedent-setting cases and because, by and large, its caseworkers were welfare liberals who wanted to keep people on the rolls rather than to cut off benefits, a telephone call from an MFY attorney was often enough to resolve a dispute.[2]

At first MFY lawyers believed that individual advocacy would correct their clients' problems. For example, in 1964 MFY announced that its Legal Unit had "solved" the problems of those welfare applicants who had been denied public assistance because they did not meet New York residency requirements by "successfully taking a case through a Fair Hearing procedure conducted by the New York State Department of Welfare."[3] When the requirement continued to be misapplied, however, MFY lawyers recognized that this sort of advocacy would help individual recipients only, not change the structural problems of the welfare system. In 1965 MFY hired a community organizer, Ezra Birnbaum, to work with the Legal Unit to organize welfare recipients into effective political pressure groups.

Birnbaum's first organizing effort was a winter clothing campaign. Scouring the welfare regulations, Birnbaum and MFY lawyers discovered that special grants of up to $150 per person (above and beyond the basic needs grants) were available in New York to buy winter clothing for welfare recipients, yet these grants were seldom requested or awarded.[4] After consultation with recipients, MFY staff members drew up a checklist of winter clothing items for clients to fill out and present to their caseworkers.

The winter clothing campaign led to the creation of an organization of welfare recipients, the Lower East Side's Committee of Welfare Families, which took primary responsibility for administering the effort. By the end of the winter, the committee had obtained winter clothing for nearly two-thirds of its 100 members—a success rate that attracted more people to the group and strengthened MFY's organizing efforts.[5]

The success of the clothing campaign was also due in no small part to the liberal leadership of Mitchell Ginsberg, New York City's new commissioner of social services, appointed by Mayor John Lindsay on February 14, 1966. A tall fifty-year-old academic, his hair graying at the temples, Ginsberg was on a leave of absence from the Columbia School of Social Work, where he taught alongside MFY's Richard Cloward and served on MFY's board of directors.

Ginsberg was open in his disdain for the existing welfare system. His first act in office was to outlaw the midnight raids on welfare recipients—a practice supported by the preceding commissioner, James Dumpson—and he asked welfare rights organizations to bring to his attention any violations of the order. Ginsberg was also a vocal opponent of the New York residency laws, enacted by the legislature in 1962. "People in this country have a right to move from one place to another," Ginsberg told the *New York Times* in early 1966, only a few hours after being sworn in to office by Mayor Lindsay.[6]

Three weeks later Ginsberg announced his plans to substitute a standardized affidavit for the "time-consuming and degrading" income assessment procedure used to determine welfare eligibility. In addition, Ginsberg proposed a plan to allow welfare recipients to keep about half of their earnings without taking a reduction in benefits. And he announced other steps designed to "bring services closer to the people," including the creation of advisory groups of clients in each welfare center, the establishment of satellite welfare centers in housing projects, and the transfer of most decisions about individual clients from the central administration to the local centers. During his first year in office Ginsberg addressed caseworkers over closed circuit television, urging them to help locate people eligible for welfare who were not yet on the rolls.[7]

Ginsberg's liberal posture attracted a particular kind of caseworker to New York City's Department of Social Services: college graduates who wanted to address the "human needs and suffering" of the poor. These workers subscribed to Ginsberg's notion that most welfare recipients' problems could be solved if larger grants were targeted to their particular needs. They exercised their discretion to readily approve, within reason, recipients' applications for special grants or to replace lost welfare checks.[8]

Although a few caseworkers relished the punitive aspects of welfare— one fellow, so the story went, spent his vacations chasing putative fathers and monitoring the homes of female recipients for a man in the house— most agreed with Ginsberg that welfare regulations should be reformed.

By interpreting the rules as broadly as possible—for example, generously granting requests for winter clothing—and by sharing internal welfare department regulations with MFY lawyers, the caseworkers contributed in their own small way to welfare law reform and, indirectly, to MFY's organizing efforts.[9] At the same time, MFY's efforts provided leverage vis-à-vis the state and federal governments for the city welfare administration, admittedly run by "decent persons," to increase their administrative budgets and the public assistance budgets of their clients.[10]

Eager to capitalize on the success of the winter clothing campaign, Richard Cloward, Ezra Birnbaum, and four welfare recipients active in the campaign traveled to Syracuse, New York, in 1966 for a meeting of the Poor People's War Council on Poverty, a gathering of grass-roots activists from around the country. They had been considering the possibility of organizing a national movement of welfare recipients. In Syracuse they met George Wiley.

An African-American raised in a white middle-class community in Rhode Island, Wiley was an unlikely leader for a poor people's movement. Far from being a revolutionary, he was the first black member of a fraternity at Rhode Island State College, which he attended on a scholarship. Wiley completed a doctorate in chemistry at Cornell in 1957 and joined the faculty of Syracuse University in 1960. There he met and married Wretha Whittle, a politically active graduate student from Texas, and began to take a serious interest in the civil rights movement.

Wiley was a natural leader who listened attentively to opposing views and then responded with convincing, well-structured arguments. His first foray into political organizing was an unqualified success: he helped establish the Syracuse chapter of the Congress for Racial Equality (CORE)—an interracial civil rights organization founded in 1942—then led the chapter in a series of demonstrations over school segregation and employment discrimination. Wiley's campaigns caught the attention of James Farmer, national director of CORE, and in 1964 Farmer offered Wiley a job as associate national director of the organization. Wiley accepted, arranged a sabbatical from his faculty post and moved his family to New York City, where CORE was headquartered.

Despite Wiley's personal popularity and administrative skill, he left CORE in the winter of 1966, shut out in a power struggle that involved not only individual egos but the issue of black separatism. Wiley's wife and several of his key aides were white, and he believed that CORE should shift its emphasis from racial to economic issues to lead an integrated movement of poor people. But CORE and other civil rights groups were beginning to advocate racial separatism and militancy—and the exclusion of whites from the organization's staff.[11] The renegade Brooklyn chapter of CORE even announced that it would abandon its civil rights advocacy to set up "a new world of [its] own," an agricultural community for its black members.[12] Under the circumstances, there was no longer any room for someone like Wiley at CORE.

Looking for a new job, Wiley returned to his home base in Syracuse and attended the Poor People's War Council on Poverty. Cloward had served on the faculty advisory committee for CORE, and he spotted Wiley across the room. Maneuvering Wiley into a corner, he described MFY's winter clothing campaign. Then Cloward gave Wiley his pitch: he believed that a new movement of welfare recipients could be organized around a strategy developed by Cloward and his sociologist colleague at Columbia, Frances Fox Piven.[13]

The strategy was simple. The new movement would obtain government benefits for every eligible welfare recipient by filing hundreds of thousands of applications with local welfare agencies. This would result, Cloward and Piven believed, in a fiscal crisis that would lead to a call for a national guaranteed minimum income. According to Cloward, "Organizing the poor around welfare was a twofold idea: You could get immediate relief for a great many people, and you might even get a more far-reaching reform that would result in a permanent income floor to protect the poor from the worst ravages of poverty."[14] The strategy assumed—as was not inappropriate in the mid-1960s—that it would be politically impossible for the government to cut back welfare payments and to award recipients less than what was already a subsistence grant. Given the public's apparent desire to end poverty through social programs, Piven and Cloward believed that a welfare crisis could result only in more money for recipients.

Wiley was sold. He resigned from his tenured position at Syracuse University, moved his family to Washington, D.C., and joined a newly formed "liberal establishment" organization, the Citizens' Crusade Against Poverty. Within a few months of his arrival Wiley proposed to the Crusade's Board that it adopt Cloward and Piven's crisis theory as the organization's plan of action. When the board turned down the plan, Wiley struck out on his own, creating—virtually out of thin air—the Poverty/Rights Action Center (PRAC).[15]

PRAC opened in May 1966 with four staff members and funding from the Wileys themselves. Its major goal was to establish a national welfare rights movement.[16] The boundlessly energetic Wiley called, wrote, prodded, and pleaded with local welfare organizations to join the movement. In short order, Wiley turned a local recipients' march from Cleveland to Columbus, Ohio, into a national media event. With 200 marchers in Ohio and simultaneous demonstrations in fifteen states, the June 1966 march was a launching pad for many local welfare organizations, including the City-Wide Coordinating Committee of Welfare Groups in New York City. And in August 1966 Wiley assembled 136 recipients from 100 welfare organizations in twenty-four cities to discuss the formation of a national welfare movement.

During the next twelve months the fledgling organization held regional workshops and established membership rules, which required welfare recipients to pay $1 as dues. In August 1967, one year after its first meeting, the group held its inaugural convention as the National Welfare Rights Organization (NWRO). One hundred seventy-eight public assistance recipients attended, representing recipients in forty-five cities.[17] They elected Wiley executive director and adopted a set of goals for NWRO:

1. Adequate Income: A system that guarantees enough money for all Americans to live dignified lives above the level of poverty.
2. Dignity: A system that guarantees recipients the full freedoms, rights, and respect as all American citizens.
3. Justice: A fair and open system that guarantees recipients the full protection of the Constitution.
4. Democracy: A system that guarantees recipients direct participation in the decisions under which they must live.[18]

The NWRO's plan for achieving these goals, at least in its early phase, was heavily indebted to Piven and Cloward's crisis theory: the plan focused on increasing benefits for NWRO members and expanding the welfare rolls with the idea that a guaranteed minimum income would result. Wiley differed from Piven and Cloward only in his emphasis on membership in NWRO as a prerequisite to participating in its campaigns. He believed that a welfare crisis would provoke the desired response only if a coherent organization voiced the demands of welfare recipients.

Piven and Cloward had not addressed the practical problems of organizing recipients: What immediate, tangible benefits would make activism attractive to poor people?[19] But a group of New York City lawyers from MFY, the Center on Social Welfare Policy and Law, and the Legal Aid Society saw the potential for lawyers to work with recipients to provoke the crisis that Piven, Cloward, and NWRO envisioned.

Beginning in 1966 a group of poverty lawyers from around New York City met in the evenings, at coffee shops or at the offices of the Center on Social Welfare Policy and Law. Sparer was one of them, along with a young Legal Aid lawyer named David Gilman and a dozen others. "The meetings got started," Gilman recalls, "because we wanted to be responsive to the political aspect of the welfare rights movement and wanted to develop a legal strategy that coincided with the movement's goals."[20]

The meetings were not always productive. According to Gilman, "Everyone was overworked; everyone was scattered." Nevertheless, they came up with an idea that dovetailed with Piven and Cloward's crisis theory: they would flood the system with cases.

Given its liberal government, New York City seemed a more likely site for a model welfare program than for confrontations and litigation between recipients and caseworkers. In spite of his promising start, however, a year after Mitchell Ginsberg assumed control of New York's welfare agency, not much had changed. The state, which provided a large percentage of local welfare funds and exercised control over most administrative procedures relating to welfare, had yet to approve Ginsberg's proposals for reform. The city welfare administration was disrupted by work stoppages organized by the Social Service Employees Union, whose members were protesting high caseloads and low pay.[21] Welfare benefits were unchanged except for a 10 percent increase in the children's clothing allowance to $9.60 per month; the average basic monthly allowance for a New York City family on AFDC was set at about $172 a month.[22] Though much higher than the average welfare payment of less than $50 per month for families in Alabama and Mississippi, New York welfare benefits were still well below $3,130 per year, the federal poverty level for a family of four.[23]

In addition, recipients were at the mercy of their caseworkers for that portion of their benefits allocated as special grants, including most household items, clothing, and special dietary supplements. Some caseworkers would extend special benefits liberally; a caseworker concerned about the public fisc or distrustful of the recipient could deny the recipient's requests for special grants. These discretionary grants, initially envisioned as a way to link benefit levels to the actual cost of a minimum standard of living, varied widely among recipients with the same level of need.

With no reforms likely to be implemented in the near future, the commissioner's good intentions were wearing thin. "People on welfare can't eat sympathy," said Virginia Snipe, leader of the Welfare Recipients League, to reporters.[24] Despite Ginsberg's conciliatory tone and willingness to talk, welfare rights leaders were beginning to believe that confrontation was the best strategy.

Numbers were crucial to the crisis strategy envisioned by the poverty lawyers. As long as only a few lawyers handled only a fraction of the welfare cases, city government was happy to resolve those cases by simply reinstating the recipient or paying the minimal sums the recipients requested. But if the lawyers began to present the city with thousands of requests for special grants and requests for fair hearings when benefits were denied, the welfare department would have to make some changes in its system. Perhaps, as Piven and Cloward anticipated, city leaders would adopt a guaranteed minimum income.

Fair hearings, administrative appeals of caseworkers' decisions, were the central prong of the lawyers' strategy. Under federal law a fair hearing could be requested each time the city dropped an AFDC recipient from its rolls or refused a recipient's request for more welfare benefits under the special grant program.[25] A pending request for a fair hearing did not reverse the administration's decision; a recipient removed from the rolls remained off until a decision was rendered. Fair hearings were, however, intended to extend a modicum of fairness and objectivity to decisions concerning welfare benefits. Conducted by a hearing officer employed by the state, the hearings—sort of mini-trials—gave the welfare recipient and the city an opportunity to present evidence, with the hearing officer deciding who was right.

Fair hearings were rare; they had been undiscovered or ignored because virtually no poor people had lawyers and virtually no lawyers were familiar with the intricacies of the welfare system. When David Gilman first requested a fair hearing in late 1965, the welfare department questioned whether such a request was ethical. But Gilman proceeded with the hearing, the first of hundreds that he would handle over the next few years, with a success rate of close to 99 percent.[26]

Gilman was a quick-moving, confident man who, like his mentor, Ed Sparer, graduated from Brooklyn Law School. Sparer steered Gilman to the Legal Aid Society after his graduation in 1965 with the intention of infiltrating its ranks with aggressive, activist lawyers.

Although many of his early welfare cases were referrals from Sparer, Gilman himself was an avid organizer. He was intensely focused when he talked to groups about welfare rights, drawing them into the spirit of the communal struggle that he felt so strongly. In the evenings, Gilman traveled around the city in a beat-up station wagon with other welfare rights activists, visiting local churches and community centers where he preached to welfare recipients about their entitlements. When people asked how to get benefits, Gilman told them to come to Legal Aid. But the Legal Aid Society made clear to Gilman that it was not pleased with this approach—it preferred to see clients who came in of their own accord, not those who were drummed up off the streets. Nevertheless, Gilman persisted and, very quickly, he accumulated an enormous caseload.[27]

Gilman and the city's other welfare rights lawyers began their coordinated "crisis" strategy in 1966 with a special grants campaign. Like the winter clothing campaign, the special grants campaign centered around mimeographed lists, prepared by the movement's lawyers, setting out the items for which special grants were available—a couch ($30), a dinette set ($27), one place setting per family member, one chair per person, an alarm clock ($3), a dust mop ($1.60), and so on. The prices were low, sometimes unrealistically so, but the welfare department's home economists were charged with helping recipients find second-hand items or sales so that they could stay within their budget.[28]

The special grants campaign, scheduled to last three months, was launched in June 1967 by Gilman, who had moved from Legal Aid to the Center on Social Welfare Policy and Law to coordinate the campaign.[29] The itemized lists, distributed in the city's poor communities, were tirelessly explained by lawyers and organizers. At the conclusion of presentations to community groups, organizers sat at card tables and tallied up recipients' needs on the prepared form.

The completed forms were submitted, hundreds at a time, to the city's welfare department. If no special grants were forthcoming, Gilman or other lawyers followed up with requests for fair hearings. Although the lawyers worked closely with organizers, "it was easy to distinguish between the two," Richard Cloward said. "The lawyers stayed in their role. Lawyers were, primarily, a great source of reassurance to the clients, who feared retribution by the welfare administration. In Brooklyn, priests performed the same function."[30]

New York's special grants campaign was quickly taken up by movement leaders at the national level.[31] George Wiley saw the campaign as a potential organizing tool for NWRO. He would begin, he thought, by organizing current recipients around special grants in the states that had systems similar to New York's, then move to organizing poor people who were not yet on the rolls. Sparer believed that publicity generated by the special needs campaign would educate the judiciary and encourage the courts to deal compassionately and realistically with the welfare issues that the Center was beginning to litigate in federal court. Both Sparer and Wiley recognized that, at least in the short term, the special needs campaign could yield real benefits for their clients.

Along with many others from the social welfare establishment, New Deal veteran Elizabeth Wickenden dissented from the crisis theory in general and the special grants campaign in particular. She wrote to Richard Cloward in 1966 to argue that the central issue for welfare rights advocates should be the level of basic benefits and that the crisis proposed by Cloward was tangential to that issue. "There is no exercise of legal rights that can answer this problem which requires either a reduction in need through preventive measures, larger appropriations, or a combination of both," she asserted. In addition, Wickenden—who recalled a time when welfare had been purely a matter of state charity—believed that the result of provoking a crisis could be dire: "As one who has worked with Congress for thirty-three years and read *The Congressional Record* daily for most of that period, I feel that the greatest danger to a better public assistance policy is the tendency of advocates to underestimate the terrible vulnerability of the program to adverse pressures." According to Wickenden, "A terrible risk is being taken in giving opponents of these rights a useful excuse for their repeal or diminution."[32]

Wickenden's fears aside, the special needs campaign succeeded as few other welfare organizing efforts had. One of the key factors in its popularity, Gilman believes, was that it was legal and within the system at a time when many attempts to effect social change were not.[33] New York City officials needed only to look across the Hudson River to see a different tactic at work: in the midst of New York City's special grants campaign, in July 1967, a bloody five-day riot erupted in the ghetto of Newark, New Jersey. Businesses were systematically looted while National Guardsmen charged through the streets, firing on housing projects and stores. Calm was finally restored when Governor Richard Hughes ordered the National Guard to withdraw. The incidents in New Jersey were replicated in cities across the country. In Detroit, the "worst American riot in a century" left 43 dead, 7,000 arrested, 1,300 buildings destroyed, and 2,700 businesses looted.[34] In all, there were 164 racial disturbances in the country in the first nine months of 1967.[35]

At the end of the summer the special needs campaign was extended into the fall. To avoid extra paperwork, lawyers began submitting fair hearing requests along with the initial requests for special grants. By September

1967, more than 1,000 fair hearing requests had been filed with the welfare administration. By the end of the year, 4,233 requests had been filed. At the same time, the city's welfare rolls rose to 764,000 relief recipients, an increase of more than 28 percent over the previous year.[36]

The autumn of 1967 also brought a changing of the guard at the city welfare administration. In August, Mitchell Ginsberg accepted an appointment as the head of the Human Resources Administration, one of Mayor Lindsay's newly created "superagencies," which was designed to rationalize city government by combining all antipoverty and welfare programs within a single agency. While Ginsberg remained ultimately responsible for the city's welfare program, his post as welfare commissioner was filled by Jack Goldberg, a forty-seven-year-old social worker.[37] Like his predecessor, Goldberg was a member of the New York circle of activist social workers and an old friend of Piven and Cloward.

Though more than 90 percent of the welfare cases filed during the special grant and fair hearing campaigns were settled before a fair hearing actually occurred, the task of monitoring and staffing the hearings was immense.[38] The welfare department scheduled more than 3,000 fair hearings between September 1967 and January 1968. To handle them, special fair hearing offices were set up in all five boroughs of New York. The department appointed four new hearing officers to assist the two regular officers and called several officers out of retirement.[39]

On the recipients' side, Gilman worked out a master plan to keep track of the hearings. In the evenings he ran training sessions for welfare advocates. Lawyers, law students, social workers, and community organizers all represented recipients in fair hearings. "They came out of the woodwork," Gilman recalls. "It was a time of high activism. Everyone wanted to help."[40]

Nevertheless, there were never enough advocates to provide competent representation to all of the welfare recipients involved in the campaign. On one occasion, the city contacted the City-Wide Coordinating Committee for Welfare Groups to schedule 731 fair hearings. At wit's end, City-Wide's staff attorney despairingly wrote to NWRO's counsel that "with the present lack of adequate volunteer support on welfare cases I don't see how we will ever be able to handle 731 hearings."[41] "These cases must be handled," was his superior's uncompromising response.[42] The staff attorney struggled to comply. But when movement leaders assessed the initial effort a few months later, they wondered whether a truly massive fair hearing campaign would ever be possible, given the uneven ratio of lawyers to recipients.[43]

The 1967 campaign was successful, however, in three ways that were important to the movement's future. First, in New York City alone, millions of dollars in benefits were paid out to welfare recipients struggling to get by on subsistence benefits of, in 1967, about $2,500 per year for a family of four, substantially below the federal poverty line. Gilman estimated that by December 1967, $5 million had been paid out in special grants, with some clients receiving as much as $1,000 in one-shot payments.[44] The liberal attitudes of the administration and many of the caseworkers contributed to the magnitude of this success, of course. But without lawyers to present grant applications to the welfare department and follow up with hearing requests, money earmarked for special grants would have stayed in the government's coffers collecting interest—just as it had in 1965 when, though much more had been budgeted for the purpose, the average special grant given out by the city was only $40 per family.

Second, the campaign built a cohesive organization of recipients around the issue of welfare rights. More recipients were willing to support, and even join, NWRO and the City-Wide Coordinating Committee because the organizations had established a track record of actually delivering increased benefits to their members.

Finally, the 1967 campaign mobilized and organized lawyers in aid of the movement. The initial success of NWRO attracted the attention of civil rights lawyers, who joined forces with lawyers from legal services, Legal Aid societies, and the Center on Social Welfare Policy and Law. The NAACP Legal Defense and Educational Fund secured a Ford Foundation grant to hire additional lawyers, sponsor conferences on poverty law, and establish a resource center for all types of litigation relating to poverty, including welfare, consumer credit issues, and landlord-tenant cases. Carl Rachlin, formerly general counsel to CORE, became general counsel to NWRO, working closely with Ed Sparer at the Center. And the ACLU made a commitment to welfare rights through litigation handled by the Roger N. Baldwin Foundation.[45]

The special needs campaign brought together all of these groups to brainstorm about the role of lawyers and legal strategies in promoting change in the welfare system. "We are moving into an era of poverty law," Jack Greenberg of the NAACP Legal Defense Fund announced, "which is in some sense comparable to the civil rights law of the mid-1930s."[46]

At the same time, George Wiley recognized that lawyers and legal strategies had limited utility in a grass-roots movement. Like Ed Sparer, he believed that lawyers, organizers, social workers, and recipients must work together. For example, on a trip to open an NWRO office in San Francisco, Wiley sized up two legal services lawyers working with the group: "The two attorneys . . . are working closely with welfare rights and . . . are both very committed to welfare rights organizing in the Bay Area and want to see it happen. However, neither of them has a particularly good grasp of what is entailed in developing organization. . . . They do not grasp the inner dynamics of organizing, and [it is] their basic legal approach to advocacy pressing for policy change—and being hung-up about the problems in California welfare law—that makes organizing difficult." To overcome the limitations of their legal training, Wiley stressed that the lawyers should rely on the organizing resources and staff of NWRO before embarking on any welfare rights project.[47]

In contrast, Wiley viewed the special needs campaign as a model for collaboration between lawyers and organizers. With Wiley's encouragement, New York's fair hearing campaign continued into 1968, but with a more aggressive edge. NWRO members were eager to push for rapid changes in the welfare system. Moreover, there were rumors that the special grant system would be discontinued, and movement leaders wanted to get as much as possible out of the system before it was too late.[48]

The new season of protests began in April 1968, when organized groups of welfare recipients demanding special grants staged demonstrations and sit-ins at welfare centers throughout New York. Following his predecessor's lead, Goldberg openly sympathized with the demonstrators and expressed his opposition to the existing welfare system: "This department ought to be providing services to people and get out of the business of having people come as supplicants and saying they need something and having an individual judgment made. We need some kind of form of a guaranteed minimum income."[49]

But without the state's cooperation, Goldberg could take no action, and the confrontations continued. At the end of June, a dozen welfare recipients staged a sit-in demonstration in Goldberg's office at 250 Church Street. A few days later, thirty-eight welfare rights demonstrators were arrested as they blocked the door to the welfare department's headquarters.[50]

Meanwhile, the welfare rolls in New York City continued to rise. By September 1968 the head count was more than 900,000. The policies of

Ginsberg and Goldberg accounted for some of the increase: a Columbia University study showed that 58 percent of the applications for AFDC were accepted in 1965; by mid-1967, during Ginsberg's tenure, the figure was up to 75 percent. In addition, community organizers had succeeded in educating many new recipients to assert their right to benefits. In July 1968, for example, the Center on Social Welfare Policy and Law sponsored publication of a handbook entitled "Your Right to Welfare," which explained in clear, understandable terms the legal rights of welfare recipients.[51]

As the welfare rolls continued to expand, the city, state and federal governments were paying out more than ever in benefits. New York City's special grant payments alone reached $10 million to $12 million a month in the summer of 1968. In late June, the state announced that something had to give. That something would be the special grants system.[52]

The state proposed that special grants be replaced by a "flat grant" system. Under the new system, scheduled to go into effect September 1, 1968, recipients would not be issued checks to cover specific, itemized needs. Instead, each recipient would receive, in addition to regular grants for housing, food, and utilities, $100 a year in four installments of $25 to cover clothing and household items.[53]

Goldberg defended the plan as the first of a series of steps necessary to eliminate unfairness in the welfare system and to set national standards for benefits.[54] And, in fact, the plan did eliminate the discretionary aspect of special needs grants to which welfare rights activists had objected. The problem was that it replaced special grants—which some recipients had parlayed into thousands of dollars of necessary benefits—with a mere $100 a year. New York state had chosen the course predicted by Elizabeth Wickenden: it ignored previously established minimum standards and acknowledged needs of recipients—such as winter clothing or household items—and, when pressed, eliminated programs designed to meet those needs dollar for dollar.

The flat grant proposal, condemned by welfare rights organizations as a thinly veiled attempt to reduce benefits, set off heated protests among welfare recipients. At the end of August, 600 relief recipients rioted near City Hall; nine of the rioters were hospitalized in a confrontation with more than 200 police officers. The month ended with disruptive tactics directed at the city's neighborhood welfare centers and the creation of a "war room" at the welfare department headquarters to monitor the disruptions.[55] These attacks were often supported by caseworkers, many of whom demonstrated alongside the recipients. In return for caseworkers' support, NWRO's lawyers agreed to represent caseworkers who were arrested during the protests.[56]

Despite their vigor, the protests had no discernible effect on the city or state administrations. The state had approved the flat grant policy, and, with more than 1.5 million recipients, it simply couldn't afford to rescind the decision. The policy went into effect in September as scheduled. And though violent protests continued until the end of the year, the system was not changed.[57]

By eliminating the welfare rights movement's principal organizing tool—itemized grants—the flat grant system thwarted efforts to organize recipients.[58] Groups had little to offer recipients in the way of tangible rewards, which were crucial to attracting and maintaining membership. The movement also lost an important public relations tool. Unlike the special needs grants, the flat grant system had the appearance of fairness—the welfare department no longer seemed to be stingily doling out largess one bobby pin at a time.

Further, the flat grant system brought an end to the winter clothing, special needs, and fair hearing campaigns—the heady, revolutionary strategies based on Piven and Cloward's crisis theory. In practice, when a backlog of fair hearings began to develop and the demands for benefits started to mount, there was no crisis. The state simply cut back benefits. Though Piven and Cloward deemed the strategy a success because of the large sums of money transferred from the government to the poor during the campaign, the introduction of the flat grant system demonstrated that a livable, guaranteed minimum income would have to be achieved through some other means.

In the late summer of 1968 NWRO issued an "action proposal" to its members. "Up to now," NWRO acknowledged, "the Welfare Rights Movement has been built by setting up mass benefit campaigns which put money into people's pockets and which lead our groups to quick successes. This attracts members, builds loyalty and helps people quickly and visibly." The new organizing techniques that NWRO proposed to replace the fair hearing and special needs campaigns testified to the welfare organization's desperation. Ideas for creating a mass movement of welfare recipients were not only scarce but, as was soon apparent, ineffectual.[59]

First, NWRO recommended that organizers try to reproduce mass benefit campaigns by searching their state laws for loopholes through which the new regulations could be circumvented—a tactic that yielded minimal results.

NWRO also proposed a Spend the Rent Campaign, recommending that recipients dramatize the inadequacy of their benefits by spending rent grants on food and clothing that were once covered by special needs grants. According to NWRO, local organizers should begin the campaign by "training people how to resist evictions (sitting on furniture, mobilizing crowds in hallways so police cannot remove furniture, and putting furniture back in building if it is put on [the] street)." The campaign fizzled, however, when recipients and their families were unwilling to risk their homes for an unwinnable campaign.[60]

Alternatively, NWRO urged recipients to spend all of their grants on rent, gas, light, and other bills, leaving insufficient money to buy food for their families. Again, however, the price expected of recipients—hunger—was unrealistically high, and the campaign was never initiated.[61]

In fact, the most effective campaign, from the standpoint of publicity, was a nationwide crusade to obtain credit for NWRO members at department stores—a campaign in the style of Saul Alinsky, the famous Chicago-based radical who advocated organizing on the community level around local issues without (in contrast to the Cloward and Piven crisis strategy) an overarching goal. Though Sears Roebuck refused to extend credit, Montgomery Ward, Brooklyn's Abraham & Strauss department store, and a number of local stores in other cities extended small amounts of credit to NWRO members. But the campaign ended in disarray when few welfare recipients applied for credit accounts for fear of defaulting on their charges.[62]

With NWRO's mass membership drives effectively over, the organization's numbers stabilized at about 20,000 members nationwide, and the locus of social change shifted to NWRO's legislative lobbying and the litigation strategy developed by Sparer—a strategy that, through the courts, had the potential to bring decisive reform to the welfare system and even increase the baseline public assistance grant available to recipients.

Chapter 5
Southern Strategy

Q: So it is your understanding that if a man is not living in the home regularly, and visited once a week for the purpose of cohabiting, that mother could be denied or would be denied or should be denied aid, because of the application of the substitute father regulation?

A: It's sort of a hard thing to say, because, you see, I don't just use my judgment. When I find a situation such as this, I go back to the office and discuss it with the case work supervisor, and then as soon as I can get all the facts together, then I try to make a decision.

> —Deposition of Jacquelyn Stancil, caseworker, Alabama State Department of Pensions and Security, March 9, 1967 (*Smith v. King*, Civ. Action No. 2495-N)

The litigation strategy to constitutionalize welfare owed much to the NAACP Legal Defense and Educational Fund and its campaign against racial segregation. Like the NAACP Legal Defense Fund lawyers, Ed Sparer and his colleagues at the Center on Social Welfare Policy and Law mapped out which issues should be litigated, in which courts they were likely to succeed, and how they should be presented. And, just as the NAACP Legal Defense Fund attempted to manage the desegregation campaign, the Center made every effort to dictate the course of all litigation in the welfare area.[1]

Sparer wanted to begin the campaign by litigating first in the South, not only because the southern states' poverty ensured that the situation for welfare recipients was worse than in the northern states, but also because of the litigation successes of the civil rights movement in the South. That movement had exposed Southern federal judges to litigation for social change, and Sparer thought that they might be more willing than northern judges to strike down offensive state laws. By converting welfare rights into a southern civil rights issue, Sparer hoped to gain some early momentum for his campaign.[2]

In addition to its regular efforts to train legal services lawyers in welfare law, the Center initiated a program to educate recipients and social workers in the South about welfare rights issues. In its first full year of operation, 1966, the Center published the "Mississippi Welfare Rights

Handbook" and the "Georgia Welfare Rights Handbook" and completed a study of the uniformity—or lack thereof—in the application of welfare law in Georgia.[3]

In the fall of 1966 Sparer conducted advocacy training in Louisiana for attorneys, community leaders, social workers, and nongovernment welfare professionals. Because copies of the state's welfare regulations were virtually impossible to obtain from the state itself, Sparer arranged for a Center attorney to visit Washington, D.C., and copy Louisiana's welfare regulations from the files of the Department of Health, Education, and Welfare prior to the training. Though attendance by lawyers was spotty, a few weeks after the program Carl Rachlin wrote that "it is clear that organization of welfare clients will take place as a result of this conference."[4]

To further consolidate its presence in the South, the Center worked out an arrangement with Jack Greenberg, legal director of the NAACP Legal Defense Fund. The fund had strong ties throughout the South as the result of its desegregation work. Under the agreement, the Center would review and, if it chose, serve as co-counsel on all welfare cases referred to the Legal Defense Fund.[5]

With this agreement in hand, the Center set about convincing the larger network of southern civil rights lawyers that poverty was a legitimate civil rights issue. Like Carl Rachlin, who joined NWRO after leaving as general counsel to CORE, many former civil rights advocates were alienated by the black power movement and by the increasing violence of civil rights groups.[6] Carl Rachlin's allegiance to the welfare rights movement was important in tapping into this network of civil rights lawyers, many of whom had been mobilized as members of the Lawyers Constitutional Defense Committee (LCDC)—organized by Rachlin, Mel Wulf of the ACLU, and others—as the legal arm of Freedom Summer in 1964.[7] Several civil rights groups had recruited more than 1,000 volunteers—mostly white northern college students—to spend the summer of 1964 in the South registering black voters and teaching at "freedom schools." Anticipating violent opposition, the LCDC enlisted dozens of northern lawyers to defend the Freedom Summer volunteers against claims brought by local authorities and to initiate lawsuits when they were harassed or beaten.

The promise of ground-breaking legal work at the Center had already attracted lawyers who, even a few years before, would not have considered poverty law. For example, one new attorney at the Center, Stephen Wizner, began his professional life at the Department of Justice after graduating from the University of Chicago Law School in 1964. While in law school, Wizner had attended an address in which Attorney General Robert Kennedy urged lawyers to join in the "unconditional War on Poverty to which President Johnson has summoned all of us. . . . Rarely if ever do the best lawyers and the best law firms work with the legal problems that beset the most deprived segments of our society."[8]

Wizner was galvanized by Kennedy's speech, but instead of joining the War on Poverty he joined the criminal division of the Department of Justice, hoping for a chance to work with Kennedy.[9] Two years later, after Sparer had mapped out a challenging constitutional campaign that provided an attractive alternative to routine welfare and housing disputes, Wizner joined the Center to begin his career in poverty law.

In fact, the Center threatened to institutionalize a two-tiered poverty bar, a potentially devastating problem for the fledgling legal services movement. Ambitious lawyers who wanted to litigate important constitutional cases would be lured only by the Center and other groups specializing in impact litigation. Neighborhood offices would be left, by and large, with the same nonactivist lawyers who had always worked at Legal Aid societies.

To address this potential problem, the federal Office of Economic Opportunity established the Reginald Heber Smith Fellowship Program, which was designed to involve neighborhood offices in impact cases while enticing bright young law school graduates to represent clients on the grass-roots, community level by giving them a prestigious fellowship. The explicit duty of all fellowship winners, known as Reggies, was to engage in legal work that would have a broad impact on poverty.[10]

The Reggie program presented yet another opportunity for Sparer to spread the gospel of his litigation strategy. In 1967 the first group of Reggies assembled at the University of Pennsylvania for an intensive five-week training session. It was an impressive group. One-third had been on their respective law reviews; many had clerked for federal or state court judges. One of the Reggies had graduated first in his class at the University of Chicago Law School, and several others were in the top 10 percent of their graduating classes.[11]

Sparer lectured to the group for a full week about welfare law and his litigation agenda. At the end of their orientation session, fully indoctrinated with Sparer's views, the Reggies dispersed to thirty-nine neighborhood legal services offices and backup centers around the country.[12]

The Center also tried to anticipate the major legal issues that would be raised by federal challenges to state welfare laws and devoted significant staff time to research and writing on those issues. Aside from the "right to live" theory itself, the question of whether the federal courts could exercise jurisdiction over states' welfare laws posed the major hurdle. It was a central issue—the prerequisite to Sparer's entire litigation strategy. The ambiguity of the Social Security Act of 1935 left much room for states to argue that they retained the prerogative to design their own welfare programs and set priorities without federal oversight.

The research on this issue began in earnest in the fall of 1966 when Robert Cover, a first-year law student at Columbia Law School, walked into the Center. At twenty-three, Cover was already a civil rights veteran; as a Princeton undergraduate, he spent nine months in Albany, Georgia, working for the Student Nonviolent Coordinating Committee (SNCC), one of the civil rights groups organizing northern students during Freedom Summer. During that time, Cover was arrested in a civil rights demonstration and jailed for three weeks. While waiting for his trial he went on a hunger strike and was beaten by other prisoners. Cover's respect for the civil rights lawyer who defended him, C. B. King, was the major factor in Cover's decision to go to law school.[13]

While seeking the same sense of political purpose and community in New York that he had found with SNCC, Cover heard about the Center and volunteered as an intern. It was a stroke of luck for the Center. Cover was one of the most talented law students at Columbia; two years later, even before he graduated, he was invited to join the law school faculty.[14]

Wizner gave Cover a writing assignment: draft a memo on federal court jurisdiction over state welfare laws and practices. Cover went away for a few weeks to work on his project. Wizner didn't have high expectations of a first-year law student, but he hoped that Cover might provide him with some useful research. Cover returned, however, with an astute memo synthesizing the most persuasive arguments available to poverty lawyers seeking to overcome obstacles to federal judicial relief. The memo placed particular emphasis on the political and judicial climate in the South, where the unfavorable experiences of civil rights litigants in the state courts lent special weight to arguments for federal jurisdiction.[15]

According to Cover, federal judicial review of state welfare laws was a necessity, particularly because administrative review—that is, review of recipients' claims by federal or state welfare agencies—was demonstrably futile. Though the federal Department of Health, Education, and Welfare was required to assess the conformity of state welfare laws to federal standards, in the thirty years since the passage of the Social Security Act it had conducted only sixteen conformity hearings; the most recent was initiated by Elizabeth Wickenden and her colleagues in 1960 when Louisiana threatened to cut off AFDC funds to more than 23,000 illegitimate children.[16] Similarly, most state welfare schemes provided no means to administratively challenge the general validity of welfare regulations. At best, recipients could request a fair hearing to address the decision affecting them and then seek individual review by courts if they were still dissatisfied.[17]

Resorting to the state courts for review of welfare laws was equally inappropriate and ineffective, according to Cover. In the South, state courts were notoriously hostile to the interests of blacks, who made up a large proportion of welfare recipients there. Cover wrote simply and persuasively that "the legal questions presented by welfare cases are, for the most part, federal. . . . Not only are federal courts likely to be more familiar with the questions presented than are the state courts, but federal interpretation will lead to a more uniform application of the Social Security Act throughout the nation."[18] Wizner promptly circulated the memo to poverty lawyers around the country so that they could incorporate the arguments into their federal court briefs.[19]

Cover's arguments were squarely tested in the first welfare case heard by the U.S. Supreme Court. In accordance with the Center's strategy, that case, *King v. Smith*, was from the deep South: Selma, Alabama, a center of civil rights activity throughout the 1960s.[20] The plaintiff, Sylvester Smith, was a poor black woman with four children living in a shack on the outskirts of the town. She earned $20 a week as a waitress. From time to time, a married man named Willie E. Williams visited Smith in the evenings, returning in the morning to his wife and nine children in nearby Tyler, Alabama.[21]

In August 1966 Smith sent a letter to President Johnson complaining about the inadequacy of her welfare grant and about other Alabama welfare policies.[22] A presidential aide forwarded the letter to welfare officials in Alabama. A few weeks later, perhaps by coincidence, Smith's caseworker became suspicious that Smith had a live-in boyfriend who was not contributing to the support of her children. On October 11, 1966, Smith received a letter from her caseworker informing her that, effective September 30, 1966, her welfare benefits were cut off under Alabama's "substitute father" rule, a variation of the man-in-the-house regulation in eighteen states. Under Alabama's law, a single mother on welfare could not "regularly and frequently cohabit" with a man, whether or not he provided any financial support and whether or not he was obligated to provide any support.[23] If the welfare department incorrectly suspected an AFDC recipient of cohabiting, she could only clear up the mistake by providing at least two references "in a position to know," such as "law-enforcement officials; ministers; neighbors; grocers."[24]

The Center attorneys, who were on the lookout for southern plaintiffs, heard about Smith from Donald Jelinek, a New York lawyer who first went to Selma to work for the LCDC.[25] When Freedom Summer was over, some of the LCDC lawyers, Jelinek among them, had stayed in the South to continue providing legal representation to poor blacks. At the urging of Ed Sparer, Carl Rachlin, and others, their focus on civil rights gradually gave way to legal work that addressed poverty as well as race.[26] The LCDC's work remained controversial, however. When Jelinek met Smith, he was facing criminal charges initiated by the state of Alabama because of his activities.[27] Because these charges prevented him from representing Smith in what might be an important test case for the Center, Jelinek called Sparer.

The *King* case was only one of several substitute father cases that the Center was working on in the fall of 1966. Others were from Georgia, Arkansas, and Michigan. Copying the NAACP's practices, Sparer and his colleagues weighed each to decide which should be litigated with a view toward creating a precedent. Because the Alabama regulation was particularly broad and harsh, and because Smith was a sympathetic southern plaintiff, the lawyers decided that *King* gave them the best shot at winning. Martin Garbus was given primary responsibility for the case.

Garbus had joined the Center in late 1966 as codirector with Sparer. A 1959 graduate of New York University Law School, he had specialized in civil liberties and first amendment litigation at a succession of small, politically influential New York City firms. Reflecting the emerging poverty law hierarchy, Garbus had declined invitations to work at the MFY Legal Unit. "I wasn't interested in that storefront stuff," he later explained. But the Center was a different matter: "Test case work was a new, rich area."[28]

Garbus' job was to relieve Sparer of most of his litigation duties so that Sparer could devote his time to the activities that he preferred: speaking and writing. At first, much of Garbus' time was spent building up the Center's form files with model litigation papers that could be quickly revised to fit a particular case. "Our idea," recalls Garbus, "was that we would get a case one day and go to court the next day."[29]

Garbus modeled his draft of Smith's complaint on a complaint filed by the Center challenging Georgia's "employable mother" regulations. During each harvest season, counties in rural Georgia closed all AFDC cases of mothers with children over three years old, forcing the mothers to work in the fields for substandard wages.[30]

The model wasn't quite right, but no one had the time to notice. The Georgia employable mother case was framed as a class action brought on behalf of all "needy Negro mothers and dependent Negro children" wrongfully denied benefits. The Center lawyers chose this class in the Georgia case because, they alleged, employable mother regulations were used to single out and deny benefits to African-American women rather than white welfare mothers.[31] By alleging that the regulations disproportionately affected blacks, the Center lawyers hoped to receive the "strict scrutiny" reserved for classifications based on race—a level of judicial review that is almost impossible to satisfy.

Garbus copied this class in his complaint for Smith, alleging that the state of Alabama had violated the rights of all "needy Negro mothers and dependent Negro children" by applying "the 'substitute father' regulation in such a manner as to disqualify Negro applicants and recipients but not white applicants and recipients."[32] In his haste to file the case and secure strict scrutiny of the regulations, Garbus put aside the messy factual issues that this allegation raised: whether more "Negro" applicants cohabited and whether the ratio of blacks to whites among those whose benefits were cut off matched the ratios of those receiving welfare.

But before the Center was ready to proceed with Smith's complaint, a group of Washington, D.C., legal services lawyers filed its own lawsuit, *Smith v. Board of Commissioners.* The suit, filed in the District of Columbia federal court, attacked the District's substitute father regulation. Garbus quickly obtained a copy of their papers and, generally critical of "young, inexperienced" legal services lawyers, he concluded that the papers were badly written. Besides, the case had been assigned to an unsympathetic judge. It seemed likely that the lawyers would lose this first attack on the substitute father rule and establish an unfavorable precedent.

Garbus used his best efforts to persuade the Washington legal services lawyers to withdraw their complaint.[33] They refused. They had their own careers to consider, and they were not about to subvert them for the glory of Garbus and the Center. More importantly, they could not ethically send away desperate clients simply because the Center felt that *Smith v. Board of Commissioners* was not suitable for test case litigation.

While Garbus and the legal services lawyers argued, the defendants asked the judge to dismiss the complaint. Because welfare benefits were merely charity, they asserted, the District of Columbia could distribute those benefits on any basis it wished, free from the interference of the federal government.

The judge agreed, writing in his two-page opinion that "payments of relief funds are grants and gratuities. Their disbursement does not constitute payment of legal obligations that the government owes."[34] The judge also ruled that federal courts had no authority to strike down state welfare practices. The case was dismissed in October 1966.

The judge's decision—the first published judicial pronouncement on the legality of substitute father regulations—created a difficult hurdle for the Center in its attempt to attack substitute father rules in the South. The Center had offered only limited assistance to the Washington, D.C., legal services lawyers, but now it stepped in to help appeal the judge's decision. While the appeal was pending, the Center filed the *King* case on December 2, 1966, in federal district court in Montgomery.[35] The defendants— Governor George Wallace; the state of Alabama; and the state welfare commissioner, Ruben King—were represented by Mary Lee Stapp, a lawyer from the Alabama Department of Pensions and Security.

The case went forward quickly under Judge Frank J. Johnson, who had used his authority to single-handedly desegregate the Alabama public school system a few years before.[36] In the last week of December, Johnson granted the Center's motion to convene a three-judge "constitutional court" to hear the case. With his ruling, Johnson recognized that the case raised significant constitutional issues and gave the parties the right to appeal directly to the Supreme Court rather than go through the time-consuming process of appealing to the intermediate Court of Appeals.

Predictably, Alabama sought to have the case dismissed. The state pointed out that the Department of Health, Education, and Welfare had allowed the substitute father regulations to stand for fifteen years, during which time similar regulations were adopted by other states. HEW's long acquiescence, Alabama asserted, indicated that the substitute father regulation was consistent with federal law. But Johnson denied the state's motion and set the case down for trial in May 1967.[37]

As the trial date neared, the lawyers and staff sociologist at the Center gathered information to bolster their claim that the substitute father regulations were racially discriminatory. Their intention was to prepare a "Brandeis brief," named after the Progressive-era trial lawyer Louis

Brandeis.[38] In true Progressive fashion, a Brandeis brief was designed to present the court with social science data—facts that might be considered by a legislature—rather than the narrow legal arguments traditionally considered by courts.

The Brandeis brief submitted in *King v. Smith* informed the court that of 184 welfare cases closed under the substitute father regulations in Dallas County, Alabama, from July 1964 through January 1967, 182 involved black families. During June 1966, in seven representative Alabama counties, every one of the more than 600 recipients cut off welfare was black.[39]

Center attorneys also anticipated that Alabama would claim that Smith had not exhausted her remedies before applying to the state court—that is, she had not requested an administrative fair hearing to challenge the termination of her benefits. They prepared two counterarguments based on Robert Cover's research: first, fair hearings were not meaningful remedies because they were held *after* benefits were terminated, and, second, welfare recipients whose benefits were terminated were not informed of their right to fair hearings. None of the 18,000 Alabama women cut off from AFDC because of the substitute father regulation had ever requested a fair hearing; in the three and a half years since state welfare commissioner King took office there had been about 75,000 welfare terminations and five fair hearings. The Center argued that Smith had no real option but to go to federal court.[40]

Because the parties disagreed only about the legal interpretation of the facts, not the facts themselves, the parties agreed to forgo a trial. Instead, on May 15, 1967, they submitted all of their evidence to the three-judge court.

A few weeks later, on June 23, 1967, the District of Columbia Court of Appeals issued its decision in the appeal of *Smith v. Board of Commissioners*.[41] The court found that because the Washington, D.C., welfare recipients had failed to request fair hearings when their benefits were stopped, the federal court did not have jurisdiction over their claims. The lower court's decision was affirmed on grounds that opened the way for a similar decision in the Alabama case.

This was unwelcome news for the Center, especially because the District of Columbia Court of Appeals was generally acknowledged to be second in status only to the U.S. Supreme Court. The Alabama federal court would likely pay special attention to the decision in *Smith v. Board of Commissioners*.

As the months passed, Garbus braced himself for a ruling against his client. Finally, on November 8, 1967, the Alabama federal district court announced its decision: a victory for Smith. Exercising federal jurisdiction to strike down the Alabama state law, the court found that the substitute father regulation violated the equal protection clause of the Fourteenth Amendment by denying aid to needy children on a basis not rationally related to the children's need for benefits—that is, whether their mother cohabited.[42] The court declined, however, to accept the plaintiffs' characterization of the case as a civil rights matter: "While the plaintiffs placed considerable emphasis upon facts strongly indicating that the 'substitute father' regulation was designed to discriminate and has the effect of discriminating against Negroes, by reason of the facts presented, this case does not rest upon racial considerations and therefore the decision should not rest upon such considerations. On the contrary, this decision should be and will be designed to enure to the benefit of all needy children regardless of their race or color. The Equal Protection Clause is not restricted in its application to the protection of the rights of Negroes. It is more far-reaching, protecting the rights of any identifiable class."[43]

In light of this decision, the district court ordered Alabama to immediately reinstate to the AFDC rolls every child who had been declared ineligible for welfare under the substitute father rule. Alabama resisted, and within a month the state appealed directly to the Supreme Court, which scheduled oral argument for April 22, 1968—the same day that the Poor People's March on Washington, organized by Martin Luther King, Jr., was to begin in Atlanta.

Alabama's brief to the Supreme Court simply reiterated the state's position that the substitute father regulation was a fair, rational rule, well within the bounds of state power to administer welfare to its residents. In addition, the state argued that it had only limited resources for welfare payments, threatening that it would be forced to reduce welfare benefits to all other recipients if the Court struck down the substitute father regulations. Alabama estimated that it would cost the state an additional $645,000 a year to support children with "substitute fathers," not to mention the cost of hiring additional caseworkers to handle their cases.[44]

In response to Alabama's arguments, Garbus raised a grab bag of constitutional issues of varying degrees of persuasiveness. In addition to asserting that the regulation violated the equal protection clause, Garbus added a new claim that the substitute father regulation violated Smith's constitutional right to privacy by giving welfare caseworkers license to pry into her personal life.[45] Garbus also inserted the argument that AFDC recipients have a right to a fair hearing before, rather than after, termination of their benefits, and he alluded to the right to live, noting that several scholars had made a "persuasive argument that the needy have a *right* to receive welfare aid."[46] Though the arguments were unlikely to be the basis of the Supreme Court's opinion in *King v. Smith*, Garbus used the brief to begin educating the Court about welfare issues that the justices would probably see in future cases.

In writing the Supreme Court brief on Smith's behalf, Garbus did not, however, abandon the race discrimination claims rejected by the District Court. Garbus noted that the only benefit program for which the substitute father policy was in force, AFDC, was also the only public assistance program in Alabama with more black than white recipients. In addition, Smith's brief noted a 1963 study of Alabama's AFDC recipients indicating that "there were 16 times as many Negro illegitimate children receiving aid as white children" and "45 times as many Negro illegitimates in Alabama as white illegitimates." According to Garbus, policies "aimed at cutting off aid to families where there were illegitimate children would strike primarily at Negro families."[47]

Garbus' colleagues at the Center felt that his draft brief was too ambitious. Because Garbus had left the Center a few months before, taking responsibility for litigating *King* with him, their input had been minimal. The brief raised an exhaustive series of constitutional issues, ranging from equal protection to self-incrimination to privacy, but made only the barest allusion to the statutory issue of whether Alabama's regulations were consistent with federal law.

Afraid that Garbus was throwing away the recipients' strongest claim in the brash hope of garnering an important constitutional victory, the Center prepared an amicus brief addressing the statutory question of whether the substitute father regulation violated the federal Social Security Act. Under that law, a needy child is entitled to benefits when the supporting parent is dead, absent, or incapacitated. Alabama's regulation stated that even though Smith's friend had not fathered any of her children and had no legal obligation to support them, he could be considered a parent, so that his occasional presence in the household disqualified Smith's children from receiving AFDC.[48] The Center asserted—in an argument ignored by Garbus—that under the Social Security Act a parent must be a person who is legally responsible for the children, not merely someone who is occasionally present in the home.[49]

Before Garbus left New York for the Supreme Court argument, Steve Wizner and other lawyers familiar with the case prepared Garbus by "mooting" him—that is, staging a mock argument, listening to his presentation, and asking questions that might be posed by the justices.

His preparation paid off: the real argument went well for Garbus. The toughest questions came from Justice John M. Harlan, who interrogated Garbus about the power of the federal government to override the welfare standards adopted by a state. In response, Garbus trotted out the arguments prepared the year before in Robert Cover's memo. Harlan seemed particularly impressed when Garbus informed the Court that a full 83% of the AFDC payments in Alabama were made with federal money. The news that HEW had ineffectively controlled state substitute father regulations was also of particular interest to the justices. Although HEW had announced more than a year before that it would cut off federal welfare funds to Alabama unless the state administered its programs fairly with regard to race, Alabama had continued to enforce substitute father regulations without any repercussions. Further, HEW had apparently taken no action against Georgia, Arkansas, and Mississippi, states with policies similar to those in Alabama.[50]

In contrast, Mary Lee Stapp, who represented the state of Alabama, faced genuine hostility from certain members of the Court. Both Justice William J. Brennan and Chief Justice Earl Warren seemed to grow impatient when Stapp was unable to defend the state's substitute father policy without making covert appeals to racism.[51]

Watching Stapp argue to the Court, Garbus counted the votes of Justice Brennan and Chief Justice Warren for his side. He also believed that he had Justice Abe Fortas' support. An old friend of Elizabeth Wickenden from their days working for President Roosevelt during the New Deal, Fortas had taken a personal interest in the emerging welfare rights struggle. In fact, in March 1966 he gave a speech at New York University Law School, entitled "Equal Rights for Whom?" that anticipated many of the issues raised in *King*.[52] But years of litigating had taught Garbus that it is impossible to tell what a judge is really thinking by his comments during oral argument. He tried not to count on anyone's vote.

Garbus returned to New York to await the Supreme Court's decision. It was not a relaxing time. Garbus had accepted a position at the ACLU's newly created Roger Baldwin Foundation. He was still feeling his way in the job; several of Garbus' co-workers privately expressed doubts about his ability to handle the demands of his new position.[53] There was also more than a little tension in the office concerning the issue of what the new foundation should actually be doing. Roger Baldwin, the aging founder of the ACLU, expressed serious misgivings about the foundation's bold attempts to address issues outside the traditional civil rights sphere—migrant workers, juvenile delinquency, and welfare.[54] While he tried to weather the storm, Garbus hoped that his successes in court would divert his colleagues' attention from office politics.

On June 17, 1968, Garbus received a telegram from the clerk of the Supreme Court telling him that Smith had won. The unanimous decision, authored by Chief Justice Warren, was based squarely on the Center's statutory arguments. The chief justice and seven of his brethren agreed that Alabama's regulation violated the Social Security Act. "Destitute children who are legally fatherless cannot be flatly denied federally funded assistance on the transparent fiction that they have a substitute father," Warren wrote, citing Cover's article in support of federal jurisdiction over the case. "Insofar as this or any similar regulation is based on the State's asserted interest in discouraging illicit sexual behavior and illegitimacy, it plainly conflicts with federal law and policy."[55]

The ninth member of the Court, Justice William O. Douglas, concurred, but, like the district court, he decided the case on equal protection rather than statutory grounds.

The Supreme Court's ruling in *King v. Smith* affected 20,000 children in Alabama alone, and about 500,000 children in the eighteen other states with similar substitute father regulations.[56]

Despite this victory, the Center began to move away from its southern strategy. The logistical problems of finding and representing clients hundreds of miles south of New York City simply proved too great. In addition, the Center seriously underestimated the desire of the southern states to avoid confrontations with northern welfare activists so soon after the violence of Freedom Summer. Too often, southern states preferred to compromise rather than litigate or, like the three-judge court in *Smith v. King*, were unwilling to inflame the tension between the races by confronting the racial impact of welfare laws. In contrast, local welfare authorities in some northern states were as eager as the welfare rights lawyers to obtain rulings that would require greater federal expenditures for welfare recipients; they would be willing participants in the Center's test case campaign.

The southern strategy was finally doomed in mid-1967 when legal services lawyers in Mississippi brought a federal case claiming that welfare benefits could not be cut off prior to a fair hearing: *Williams v. Gandy,* filed June 9, 1967.[57] The lawyers at the Center who were assisting with the case believed that it would be the perfect vehicle to test the issue of due process rights in the welfare context.[58] Thousands of Mississippi welfare recipients had been removed from the rolls over the years without receiving a meaningful opportunity to challenge the caseworker's decision before their benefits were cut off.

But instead of defending its policies, the state promptly acquiesced to the plaintiffs' claims. The case was settled out of court and, at least on paper, Mississippi became the first state to provide fair hearings before termination. It seemed like a favorable result. Without a court decision, however, the Mississippi case created no precedent on which the Center's lawyers could rely in future cases, and though Center attorneys had little faith that the state would comply with its agreement, monitoring compliance from New York was certain to prove impossible. In fact, Mississippi soon promulgated rules providing that fair hearings were *not* available when benefits were suspended or reduced rather than terminated.[59]

After reaching this impasse in the South, the Center focused most of its resources on cases in the North—Connecticut, Pennsylvania, Maryland, and, most of all, New York—where it was familiar with the political climate, more closely connected with recipients and better able to anticipate the ins and outs of any welfare litigation it initiated.

Chapter 6

The Middle Years

As members of a National Welfare Rights Movement . . . we are not willing to exchange our rights as American citizens
   · our rights to dignity
   · our rights to justice
   · our rights to democratic participation
In order to obtain the physical necessities for our families
   · their food, their shelter, their clothing
Which the conditions of our society and our lives
   · our age
   · our disability
   · the absence or death of a family's breadwinner
   · our lack of economic opportunity
Have made us no longer able to provide for our families.

—Goals for a National Welfare Rights Movement, 1966

By 1967 the confidence that marked the early years of federal antipoverty efforts was beginning to wane. Even Sargent Shriver, the eternally optimistic head of the Office of Economic Opportunity, conceded that eliminating poverty would take longer than originally anticipated. Despite growing criticism of the federal spending entailed by the War on Poverty, President Johnson continued to support the program. "Poverty is curable," Johnson told a group of antipoverty volunteers in May 1967. "We are not backing off from our commitment to fight poverty, nor will we so long as I have anything to say about it."[1]

With the Vietnam War diverting federal funds from domestic programs, however, Johnson's support amounted to little more than lip service. Senator Robert Kennedy repeatedly reminded the administration that no fundamental improvements in welfare were likely until the government committed "vastly greater resources" to antipoverty efforts.[2] But no such resources were forthcoming. Given the initial failure of government programs to cure poverty and the increasing militancy of welfare recipients, public support for increased expenditures was limited. Instead, the new federal initiatives consisted of cost-cutting measures and inexpensive improvements to the existing system. For example, Johnson signed legislation in early 1968 that allowed recipients to keep up to $150 a month in earnings while still receiving welfare, at the same time freezing federal welfare grants. States and cities focused on trimming the costs of administering the welfare system by increasing efficiency and stretching federal grants to reach as many families as possible.[3]

The welfare rolls nevertheless continued to grow, in part because the welfare rights movement had reduced the stigma of receiving welfare; a greater percentage of the eligible poor applied for public assistance. Recipient militancy was at its height. According to a legal services attorney in Newark, New Jersey, many clients who came into her office after reading NWRO pamphlets were "much more eager to stand up for their welfare rights than [clients] were" even two years before. The attorney also noted "a corresponding change in the attitudes of the [welfare board]; many caseworkers and supervisors no longer receive objections by clients or their attorney as an intrusion upon their hallowed prerogatives, but are quite willing to discuss the problems of the recipients in a more objective fashion."[4]

From the perspective of the government, a new approach to welfare was needed to bring the welfare rolls and recipients under control. The impetus for developing such an approach was the 1968 election campaign; candidates Richard Nixon, Hubert Humphrey, and George Wallace were groping for ideas and social scientists were eager to suggest them. One of the most talked-about proposals for welfare reform, variously known as a "family allowance," "negative income tax," or "guaranteed minimum income," was promoted as a means to eliminate duplication of effort at the federal and local levels while streamlining the delivery of benefits. Each of these variations guaranteed payment of cash benefits by the federal government, rather than the state government, an approach that would eliminate the outmoded distinctions between AFDC and state relief programs.

The notion of a guaranteed minimum income was not purely theoretical: in November 1967 the OEO initiated a program in New Jersey to test the negative income tax concept. One thousand families were chosen to receive between $80 and $120 per month from the federal government, depending on their income and size.[5]

Despite serious attention from social scientists, the possibility that a guaranteed minimum income would be established remained remote, at least during the Johnson administration. According to the president's 1967 economic report to the nation, such schemes—which would cost about $11 billion per year just to maintain the nation's poor at poverty-line levels—"are almost surely beyond our means at this time." Even so, re-ported *Newsweek*, "the consensus among welfare officials, from high-level Federal officials in Washington to embattled recipients . . . is that some kind of basic-allowance system is the only answer to one of the Great Society's most contentious problems."[6] And by late 1968, in a scene hark-ing back to the days leading up to the federal programs of the New Deal, New York Governor Nelson Rockefeller admitted that his state was over-whelmed by the numbers on its welfare rolls and could no longer bear its share of the costs. He called for the federalization of welfare and for uni-form benefits nationwide.[7]

Under the circumstances, the lawyers at the Center on Social Welfare Policy and Law grew more cautious in setting their legal priorities. Social change through law, they believed, required patience and planning—case after case to establish preliminary principles and legal scholarship to legit-imize novel arguments. As Center staff attorney Henry Freedman wrote to NWRO general counsel Carl Rachlin in 1968, "An attempt to deal at the outset with economic issues posed in their broadest form is likely to make the most liberal judge reluctant to grant relief. We, as lawyers, know that the legal process can be used to our advantage only by the development of precedent. . . . The political goals of the welfare rights groups would be ill-served by our closing off the possibility of substantial victory on any eco-nomic issue by bringing a case on too broad a scale and losing."[8] The legal strategy could not and should not be rushed, the Center concluded. The NAACP Legal Defense and Educational Fund had taken decades to achieve its goals in the desegregation campaign. The Center's campaign, arguably more ambitious than that of the Legal Defense Fund because it called on courts to expand economic rather than political and civil rights, was only three years old.

The pressing needs of the recipient movement, however, made it diffi-cult for welfare rights lawyers to move slowly. As Freedman acknowledged, "Adequacy of the grant is pretty much the key 'political' issue the welfare rights groups wish to pursue . . . [yet] we lawyers have litigated in this area very little."[9] Instead, the Center's lawyers had focused on eligibility is-sues, such as that raised by *King v. Smith*, where the question was whether a particular criterion for welfare eligibility was valid. These cases involv-ing access to welfare, the lawyers believed, were easier to win than were direct challenges to the adequacy of the grant. By starting with efforts to expand eligibility, the Center could begin to educate judges about welfare issues; build momentum for the next stage of the campaign; and increase pressure on local, state, and federal governments by expanding the welfare rolls—an extension of Cloward and Piven's crisis theory but without the problem of organizing recipients.

The difference in the approaches of NWRO and the Center contributed to the rift between the two organizations, particularly after 1967, when Sparer left the Center and began a teaching career that took him first to Yale and then to the University of Pennsylvania.

Sparer, according to legal services veteran Gary Bellow, was one of the few poverty lawyers who understood that a legal campaign was an organizing tool for a social movement, not the other way around. According to Bellow, "Sparer always performed the bridge between mobilization and test case work."[10] Sparer's background as a Communist Party organizer and labor lawyer attested to his commitment to movement politics. While Sparer was at the Center its function was, more or less, to act as counsel for NWRO.[11]

This vision of the Center was not widely shared by the new lawyers who Sparer hired. They saw the Center as a sort of high-powered think tank, generating its own legal strategies and agenda. In fact, many on the Center staff believed that Sparer's skills were not well suited to a public interest law center engaged in complex test case litigation. According to one Center attorney, Sparer was an organizer. "We would make legal arguments; he'd say, 'It's unfair, it's horrible.'"[12] Sparer "didn't really understand litigation," recalls Martin Garbus, former codirector of the Center.[13] In David Gilman's words, "Ed Sparer was a thinker and energizer rather than a litigator."[14]

Despite this evaluation by his staff, Sparer on more than one occasion used legal arguments to rein in the feisty Rachlin. Because of his close connection with NWRO, Rachlin had difficulty following the Center's measured approach to litigation. Sparer often reminded Rachlin that attempts to rely solely on constitutional grounds when, in fact, a case could be resolved on a statutory basis, were likely to backfire. "No matter how quiet you are on the issue, these facts will quickly become known to the court [and] . . . will simply lower your standing and credulity," Sparer told Rachlin, urging him to approach welfare rights litigation one issue at a time.[15]

Sparer's colleagues were correct, however, in observing that his primary allegiances were to the movement. When Sparer left the Center he appointed Brian Glick, a civil rights activist and former organizer with the Students for a Democratic Society (SDS) as his replacement. Glick shared

Sparer's ideal that the welfare rights legal strategy must be an outgrowth of the recipient movement and must be responsive to recipients' concerns, expressed both through NWRO and through the clients of neighborhood legal services offices. But Glick was less than two years out of law school, and the Center staff refused to take directions from such an inexperienced leader. Stephen Wizner left the Center to join MFY; another attorney, Johnny Weiss, soon followed. The Center's board of directors, led by Columbia Professor Paul Dodyk, intervened to avert a crisis, and within a few months Glick was asked to step aside in favor of Lee Albert.[16]

A slight man with sandy blond hair, Albert was close to the antithesis of Sparer and Glick. He had been an outstanding student at Yale Law School and editor of the law review. After graduation Albert clerked for Justice Byron R. White of the Supreme Court, spent a year teaching law at the London School of Economics and, for a few months before joining the Center, worked as an assistant U.S. attorney in New York City. During those years Albert made all the right connections: Wizner and Weiss were old friends, and Dodyk had clerked for Justice Potter Stewart the same year that Albert clerked for White.[17]

Albert made his own enemies once he joined the Center, however. Some neighborhood poverty lawyers were put off by his faintly superior manner and the unnerving British accent that the Jersey City–raised Albert acquired during his year in London.

More fundamentally, Albert had little interest in nurturing a social movement centered on welfare rights. He had never handled a fair hearing or worked with welfare recipients. His interests centered around legal principles; his ambitions involved Supreme Court arguments rather than revolution. According to Albert, "I believed in using lawyer's expertise to provide a leadership role in the movement of cases through higher courts."[18]

With Albert's arrival, the Center moved its quarters from the Columbia School of Social Work to the Columbia Law School. The move was more than symbolic; the Center's newly reinforced affiliation with the law school virtually assured that its activities would be focused on traditional law reform rather than on organizing or on investigating social policy questions.[19] One observer favorably described Albert's vision: "The Center plans to increase the number of 'ground-breaking' cases which are handled by Center attorneys. Because of the greater control the Center will have over 'test cases' in which Center attorneys have formulated the issues and initiated the litigation, I believe that the Center will be in a better position than ever to obtain decisions on the complex and novel legal problems of the poor—issues which must be subject to extremely close analysis and scrutiny if favorable decisions are to overcome the weight of past authority and practice."[20] At the same time the Center expanded its docket to include housing cases—challenging, for example, the procedures for eviction from public housing—and made plans to take up issues relating to the differential treatment of poor children in public schools, the treatment of welfare recipients by public hospitals, and the administration of family courts.[21]

As Albert's litigation style took hold, the Center's work on behalf of NWRO diminished. The task of communicating with Rachlin was delegated to senior staff attorney Freedman, a congenial peacemaker who stayed on after Sparer's departure, and Ron Pollack, a staff attorney who, despite the shifts at the Center, was determined to maintain a connection between his work and the recipient movement.[22]

Even from his vantage point at Yale Sparer could see that the Center was shifting its focus from the social work and political organizing components of welfare rights law. But Sparer didn't interfere, at least not directly. Instead, he went about his teaching and consulted widely with legal services and welfare rights groups. Embittered by Glick's ouster, Sparer rarely spoke to Albert. When he did, both men recognized that their different orientations made real communication or collaboration impossible.[23]

One of the most ambitious new campaigns, and one of the few that combined political organizing with legal theory, was a series of cases in which Pollack challenged the administration of the Food Stamp Act of 1964.[24] Because of its local focus, the campaign held promise as a tool for mobilizing recipients, and Pollack coordinated his efforts with Rachlin and George Wiley at NWRO. Through the Food Stamp Act the federal government had extended to local authorities millions of dollars earmarked to feed the poor, but more than one-third of the poorest counties in the United States had failed to join the program. The availability of food stamps in a county depended entirely on whether that county participated in the program.

On November 19, 1968, Pollack issued a press release with the headline "Can Starvation Be Outlawed in the United States?" and filed lawsuits in nineteen states claiming that once one county in a state provided food stamps to the poor, every other county in that state must do so or be in violation of the federal equal protection clause. The following day Pollack and NWRO assembled two dozen recipients to meet with the press and

Department of Agriculture officials to discuss the recipients' claims that "starvation is illegal in America."[25]

The food stamp campaign was a success. Though the use of the equal protection clause in support of the recipients' claims was unorthodox, courts were distressed by the evidence of widespread hunger resulting from the failure to accept federal money. Federal courts in Texas, California, and Missouri quickly mandated that every county in each state participate in the program; in states where court challenges moved more slowly, public pressure provoked change. Eventually, all but eight of the nation's 1,000 poorest counties were brought into the program; by January 1970, little more than a year after the campaign began, food stamps were available in 2,731 of the 3,049 counties in the country.[26]

Though the food stamp campaign yielded significant results for recipients, the cases had little precedential value for future welfare litigation. The bread and butter of the Center's practice remained test cases systematically raising the issues set out by Sparer in 1965.

The order in which these issues should be litigated was debated endlessly. For example, Freedman asked Rachlin to edit several claims from a draft complaint attacking Ohio's maximum grant regulations because "we should not at this time attack the . . . variation from county to county arising from matching funds provided by counties, and allegations of different treatment by other states." According to Freedman, raising too many issues in one lawsuit "will at best delay and confuse matters and will likely cause defeat."[27]

In time the Center initiated cases to establish welfare recipients' rights to a fair hearing before their benefits were terminated; cases to determine the particulars of the fair hearing procedure; and cases designed to establish recipients' rights to privacy. The lawyers were still skirting the issue of the adequacy of the welfare grant while continuing their efforts to build precedents for the constitutionalization of welfare. Despite the Center's deliberation, most cases washed out before they even got to federal court— that is, the state or city would simply restore benefits and moot the proceeding. The problem of washing out, combined with the Center's increasing inability to control the experienced neighborhood legal services lawyers around the country, rendered debates concerning welfare rights litigation strategy largely theoretical. The Center could no more dictate the order in which cases were presented to the Supreme Court than it could control the Court's decisions.

In fact, the second welfare rights case to be heard by the Supreme Court was not brought by the Center but by neighborhood legal services lawyers. In *Shapiro v. Thompson,* which followed the oral argument in *King v. Smith* by only one week, three consolidated cases challenged welfare residency laws in Connecticut, Pennsylvania, and the District of Columbia. In these jurisdictions and in thirty-seven other states an individual was required to complete a minimum residency before receiving welfare. If the individual applied for welfare too soon, he or she would be sent back to the state of origin. The Connecticut statute, for example, stipulated that "when any person comes into this state without visible means of support for the immediate future and applies for aid to dependent children . . . or general assistance . . . within one year from his arrival, such person shall be eligible only for temporary aid or care until arrangements are made for his return."[28] This state law implemented a federal statute that allowed states to require residency of up to one year as a condition of eligibility for AFDC.[29]

Nineteen-year-old Valerie Thompson, the plaintiff in *Shapiro v. Thompson,* felt the brunt of this statute in late 1966 when she moved to Connecticut from Massachusetts with her two young children to be near her mother. Because she was solely responsible for the care of her children, Thompson was unable to work; her mother was also unable to support the family on her own small income. Thompson's application for public assistance was turned down, however, because she had resided in Connecticut for less than one year.

Using materials prepared by the Center but taking care not to relinquish control of the case, Thompson's lawyers and legal services attorneys representing similar clients in Pennsylvania and in the District of Columbia raised two key issues before the Supreme Court. First, they asserted that residency requirements frustrated their client's constitutional "right to travel." Second, they argued that the residency requirements violated the equal protection clause of the Constitution because they discriminated between those welfare applicants who had resided in the state for more than a year and those who had not. The Washington, D.C., recipients also devoted several pages of their brief to a discussion of the as yet unrecognized constitutional right to welfare—the "right to live"—in hopes that the Court might use their case as a vehicle for adopting this controversial theory.[30]

The *Shapiro* lawyers, unlike those who argued *King,* did not attempt to gain the "strict scrutiny" afforded racial classifications by claiming that residence laws had a differential impact on blacks. In *Shapiro* the issue was poverty, not race. The lawyers framed their arguments to allow the Court to find that poverty itself was a classification that required strict scrutiny.

Elizabeth Wickenden happened to be in Washington on May 1, 1968, the day of the oral argument in the three *Shapiro v. Thompson* cases. She stopped by the Supreme Court to hear the argument and, at her old friend Justice Abe Fortas' invitation, was ushered into the section reserved for the justices' family members.

The Shapiro argument was was not an impressive sight, Wickenden recalls. All of the plaintiffs' lawyers were young and inexperienced; the lawyer arguing the Connecticut case was barely two years out of law school. Midway through the argument Fortas motioned to one of the Supreme Court pages and handed him a note to deliver to Wickenden in the gallery. "Wickie," it said, "the welfare mothers are crying out for your help. Come down and rescue this case."[31]

The votes on the residency law case broke down along unusual lines. Chief Justice Earl Warren was convinced that Congress could limit welfare on the basis of residence and, because the state statutes conformed to federal law, voted to uphold them. In his draft majority opinion, he categorically rejected the claim that the residency law violated the constitutional right to travel—it merely "imposes a burden of uncertain degree on the welfare recipient who chooses to travel," he wrote. Warren also rejected the plaintiffs' equal protection claim. Refusing to use strict scrutiny to evaluate the relationship between statutory means and ends, he asked simply if residence requirements were reasonably related to a legitimate legislative purpose. Because residency laws encouraged states to participate in the federal welfare scheme by limiting the number of residents likely to move to the state, Warren concluded that residence laws were sufficiently rational to pass muster under the equal protection clause. His opinion was joined by Justices Stewart, White, Hugo L. Black, John M. Harlan, and William J. Brennan.[32]

Justice William O. Douglas drafted a short dissent stating that residency laws violated the right to travel. The principal dissenting opinion, however, was drafted by Fortas. Cutting through the legal jargon employed in the draft majority opinion, he wrote that the real purpose of residence laws was to discourage poor people from coming into the state, not, as the majority suggested, to promote state participation in welfare programs. Fortas asserted that the laws' purpose did not justify the serious impediment that residency requirements posed to the constitutional right to travel. Further, he argued, residence laws distinguished between rich and poor without a "reasonable basis" sufficient to meet the requirements of the equal protection clause. The rich could move and live where they pleased; the poor could not. Though he analyzed the residency laws as "poverty-based" classifications, Fortas stopped short of employing the strict scrutiny test used to assess race-based classifications.[33]

After Fortas circulated his draft dissent, Brennan decided to shift his vote to the Fortas opinion. Stewart also withdrew his vote but refused to recast it. With the decision deadlocked, the justices set the case down for reargument the following term.

The announcement that *Shapiro v. Thompson* would be reargued sent a wave of panic through the welfare rights community. The lawyers knew that they would lose *Shapiro v. Thompson* unless they made a strong showing at the second argument. Using the threat of imminent defeat to pressure the recipients' lawyers, the Center wrested control of *Shapiro* from the legal services attorneys and, after much debate, asked Archibald Cox, Harvard Law School professor and solicitor general under Presidents Kennedy and Johnson, to handle the argument. Cox agreed, though he had no experience with welfare litigation. Like a good advocate, he immersed himself in the issues and, in the autumn of 1968, traveled to Sparer's rural home in North Madison, Connecticut, for an intense day of preparation in Sparer's study.[34]

Cox's presentation on October 23, 1968, was virtually seamless; for much of his argument, the justices sat rapt.[35] Stewart, in particular, was swayed by Cox, and at the justices' conference on October 25, he voted to strike down the residency laws.[36] With the majority of the justices now favoring Fortas' position, the drafting of the majority opinion was reassigned to Brennan.

Justice Brennan's draft opinion took a new tack, abandoning Fortas' "reasonable basis" standard and arguing that the government can justify the restriction of a fundamental right—such as the right to travel—only when a "compelling interest" of the government is at stake. A "reasonable" relationship between the means and ends of the statute was not enough. "We recognize that a State has a valid interest in preserving the fiscal integrity of its programs," wrote Brennan. "It may legitimately attempt to limit its expenditures, whether for public assistance, public education, or any other program. But a State may not accomplish such a purpose by invidious distinctions between classes of its citizens."[37] In short, a state's desire for fiscal integrity was not a sufficient basis for it to violate the fundamental rights of its poor citizens. Douglas, Marshall, Fortas, White, and Stewart joined Brennan's opinion.

Warren and Black dissented on the ground that the federal statute allowing residency laws was a valid exercise of Congress' power under the constitution's Commerce Clause and could not be second-guessed by the Court. Harlan's separate dissent argued that Brennan's opinion was an unwise extension of the "compelling interest" doctrine beyond traditional racial classifications that went "far toward making the Court a 'super-legislature.'"[38]

The *Shapiro v. Thompson* decision was finally issued on April 21, 1969, to a euphoric reception from welfare lawyers. Whereas *Brown v. Board of Education* suggested that courts would exercise strict scrutiny only over laws involving race, *Shapiro* made clear that laws restricting any fundamental right would be strictly scrutinized and struck down under the equal protection clause. In May 1969 Freedman rated *Shapiro* as the Center's most important case to date, writing that "since there are now so many other equal protection claims abroad in welfare . . . the impact of this decision in the development of the law is profound."[39]

Supreme Court watchers also believed that *Shapiro* might signal the creation of a new version of substantive due process, the discredited doctrine developed by the Supreme Court in 1905 with *Lochner*, that would use a fundamental rights analysis under the equal protection clause to police a wide variety of state and federal laws. Sparer hoped that the opinion presaged a dramatic change in welfare law—that strict scrutiny would soon be extended to state welfare law classifications, heralding the end of geographic differences in welfare grants and moving inexorably toward a constitutional right to live.[40]

Most significantly, the Department of Health, Education, and Welfare predicted that the *Shapiro* decision and the demise of residency laws would lead to greater payments to recipients, amounting to $125 million to $175 million a year. This redistribution of funds to the poor, as Freedman wrote in 1969, undoubtedly would result in increased pressure for a uniform, federal welfare system.[41] Through litigation or lobbying, it appeared that a minimum guaranteed income was within reach.

Chapter 7

Life, Liberty, Property, and Welfare

Mrs. Theresa Negron received AFDC for herself and her five children to supplement her salary as a superintendent of her building. She advised her caseworker that she would be out of town to visit a friend in Philadelphia. Nonetheless, the caseworker wrote to her during her absence asking her to come in for an interview and, when the appointment was not kept, suspended aid without any notification whatsoever. When Mrs. Negron did not receive her check, she twice tried to contact the caseworker by telephone but the calls were never returned. She kept a June 6, 1968, appointment with another employee of the department and was advised that the department believed that Mrs. Negron's husband was visiting her. This was denied by Mrs. Negron. Four days later Mrs. Negron went to a local welfare rights organization which telephoned the department on her behalf. An employee then consulted the case record and found that the reason stated was that Mrs. Negron was living in Philadelphia. Mrs. Negron was reinstated to full assistance only after her complaint had been filed in this action on June 17.

—Brief for Appellees, *Goldberg v. Kelly* (U.S. Supreme Court, October Term, 1969)

For centuries welfare had been viewed as a gift from the state to the poor. The Social Security Act of 1935 did not alter this basic premise.[1] The welfare recipient had no legal *right* to receive welfare; the state could give it or not so long as it did not violate any federal laws (after the Supreme Court decision in *King v. Smith*) or infringe on the recipient's fundamental constitutional rights by the manner in which it dispensed its largess (after the decision *Shapiro v. Thompson*).

The legal status of welfare as a gratuity was directly at odds with Sparer's plan to create a *right* to welfare or, as he called it, a right to live. These two conceptions of welfare were theoretically incompatible. Center lawyers believed, however, that it would be too risky to directly raise the issue of whether welfare was a gratuity or a right. Instead, the lawyers stopped short of claiming that welfare was a constitutional right and argued that once an individual established *statutory* eligibility to receive welfare, public benefits must be dispensed in accordance with constitutional protections. An individual could not be denied benefits if that denial violated, for example, the individual's rights to travel, to equal protection or, most problematically, to due process.

Establishing that the due process clause protected welfare recipients posed a special problem in that an individual was constitutionally entitled to due process only if the state took, or threatened to take, an individual's "life, liberty, or property." As long as welfare was viewed as a mere gratuity it did not fall into any of those categories. But if welfare rights lawyers could obtain a court ruling that benefits were more than a gratuity, not only would recipients qualify for procedural protections, the constitutional right to welfare would be one step closer as well.

The scholarly groundwork for this next step in the welfare rights campaign was laid by Yale Law School professor Charles Reich in 1964, a few years before he gained notoriety as author of the bestseller *The Greening of America*. Reich, a New York intellectual who never practiced poverty law, was an unlikely source of insights about welfare. But as a boy Reich had befriended a remarkable family of legal activists, the Poliers, who greatly influenced him. Through Jonathan Polier, a friend from school, Reich met Jonathan's mother, Justine Wise Polier, a judge on the New York City family court and the first woman in the state to hold a judicial office above magistrate. Jonathan's father, Shad Polier, was a civil rights lawyer who, in the 1930s, defended the "Scottsboro boys"—nine black youths accused of raping two white women in Scottsboro, Alabama.[2]

As Reich grew older he became friends with Justine Polier in his own right. "By the time I was twelve," Reich recalls, "we would debate current events as if I was an adult." And through Justine Polier, Reich met Elizabeth Wickenden. Polier and Wickenden were close friends who shared a commitment to improving social welfare policy—Polier as a judge and Wickenden as a lobbyist, consultant, and writer.[3]

Reich left New York in 1946, going first to Oberlin College and then to Yale Law School. When he graduated from law school in 1952, Reich applied to clerk for Justice Hugo L. Black on the Supreme Court. Black, a native of Alabama appointed to the Court by Franklin Roosevelt, was known as a principled defender of the Bill of Rights. At Black's suggestion, Reich postponed his clerkship for one year and worked at the Washington, D.C., office of the prestigious law firm of Cravath, Swain & Moore.

Reich developed a close relationship with Black, who liked to talk with his clerks for hours about the cases pending before the Court. One case that occupied much of their attention during the 1953 term was *Barsky v.*

Board of Regents, involving a doctor in New York whose medical license was suspended when he failed to respond to a subpoena issued by the House Un-American Activities Committee. The committee was investigating the Joint Anti-Fascist Refugee Committee, of which Barsky was chairman.[4]

Reich felt strongly that Barsky's rights had been violated and, during one of his long conversations with Justice Black, suggested that Barsky's medical license should be viewed as a type of property rather than as a mere gratuity from the state. Like real property, such as land, it had value; and, like real property, it gave Barsky status in the community. A medical license should be protected by the Constitution's due process clause, Reich argued, and New York state should not be able to suspend Barsky's license for reasons unrelated to his medical practice any more than it could confiscate an individual's land because he or she voted for the "wrong" political party.[5]

Black agreed with Reich, but the majority of the Court believed that the suspension of Barsky's license was a valid exercise of the state's power to rescind the license at whim. Black's dissent was based on the grounds he had discussed with his clerk. "The right to practice is . . . a very precious part of the liberty of an individual physician or surgeon," he wrote. "It may mean more than any property. Such a right is protected from arbitrary infringement by our Constitution, which forbids any state to deprive a person of liberty or property without due process of law."[6]

At the end of his clerkship, Reich resumed his law practice, in Washington, D.C., first with Wilmer & Broun and then with Arnold, Fortas & Porter. Practicing corporate law, Reich was daily reminded how valuable government benefits such as defense contracts or Federal Communications Commission licenses could be. At the same time, he saw cases in which those benefits were used to coerce certain behavior, as in *Barsky.* In some states, for example, lawyers were still denied licenses to practice unless they took an oath pledging their support of the U.S. government and denouncing communism.[7]

One of Reich's friends at Arnold, Fortas & Porter was Walton H. Hamilton, a former professor of economics and law who was spending his retirement as a practicing lawyer. In his earlier academic incarnation, Hamilton had written the entry in the *Encyclopaedia of the Social Sciences* on property, defining it, like Reich, in a functional way. "An owner is concerned with trinket, vineyard or power, not for what it is in itself," wrote Hamilton, "but for what the community allows him to extract from it." During his time at Arnold, Fortas & Porter, Reich honed his views on property over lunches with Hamilton.[8]

Reich returned to Yale Law School in 1960, this time as an associate professor. He was assigned to teach property law, and he set about constructing a new curriculum that would focus on the meaning and function of property rather than on the arcane legal rules governing its use.[9]

While Reich was immersed in this task, Justine Polier asked him to accept a consulting job for the Field Foundation, a progressive organization established by Chicago department store magnate Marshall Field. Through Wickenden, Polier had learned about the welfare department's practice of conducting midnight raids of welfare recipients' homes. For a consulting fee of $500, Polier asked Reich to prepare a report on the legality of the raids.

Reich accepted the job. Before settling down to write, however, he attended a series of meetings convened in Wickenden's living room to strategize about developing a body of welfare law. In the 1930s and 1940s in Washington, D.C., Wickenden and her husband, Tex Goldschmidt, had been members of a similar policy circle of New Dealers that included Abe Fortas, Clifford and Virginia Durr, William O. Douglas, Reich's friend Walton Hamilton, and, occasionally, Lyndon and Lady Bird Johnson.[10] This time, Wickenden invited Shad and Justine Polier; ACLU attorney Mel Wulf; Norman Dorsen and Charles Ares, professors at New York University Law School; Marvin Frankel, a professor at Columbia Law School; Bernice Bernstein, a lawyer with the Department of Health, Education, and Welfare; Sparer, who had just joined the MFY Legal Unit; and Reich. To stimulate the discussions, Wickenden (despite her lack of legal training) prepared a seminal paper outlining possible avenues for welfare litigation—a paper on which Sparer relied a few years later when he developed his own welfare litigation agenda.[11]

Reich was enormously influenced by his exposure to practicing poverty lawyers and by the recognition that his work fit into a movement to improve conditions for welfare recipients. Hoping to contribute to the debate and to provide a tool for practitioners, Reich published his report to the Field Foundation as a law review article, "Midnight Welfare Searches and the Social Security Act." Midnight searches were a violation of welfare recipients' constitutional right to privacy, he believed. But the practice continued because government benefits were routinely used to coerce certain behavior. According to Reich, "Welfare implies dependence. And dependence means that people may more easily be induced to part with rights which they would ordinarily defend. . . . They may be asked to observe standards of morality not imposed on the rest of the community. They may be forced to endure official condescension and prying. If the welfare state is to be faithful to American traditions, government must recognize its duty, even as it hands out benefits, to preserve the independence of those it helps."[12]

Reich's work on midnight raids gave him new insight into his ongoing study of property. "I began to see that [the functional view of property] had much more profound implications than I'd first realized," he recalls. "It was linked to class; the lower on the totem pole you are, the fewer rights you have. To have one rule for television licenses, for example, and another for welfare violates principles of equality." Echoing Walton Hamilton and Jacobus tenBroek, Reich found that "the functional view of property is linked to power and powerlessness."[13]

Reich had already started drafting his next article, "The New Property." Now he revised it, incorporating references to the welfare rights struggle. It was a solitary project, and Reich refused to share drafts of the article. In fact, the students on the Yale Law Journal staff had difficulty wrenching the final version away from Reich, who was content to keep tinkering with it indefinitely. But once Peter Strauss, the editor in chief of the law journal, had the article in hand, he recognized that it was "so in tune with the way the world was going" that he decided to publish it quickly without significant revisions.[14]

In "New Property," published in 1964, Reich examined the myriad forms of government benefits, from licenses to jobs to welfare payments, and christened this array the "public interest state." Cases such as *Barsky*, he wrote, established the doctrine that such government benefits are "held by . . . recipients conditionally, subject to confiscation in the interest of the paramount state."[15]

After defining this status quo, Reich argued for a new vision of government benefits that would give them the status of more traditional property and preclude their use to coerce recipients. "A first principle should be that government must have no power to 'buy up' rights guaranteed by the Constitution," Reich stated. "It should not be able to impose any condition on largess that would be invalid if imposed on something other than a 'gratuity.' "[16]

Reich closed his article with a call for a new social compact: "If the individual is to survive in a collective society, he must have protection against its ruthless pressures. There must be sanctuaries or enclaves where no majority can reach. To shelter the solitary human spirit does not merely make possible the fulfillment of individuals; it also gives society the power to change, to grow, and to regenerate, and hence to endure. These were the objects which property sought to achieve, and can no longer achieve. The challenge of the future will be to construct, for the society that is coming, institutions and laws to carry on this work. . . . We must create a new property."[17]

Reich's transformative ideas were quickly taken up by legal services lawyers. In the welfare rights litigation campaign, the question of whether welfare constituted property or a gratuity was starkly presented in the context of welfare suspensions and terminations.[18]

Under federal and state laws welfare benefits could be cut off as soon as a caseworker determined that the recipient was ineligible. According to former MFY attorney David Diamond, the threat of termination was used to control recipients: "Termination was the device that the welfare department used to shake people up. The feeling that you can get terminated any time for anything makes you much more subservient and pliable to whatever caseworkers want."[19] Though a recipient could challenge the decision later through a fair hearing, in the interim weeks or months he or she would receive no benefits. According to the Center, the length of time between a request for a fair hearing and the commencement of the hearing ranged from 20 to 260 days.[20] Only if welfare benefits qualified as property under the due process clause would the recipient have a constitutional right to be free of the fear of coercive or mistaken termination. If welfare benefits were considered property, due process would require a hearing *before* benefits were terminated.

Recognizing that it was time to move from statutory eligibility issues to questions closer to the core of the welfare debate, in late 1967 lawyers at MFY, assisted by the Center, prepared draft briefs challenging the cutoff of welfare benefits without a hearing. The lawyers decided to file the lawsuit in New York because the relatively liberal state and city governments might concede the applicability of the due process clause to welfare benefits—a major victory in itself—and focus simply on the question of what sort of hearing the due process clause required. Lawyers and social workers at MFY began looking for potential clients.

On January 24, 1968, Peter Darrow was on intake duty at the Third Street office of MFY.[21] Darrow was one of the first volunteers to be assigned legal work through the federal VISTA program. While he was, in principle, committed to working with the poor for a year, Darrow also was eager to get the deferment from serving in Vietnam that his draft board had promised. When his year at MFY was over he planned to join a Wall Street law firm.

At the MFY Legal Unit, Darrow was assigned welfare rights cases under the supervision of David Diamond and Marianne Rosenfield. It was at the height of the recipients' fair hearing campaign, and the unit spent much of its time handling such hearings. Virtually every morning, Darrow, a thin blond man who looked like a prep-school fugitive, walked from his apartment across the Bowery and south past Manhattan's City Hall to the hearing office on State Street in lower Manhattan, his arms filled with files of the cases he would handle that day. And every afternoon Darrow returned to the MFY office to pick up the next day's files.

One of the potential clients who was waiting to see Darrow on January 24 was John Kelly, a twenty-nine-year-old homeless black man. Darrow greeted Kelly and ushered him from the waiting room to his small office. After taking down some preliminary information—how he could be contacted, his income—Darrow asked Kelly to tell his story.

According to Kelly, a hit-and-run driver struck him in 1966. Disabled by the accident, Kelly qualified for New York's home relief program. He received a check for $80.05 in the mail every two weeks. It was his only income.

Kelly told Darrow that on December 16, 1967, he had an appointment with his welfare caseworker at the Gramercy Center. They went over the usual information, then the caseworker asked Kelly to move out of his home at the Broadway Central Hotel to the Barbara Hotel, also on the Lower East Side. Kelly knew the Barbara Hotel. It was filled with drug addicts and drunks. He didn't want to move, but he obeyed his caseworker's order because, if he didn't, she might cut off his benefits. After a few sleepless nights at the Barbara Hotel, however, Kelly moved again, this time to a friend's apartment.

When he left the Barbara Hotel, Kelly tried to cover his tracks by continuing to use it as his mailing address; on January 8 he went to pick up his mail from the desk clerk. But the clerk, who had been in touch with Kelly's caseworker, told Kelly that because he had moved away from the Barbara Hotel his welfare checks were terminated. In addition, the clerk told Kelly that the hotel had returned a supplementary welfare check issued to Kelly to pay for a winter coat.

Baffled by his caseworker's vindictive behavior and the clerk's complicity, Kelly took a subway uptown and tried to see the caseworker. She refused to see him. He waited a few hours but finally, confused and defeated, he returned to the Lower East Side.

For the next week, Kelly lived on what he could borrow. He couldn't continue staying with his friend without sharing expenses, so he slept on the street. After a hard week, Kelly thought that his January 16 welfare check might yet come. It did not. Kelly again tried to see his caseworker, and she sent him away.

On January 23, Kelly contacted Cynthia Smith, an MFY social worker. She got no further than Kelly had; when she called the Gramercy Center, she was simply informed that Kelly's case was closed. Smith recommended that Kelly talk to an MFY lawyer, and Kelly made his way to Darrow's office the next afternoon.

When Kelly had finished, Darrow ran to the next office and grabbed Diamond. "I think we've got a client for the fair hearing case," Darrow whispered as they reentered Darrow's office. Darrow continued with the interview while Diamond looked on. "You have a choice," Darrow told Kelly. "It sounds as if your caseworker has arbitrarily cut off your benefits without giving you any opportunity to prove your side of the story." Kelly nodded and Darrow continued. "We want to bring a lawsuit to prevent caseworkers from cutting off benefits before a hearing. Your case could be a part of that lawsuit. It might mean that you would not get your checks again for quite a while, and we can try to help you get by in the meantime. But unless we can get people like you to join in this suit, caseworkers will continue to have the power to cut off welfare recipients without any explanation."

Darrow paused. "Will you join this lawsuit?" he asked.

"Yes, I'll join," Kelly said quietly.

Darrow smiled. "We'll put your name up in lights," he told Kelly.[22]

Kelly and Darrow agreed to meet a few days later to go over Kelly's story in more detail. In the meantime, Darrow gave him a $10 loan from MFY to tide him over.

Experience had taught MFY lawyers never to bring a case against the welfare department with a single plaintiff. It was too easy for the government to quickly reinstate the individual's benefits and resolve the case. A few years later, notably in the 1973 case of *Roe v. Wade,* the Supreme Court would hold that federal courts should decide claims "capable of repetition but evading review" whether or not the particular plaintiff was still in jeopardy.[23] But in 1968 MFY and the Center needed as many plaintiffs receiving as many varieties of welfare benefits as possible to maximize the chances that the case would remain alive until a decision was reached. During the next few days MFY lawyers spread the word among welfare activists and neighborhood law offices that more plaintiffs were needed.

It took only a few days to find five more plaintiffs: Randolph Young and Juan DeJesus, home relief recipients, and Pearl McKinney, Altagracia Guzman, and Pearl Frye, AFDC recipients. Young was cut off when $25 of his welfare money was unaccounted for, despite his explanation that the money had been stolen. DeJesus' benefits were cut off because, according to his caseworker, he drank and took drugs, charges that DeJesus denied. The welfare benefits of McKinney and four of her children were terminated because her caseworker was suspicious that the family had extra, unreported income. Guzman and her four young children lost their benefits when Guzman refused to consent to a lawsuit to increase the voluntary child support payments of her estranged husband by a few dollars a week, even though her consent was legally unnecessary. Frye and her eight children lost their benefits because the caseworker discovered that they lived rent-free in a house owned by the father of six of Frye's children and his wife.

Most of these new plaintiffs were referred by the city's growing number of legal services lawyers, but Frye was a client of Louise Gans, a Legal Aid attorney. Because the Legal Aid Society management viewed law reform litigation as "making trouble," Gans did not tell her supervisors about her contact with the legal services lawyers planning the due process case.[24]

Under the rules governing federal litigation, a complaint need only give the defendants "notice" of the plaintiffs' claims.[25] This requires no more than some succinct passages explaining the facts and citing the legal principles that support the lawsuit. The MFY complaint, however, was unusually long: twenty-eight pages detailing the stories of each plaintiff. The lawyers felt that they had to put in as many facts as possible because at first blush, what with all the rules and regulations governing welfare, the fair hearing procedure looked fair enough. Only when recipients' stories were told did it become apparent that the system of holding hearings *after* termination resulted in extreme hardship.

Once the plaintiffs' stories were written, the lawyers still had to decide who to sue: the federal, state, or local governments. The federal government provided aid to the states for AFDC, approved state welfare plans, and wrote the federal regulations governing AFDC—regulations that implied that a hearing after termination of welfare benefits was sufficient.[26] The

New York state government administered the AFDC program and wrote the rules applicable to home relief benefits; the state regulations provided only for post-termination hearings in AFDC cases and, until new regulations were issued on January 16, 1968, no hearings at all for home relief recipients.[27] The New York City Human Resources Administration administered the AFDC and home relief programs on the local level and employed the caseworkers who actually enforced the state and federal regulations.

After some debate the plaintiffs' lawyers concluded—as welfare rights lawyers had in both *King* and *Shapiro*—that suing the federal government directly was too dangerous. MFY and the Center were not certain what position HEW would take on the fair hearing issue. If HEW told the judge that pretermination hearings were unnecessary, the judge would likely give substantial weight to that position. It was less risky to challenge the federal regulations indirectly by litigating against state and local authorities. Named as defendants were George Wyman, the New York state welfare commissioner; Jack Goldberg, the welfare commissioner of New York City; and the members of the State Board of Welfare.

Preferring a behind-the-scenes role rather than direct contact with clients, the soft-spoken Diamond supervised the preparation of the brief, affidavits, and other papers to be filed with the complaint. Brief writing was what Diamond, a former Reggie, liked best about his job. "I wanted John Kelly to get some money," he later recalled, "but John Kelly was not a real person to me. He was an occasion."[28]

The emotional chaos of working directly with welfare recipients and the stress of constant confrontations with the welfare bureaucracy were often too much for Diamond. "Five people were always calling," he remembers. "One day there were so many people calling that I told the secretary that I wasn't going to take more calls unless someone was going to be thrown out of their house tomorrow or had their welfare cut off today. The telephone calls didn't slow down."[29]

Diamond was also torn by the moral ambiguity of being a welfare lawyer. Often he was on the right side of a case, and his poor client was an innocent victim of the state. But at times he found himself representing a client who was cheating the system. One MFY client, for example, had been fired from his job at the post office for pilfering mail. He received about $5,000 in severance pay when he left the job. The client lived it up for a few days, gambling and drinking away his money. Then he came to Diamond for help in applying for welfare. The welfare department had turned him down because he had just received the $5,000, but the reality of the situation was that the money was gone and the man's wife and children were starving.

Diamond was so outraged by the man's story that he had to excuse himself from the interview. "I often sympathized with the welfare department," he recalls. "I didn't feel that they should be abused by this guy, and I didn't want to help him abuse them." Diamond stepped into the next office to see Harold Rothwax, legal director at MFY. Rothwax listened to Diamond, then asked him to go back and finish the interview. "The products of a system of poverty are not necessarily nice things to look at, but the system still has to be made accountable," Rothwax said impassively. Diamond calmed down, went back into his own office and, concentrating on the client's wife and children, finished the interview.[30]

This ambivalence about the utility of legal services was, not surprisingly, often shared by clients. According to one MFY lawyer, "The clients knew that their poverty wouldn't go away even if they won their case. They would be back in nine months with a new problem, or maybe the same problem."[31]

In preparing the *Kelly v. Wyman* papers Diamond relied on models from an unsuccessful San Francisco case challenging the fair hearing system. That case, *Wheeler v. Montgomery*, was filed two months before *Kelly v. Wyman* by one of Diamond's fellow Reggies, a legal services lawyer named Peter Sitkin. In *Wheeler* the California federal court decided that a hearing was not constitutionally required prior to termination of welfare benefits.[32]

As he prepared his papers, Diamond tried to avoid the problems he saw in *Wheeler* and to emphasize the hardship that prehearing termination of benefits caused for his clients. At Diamond's direction, Sparer prepared an impassioned affidavit to submit with the briefs. "I have seen, again and again, the dire and irreparable effects of the failure to grant administrative 'fair hearings' prior to the termination of welfare assistance," wrote Sparer. "Recipients are terminated from assistance they desperately need for their survival and that of their children; they are cast into deep fear, anguish and physical suffering; if they are fortunate enough to be informed of their right to a hearing and obtain assistance in the hearing they may—and often have—won a determination that their cutoff was illegal. In no case, however, is there a mechanism for making them whole from the anguish and physical suffering caused."[33]

Diamond also wanted to stress that caseworkers' initial decisions to cut off benefits were often wrong, and he edited the affidavits to reflect that fact. Of the fair hearings in which he had represented welfare recipients, Sparer wrote, "I do not recall a *single* case in which public assistance aid was not restored, either as a result of a hearing decision or settlement by the local welfare agency prior to the scheduled hearing."[34] Darrow concurred, noting that of the approximately one hundred fair hearings he had handled, "in every case, the decision to terminate [benefits] has been made by the caseworker and supervisor based either on improper conclusions as to the requirements of the statutes or on an incomplete examination of the evidence."[35]

The complaint and supporting papers were filed in New York federal district court on Monday, January 29, 1968. The city and state quickly moved to dismiss the case. First the defendants argued that the plaintiffs' stories were misleading. Randolph Young, according to one of the city's attorneys, Merrill Charlton, "has a substantial history as a narcotic user and an alcoholic." Charlton charged that "John Kelly changed his address so often that it was almost impossible to keep contact with him to send him his grants. . . . He was never told to move out of any hotel—he was told that he must obtain a permanent address in order for his public assistance to continue steadily."[36]

"As to plaintiff Juan De Jesus," wrote Charlton, "his case was closed because he refused to attend narcotics counseling or any rehabilitation clinic or center. He also refused to look for any kind of work." Pearl McKinney's benefits were terminated "because her son, Marvin, failed to submit verification of his employment and income." Pearl Frye's case was not closed but merely suspended pending an investigation into the ownership of her home. And, wrote Charlton, Guzman's benefits had never been terminated at all.[37]

At least some of Charlton's assertions were based in fact. One of the plaintiffs had a low-paying part-time job that she had hidden from the welfare department. Another was an addict in need of treatment. In fact, the plaintiffs' lawyers were concerned that if their clients were actually given fair hearings some of them would lose. According to Lee Albert, "We were very relieved when the court put some of our clients back on the rolls without conducting fair hearings."[38]

As a precaution, the plaintiffs' lawyers continued looking for new welfare recipients to add to the lawsuit, and on February 29, claims on behalf of AFDC recipients Ruby Sheafe and Esther Lett were filed by Martin Garbus of the ACLU; Rachlin of NWRO; MFY; the Center; and the Legal Aid Society. A few weeks later, twelve more plaintiffs were allowed to intervene in the case: Theresa Negron, Cynthia Fuller, Alma Coldburn, Magdalena Mulei, Maria Fuentes, Minerva Rodriguez, Ina Sidor, Angelina Velez, Mary Holmes, and Felix Gomez, all AFDC recipients, and Leroy Pavey and Antonio Soto, home relief recipients.

As the plaintiffs' lawyers had hoped, the defendants conceded that welfare benefits were protected by the due process clause and that, as providers, they were required to grant a review before benefits were terminated. The lead city attorney on the case, John Loflin, recalls that "nobody in our group had a taste for making conservative arguments that would be uncomfortable to defend."[39] Although the court might still raise the property issue itself, it was now much more likely that the court would find that welfare benefits were protected by the due process clause.

But the defendants disagreed with the plaintiffs over how extensive the process must be. According to the defendants, welfare procedures must be extremely flexible in light of financial constraints on the government. Despite "thousands of personal tragedies behind the statistics of public assistance," they argued, the system must be operated with "some regard for fiscal and administrative control."[40]

The defendants could not, however, agree between themselves on what type of review should be offered. In the wake of the lawsuit, the state had proposed new regulations entitling both home relief and AFDC recipients to seven days' notice of the termination of their benefits and allowing them to request that an independent supervisor review the decision prior to the termination. The recipient had the right to present evidence at the supervisor's review and to be represented by an attorney. If the supervisor agreed with the decision, and the benefits were cut off, the recipient could still request a full-fledged fair hearing after benefits were terminated.[41]

The state pressured New York City to adopt these new procedures but did not offer to appropriate funds to implement the process. The formal reviews proposed by the state would require clerks, stenographers, and additional administrative personnel to handle scheduling and other logistical issues. The question of who would pay for these procedures was crucial to the city. Because of the welfare rights movement's success in organizing recipients, the cost of offering hearings had skyrocketed by the time *Kelly v. Wyman* was filed. In 1968, about 14 percent of the population of New York received welfare. In 1967–68, recipients claimed $839,155,551 from the city, up from \$587,807,056 in 1966–67.[42] The city was already in dire financial straits, and city officials were concerned that the state's fair hearing regulations would result in still more welfare expenses.

Urged by the city's welfare administration to come up with a cheaper alternative, city attorney John Loflin proposed a "paper" review. The recipient would be given seven days' written notice of termination, and the notice would specify the reasons for termination. Although the recipient would not be permitted to present witnesses or oral testimony to the welfare department, the recipient or a representative could submit written evidence to explain why the grant should continue. The supervisor of the caseworker who made the initial decision would then review the evidence and decide whether to terminate benefits. Loflin was proud of his "Option B" and was convinced that it conformed to the requirements of the due process clause.

A three-judge court was designated to hear the case in recognition of the important constitutional issue at stake.[43] The judges were district court Judges Frederick Van Pelt Bryan and Edward C. McLean and Second Circuit Court of Appeals Judge Wilfred Feinberg.

For the plaintiffs, the appointment of Feinberg, a relatively young jurist elevated to the court of appeals only two years before, was an encouraging sign. He was the most liberal of the three judges and, as the only court of appeals judge on the panel, its highest ranking member. But Feinberg, on the other hand, viewed the assignment as something of a chore. He was well aware that junior members of the court of appeals were often assigned to three-judge panels in the summer when the more senior judges were on vacation. And because a three-judge lawsuit involved constitutionally complex issues, *Kelly v. Wyman* meant extra work for each of the three judges.[44]

Oral argument was scheduled for June 26, 1968. Lee Albert, who had been the director of the Center on Social Welfare Policy and Law since March, represented the plaintiffs; Loflin appeared for New York City; and Joel Sachs was the state's attorney.

During his brief tenure Albert had shifted the locus of *Kelly v. Wyman* away from MFY. Handling a big case would, he felt, give both him and the Center much-needed credibility after Sparer's departure. David Diamond did not put up a fight. "I'm a very good second-in-command," Diamond later explained. "Lee would call a meeting and everybody would go to the Center. I could have said, 'We're not going to the Center. This is an MFY case. You come down here.' But you have to fight those battles early. And I was happy to let control slide over."[45]

When Feinberg convened the argument, Albert spoke first. He was very nervous, and Feinberg quickly intervened. "Mr. Albert," he said, "I think it would be wise if you got right to the guts of your case and told us why you think the regulations are unconstitutional."

Still trying to get his argument off the ground, Albert's response was opaque. "Your honor," he said, "our first proposition is that we think and we'd like to show that the need for procedural regularity, traditional procedural regularity, a hearing and opportunity to be heard, a trial-type hearing before an impartial fact-finder prior to government action which adversely affects an individual, where that action, where that government action is based upon a particularized set of fact-findings about that individual—we are not talking about general rules or general standards at all—we are not challenging them; we are talking about the decision of the Welfare Department to terminate which is based upon a series of fact-findings about a particular person." Feinberg interrupted again: "Mr. Albert, all of that is set forth very well in your brief which we have all read. I would still like to know . . . what is it about the regulations now that you say is unconstitutional."[46]

Finally, Albert focused on the question. The notice is inadequate, he told the judges. In addition, the review of the caseworker's decision to terminate benefits is not conducted by an independent adjudicator, but by the caseworker's immediate supervisor, who may have been involved in making the initial decision to terminate.

"Wait a minute," Bryan interjected. "As I understand it, there were two alternatives presented to the city of New York."

Feinberg joined in. "Do your objections go equally to both procedures?" he asked.

"No, your honor," answered Albert. "On its face, Option A is far superior to Option B." Option A provides a greater opportunity for cross-examination, he conceded. It contemplates that the hearing officer will be an independent referee. Its notice provision of seven days, though very short, does not rise to the level of unconstitutionality.

"Is it fair to say," asked McLean, "that the plaintiffs do not contend that Option A . . . is unconstitutional on its face?" Albert's answer sounded evasive: "We do contend, Judge McLean, that on its face it raises questions."[47]

Seated in the gallery, Albert's colleagues cringed. By conceding, in essence, that the state's regulations were constitutional, Albert had invited the judges to adopt the particulars of those regulations as a constitutional floor. The plaintiffs would now be hard pressed to ask the court to require a pretermination notice of more than seven days. Some later felt that Albert's concession in this initial argument was the most decisive point in the entire case.[48]

Loflin spoke next. His nervousness stemmed not from inexperience but from the fact that other city business had kept him from adequately preparing for the argument.

In contrast to Albert, Loflin immediately and succinctly stated the city's position: "We must meet whatever minimal standards of due process are applied, and as humane individuals we should cause the least personal damage that we can while we are spending the public's money in trying to carry out the purposes of the system." Option B met due process standards, Loflin contended, while protecting the public fisc. "We could have [pretermination hearings] . . . if the state or someone else would appropriate sufficient money to name the hearing officers and provide the facilities. I think it is simply a question of economics."[49]

When Loflin returned to his chair, Sachs rose to defend the state's position. "I am a little surprised at Mr. Albert's statement today," Sachs told the court, "that he is completely satisfied with the state fair hearings and that all he is asking the Court at this point to do is to require the state to hold the fair hearing prior to the termination of assistance."[50]

At the close of Sachs' argument, Bryan asked for some additional information: "Before you sit down there is one other thing I would like to get in an affidavit from you or from Mr. Loflin—or from both of you—and that is the percentage of cases in which recipients win at the local level and at the state level."

Loflin rose from his chair to address the judge: "I might say on this serious matter—but in a moment of levity—that I am not sure which is better for my side, whether we should win or lose."

"Well, I am not going to tell you," replied Bryan with a thin smile.[51]

Albert stood before the court again to rebut the defendants' presentations. This time, he tried to focus on the plaintiffs themselves. "The way the state and city avoids too many people asking for [a fair hearing] is by putting it out of time and putting it in such a manner that most people cannot afford to wait that long," Albert asserted. "For example, let's ask Mrs. Lett and her children, who were cut off welfare, about it. She has been hospitalized because she ate spoiled food that she managed to forage from a neighbor. Let's ask Mrs. Velez about it, who was evicted from her apartment because she was terminated from welfare."[52] In such cases, Albert argued, retroactive payments received long after the termination of benefits were not good enough.

Feinberg interrupted to ask a question: "Mr. Albert, you and some of the other attorneys have been active in a number of these cases. Is it true that HEW has not appeared in any of them?"

That was what the plaintiffs had hoped to avoid by suing only the state and city rather than the federal government. Albert answered, "To my knowledge, your honor, HEW has not appeared."[53]

The argument was over moments later.

During the remainder of the summer and fall, the parties inundated the court with information. Statistics submitted by the defendants indicated that from April through August 1968, only fifty of seventy-eight fair hearing decisions statewide—or 64 percent—affirmed the caseworker's initial decision to terminate benefits.[54] The Center exhaustively analyzed the availability of retroactive payments when a recipient won a fair hearing. Finally, Bryan put a stop to the submissions. "I think we have the entire picture," he pointedly told the parties.[55]

In October 1968, in response to a request from Feinberg, HEW filed an amicus brief in *Kelly v. Wyman*. Prepared by an Assistant U.S. Attorney in Manhattan, the brief avoided taking sides and instead simply set out "certain relevant Federal policies and how they operate."[56]

The government's mild-mannered brief was a relief to the plaintiffs, who feared that HEW would take a strong stand in favor of the city and state. Instead, the tentative observations from HEW were not likely to have much impact on the judges' thinking in the case.

In fact, the judges' thinking was revealed shortly afterward. On November 26, 1968, the three-judge court issued its opinion, finding in favor of the plaintiffs.

The opinion, written by Feinberg, was virtually all that the plaintiffs could have asked for. First, he ruled that welfare benefits fell within the purview of the due process clause. Then, while Feinberg upheld Option A as "constitutionally sufficient" provided it was properly implemented— the position that Albert had conceded during the oral argument—he struck down the city's procedures contained in Option B. "The stakes are simply too high for the welfare recipient," wrote Feinberg, "and the possibility for honest error or irritable misjudgment too great, to allow termination of aid without giving the recipient a chance, if he so desires, to be fully informed of the case against him so that he may contest its basis and produce evidence in rebuttal."[57] Feinberg particularly noted the "startling statistic" provided by the defendants that "post-termination fair hearings apparently override prior decisions to terminate benefits in a substantial number of cases."[58]

Feinberg wrote at length about the cases of Angelina Velez and Esther Lett, two plaintiffs who had been cited by Albert during oral argument. Velez had been restored to the welfare rolls after a fair hearing revealed that her termination was erroneous; Lett, according to Feinberg, also appeared to have a strong argument against termination. "Suffice it to say," the judge continued, "that to cut off a welfare recipient in the face of this kind of 'brutal need' without a prior hearing of some sort is unconscionable, unless overwhelming considerations justify it."[59]

The phrase "brutal need" was borrowed from an article on welfare hearings published in the *Yale Law Journal* the previous year.[60] Feinberg later recalled, "I wanted to get some of the individual case histories into the opinion. And I wanted to use the term 'brutal need.' I didn't think of it as a legal standard, but found it to be a very evocative, dramatic phrase. It summed up all the considerations on the side of the plaintiffs."[61]

There were also considerations on the government's side, Feinberg carefully observed, and the arguments against more elaborate hearings were made stronger because the numbers of recipients involved were so great. Feinberg worried about the cost of these procedures for the city and state. But, he later acknowledged, "I felt compassion for the plaintiffs. The stakes for the plaintiffs were high—higher than in most situations where the 'new property' was at issue."[62]

Chapter 8

The Road to Washington

Mrs. Pearl McKinney received an AFDC grant for herself and four of her five children. In November–December, 1967, her caseworker requested information concerning her eldest son's earnings. The son visited the caseworker and Mrs. McKinney's attorney sent a certified letter (receipt acknowledged) advising the caseworker of the amount of the son's earnings, that the son had not contributed anything to the household and was not a legally responsible relative, and that the son was saving up to be married. A week after this letter was sent, Mrs. McKinney received notice that her AFDC grant had been suspended for "failure to get us information concerning your son's employment." Despite his efforts, her attorney was unable to have her family restored to the rolls until after the filing of this action.

—Brief for Appellees, *Goldberg v. Kelly* (U.S. Supreme Court, October Term, 1969)

In their seminal article setting out a blueprint for federal legal services, "The War on Poverty: A Civilian Perspective," Edgar and Jean Cahn rejected lawyer-driven test case strategies as a means for social change. Instead, they argued that it was imperative for poor people to participate in their own representation and for poverty lawyers to respond directly to the needs of their clients.[1]

The goal of the Center on Social Welfare Policy and Law, in contrast, was to create a corps of lawyers who would be removed from the community and have the leisure to think strategically about welfare issues nationwide. These lawyers would not only advise neighborhood centers, they would bring their own test case litigation as well. To counterbalance the inherent elitism of the Center, Sparer felt that the Center should be directly tied to the community of welfare recipients both through its direct representation of NWRO and as part of a two-tiered legal services system.[2]

As the Center developed and its leadership changed, however, Sparer's blueprint was modified. The Center did not just back up local offices. It tried, as in *Shapiro v. Thompson* to dictate the legal strategies pursued by neighborhood welfare lawyers. This happened in part because storefront lawyers did not have the time or inclination to handle complex federal litigation alongside their heavy load of more routine cases. In addition, the

Center attorneys did not always trust lawyers outside their small circle to exercise good judgment in important cases. According to Martin Garbus, "The caliber of lawyering was very low. They were well-meaning, but almost all of these attorneys were totally green. I spent about a third of every day on the phone giving nuts-and-bolts advice."[3]

The Center's evolution into an independent force in the movement was made explicit when Lee Albert deliberately cut back on the Center's work for NWRO. From the perspective of NWRO, the Center had set itself up as a "separate base of power and interest," a trend that would have been "even stronger" had other lawyers at the Center not prevented Albert "from using all the power he had."[4]

Though the Center and NWRO continued to collaborate on some projects, relations were strained. In a letter to NWRO general counsel Carl Rachlin in early 1969, Albert accused Rachlin of aggravating "petty conflict, wasteful backbiting and fragmentation" within the movement. "I do think that this field is quite large enough for your organization and mine," Albert wrote. "But that does require at least a molecule of cooperation and, I must add, mutual respect."[5]

Rachlin responded with a detailed list of the instances in which, he asserted, the Center had ignored or rejected the participation of NWRO. The cases ranged from *Kelly v. Wyman* to Ron Pollack's challenges to the food stamp policies of the Department of Agriculture. Rachlin knew, however, that NWRO could not risk cutting off all ties to the Center. "What has happened," Rachlin wrote Albert in an attempt to make peace between their groups, "is a simple failure in communications. . . . We will continue to work together, I know, with great joy in what we do."[6]

The peace between the Center and NWRO was superficial at best, and NWRO began to look for its own lawyers rather than continue relying on the Center. Rachlin made plans to hire a staff attorney and to fill out his legal department with a Reggie, one or two VISTA lawyers, several law students and a legal secretary.[7] Meanwhile, with neighborhood legal services lawyers and the welfare recipient movement relegated to the background, the Center's lawyers handling *Kelly v. Wyman* continued to pursue their litigation strategy.

Even before Feinberg's decision was handed down the plaintiffs' attorneys in *Kelly v. Wyman* were jockeying to get the case before the Supreme Court. The race was against the plaintiffs in the California fair hearing case *Wheeler v. Montgomery*.

From a litigator's perspective, the facts in the *Wheeler* case were less compelling than those in *Kelly v. Wyman*. Plaintiff Mae Wheeler received welfare benefits under the federal Old Age Assistance program. She was better off than many welfare recipients because she also received Social Security payments and her son could support his mother if necessary.

Further, the regulations in effect in California were more solicitous of recipients than was Option B—and perhaps less likely to be struck down. In California, welfare recipients could request a face-to-face interview at least one day prior to termination with a "responsible person" in the welfare department. This opportunity for a personal conference gave the California procedure a veneer of fairness that the New York City regulations lacked.

Nevertheless, on June 14 the plaintiffs' lawyers in *Wheeler v. Montgomery*—Peter Sitkin, a former Reggie, and Steve Antler, previously with MFY—filed an appeal to the Supreme Court. The Court tentatively accepted jurisdiction and set a briefing schedule for the October 1968 term.

On the opposite side of the country, Albert was concerned that the *Wheeler* appeal would upset the Center's grand strategy. He believed that if *Wheeler* was heard by the Supreme Court there was a good chance that welfare rights advocates would lose their claim for pretermination fair hearings.[8] In addition, Albert was eager to make his own mark in the Supreme Court and did not appreciate being outmaneuvered on this important issue by a group of neighborhood legal services lawyers in California.

By the time the briefing for *Wheeler* was under way Feinberg had issued his decision in *Kelly v. Wyman*. The plaintiffs' lawyers in *Kelly* expected the city and state to appeal, but they had no control over the defendants' timing. As each day passed, it grew more likely that the Supreme Court would proceed with *Wheeler* while *Kelly* languished in the lower court. Before it was too late, however, the Center's lawyers, led by Albert, hit on a novel and brilliantly aggressive tactic: they filed an amicus brief in the *Wheeler* case on behalf of the Center, MFY, and all of the other organizations involved in representing plaintiffs in *Kelly v. Wyman*.[9]

Amicus briefs are generally filed by organizations that are not parties to the litigation but have an interest in the subject matter of the case. The role of the brief is to bring to the attention of the court data or perspectives that the parties themselves might not raise. The Center, however, used its amicus brief to advise the Court of the proceedings in *Kelly v. Wyman* and to suggest that "this Court may in its discretion be disposed to hear *Wheeler v. Montgomery* and *Kelly v. Wyman* on their merits together."[10]

Martin Garbus volunteered on behalf of the Roger Baldwin Foundation of the ACLU to pay the bill for printing the brief. But ACLU Legal Director Mel Wulf was not pleased when the $713.65 charge came to him for approval. He refused to approve payment for the unusual—and, Wulf believed, inappropriate—brief, icily informing Garbus that "from here on in, in *all cases* of whatever nature in which RBF proposes to make an appearance . . . [I will do] *everything* that has to do with litigation."[11]

The city and state, meanwhile, were working out the mechanics of their appeal of *Kelly v. Wyman*. On December 23, 1968, the City of New York applied to Supreme Court Justice John M. Harlan, who was assigned to handle emergencies in the Second Circuit, asking that the city not be required to comply with Feinberg's opinion until the Supreme Court had reviewed the case. The city argued that it should not be forced to incur the expense of setting up pretermination hearing procedures until it had an opportunity to seek Supreme Court review.

On January 10, Harlan denied the city's request in a two-sentence opinion, and the city had no choice but to begin complying with Feinberg's ruling.[12]

Almost immediately after the ruling the state of New York decided not to appeal to the Supreme Court. In fact, the state had little to gain by appealing. Because Feinberg had essentially upheld Option A, only the provisions of the city's Option B were really still at issue. The state abruptly dropped out of the litigation, leaving the city to argue that, despite the state's apparent lack of interest, a fiscal crisis would erupt unless the less expensive Option B was approved.

As the plaintiffs had hoped, the Supreme Court accepted the city's appeal of *Kelly v. Goldberg* and consolidated it for argument with *Wheeler*. The city was first to file its brief with the Supreme Court. It was a mere nine pages; clearly the city was not devoting substantial resources to the litigation. Nevertheless, according to John Loflin, the appeal "wasn't a cynical exercise. We really thought that the system the city had adopted had enough elements of fairness to meet due process standards. Though I will admit that the primary motivation behind Option B was to save money, I don't think any of us could be characterized as right-wing conservatives who wanted to get welfare mothers off the rolls."[13]

Despite the city's minimal defense, the lawyers at the Center were not sanguine about their chances of success. The Center lawyers crafted their arguments to speak directly to the concerns they anticipated from the justices rather than to respond point by point to the city.[14]

The task of coordinating the production of the plaintiffs' brief fell to

Sylvia Law, a recent graduate of New York University Law School. Employed in an administrative position at MFY as a student, Law was now a Reggie spending a year at the Center. Because she was both a protégé of Sparer and a good friend of Albert, Law mediated between warring camps in the welfare rights movement during the delicate process of committing the fair hearing arguments to paper.[15]

The key substantive question—What constitutional protections should entitlements get?—had been thoroughly debated by the Center's lawyers. There were some additional strategic questions to be settled: Should the plaintiffs address the underlying issue of whether welfare benefits are property even though the defendants had conceded the point? Should they cite Charles Reich's seminal but theoretical articles? Should their brief rely on the controversial right to live doctrine?

While Law skipped the Woodstock Festival to research the legal issues in the case, Albert went home to work on the plaintiffs' brief.[16] Now that the case was certain to be heard by the Supreme Court, Albert was even more worried that it would be wrested from his control. He reasoned that the best way to ensure that he would present the oral argument to the Court, and that the argument would conform to his vision of the case, was to exercise firm authority over the writing of the brief. For example, Albert felt strongly that the plaintiffs must address the basic question of whether welfare qualified for due process protection in the first place. Over his colleagues' objections, Albert began the brief by arguing that welfare constituted property within the meaning of the due process clause.[17]

After a few days of writing and revising at home, Albert brought the draft brief into the Center for review. Albert had a baroque way with words, so Law's principal task was to tone down the prose. "The Huns of welfare are not likely to invade the treasury," Albert had written; his colleagues insisted that the flowery language be deleted.[18] Law also tried, after consulting on the phone with Sparer, to inject some of the passion for the plight of individual welfare recipients that had informed the litigation when MFY drafted the complaint. Quoting Feinberg's opinion below, Law wrote, "There is one overpowering fact that controls here. . . . [A] welfare recipient is destitute, without funds or assets."[19] To drive home the point the Center lawyers outlined the stories of each of the plaintiffs in an appendix to the brief.

Despite Law's mediation, Sparer and Albert were polarized around the question of how to treat the right to live. Albert maintained that it was a kooky idea that would never be adopted by the Supreme Court; Sparer felt that it was imperative that the Center use *Goldberg v. Kelly* to advance the theory.[20]

Sparer was particularly adamant in light of evidence that the theory was beginning to gain acceptance. Only a few days before the appellees' brief was due, a New York federal court issued its opinion in *Rothstein v. Wyman*, a case handled by the Center.[21] The issue in *Rothstein* was whether a state law allowing higher payments to welfare recipients in New York City than to recipients in surrounding counties violated the equal protection clause. Adopting the strict scrutiny standard put forward in *Shapiro v. Thompson*, the federal district court struck down the inequitable law. In the process, it came close to recognizing welfare as a "fundamental right": "Receipt of welfare benefits may not at the present time constitute the exercise of a constitutional right. But among our Constitution's expressed purposes was the desire to ensure domestic tranquility' and 'promote the general Welfare.' Implicit in those phrases are certain basic concepts of humanity and decency. One of these, voiced as a goal in recent years by most responsible leaders, both federal and state, is the desire to insure that indigent, unemployable citizens will have the bare minimums required for existence, without which our expressed fundamental constitutional rights and liberties frequently cannot be exercised and therefore become meaningless."[22] Sparer sensed that there might be a future for the right to live provided welfare lawyers did not abandon the theory.

In the end, the plaintiffs' lawyers compromised. Even Albert could see the value of referring to the right to live in case one of the justices chose to address the theory. So on page 39 of the brief the plaintiffs paraphrased the *Rothstein* opinion and noted that without "the bare minimums essential for existence . . . our expressed constitutional liberties become meaningless."[23]

The Center's lawyers downplayed Charles Reich and Jacobus tenBroek's theories for essentially the same reasons. Reich's idea of the new property was so all-encompassing that the lawyers were afraid that it would scare the justices, and tenBroek's writings were too strident and political. Albert wanted to argue *Goldberg v. Kelly* from the narrowest possible grounds. Though their theories were crucial to the formulation of the plaintiffs' position, direct citations to Reich and tenBroek were limited to unprovocative footnotes.[24]

The plaintiffs stressed that they sought only minimal due process protections for welfare benefits, establishing a recipient's right to know the case against him or her, to present evidence, to confront witnesses, and to receive a decision free from bias.[25] Afraid that the Supreme Court might choose to leave the states alone to experiment with different fair hearing systems, the plaintiffs took pains to minimize the magnitude of their claims: "Appellees are not asking for any special or novel constitutional rule because of their circumstances. They seek only traditional constitutional safeguards, safeguards which themselves embody the government's respect for the elementary rights of individuals."[26] After two months of drafting and redrafting, the plaintiffs filed their seventy-four-page brief, with twenty-five pages of appendices, on August 30, 1969.

The Supreme Court also requested that the U.S. government file an amicus brief. The government brief was vastly different from that filed in the district court. Drafted by Peter Strauss of the solicitor general's office (he edited "The New Property" when he was a student at Yale Law School), the brief argued that pretermination hearings were not required by the due process clause. And, the government argued, money diverted to the administration of fair hearings would reduce the sum available for actual welfare payments. Congress budgeted a certain amount for welfare administration, the government asserted, and that money could be spent on public assistance payments or on fair hearings, but there wasn't enough for both.[27]

The brief was a much-needed boost for the city and a devastating surprise to the *Goldberg* plaintiffs, who knew that the Court would give substantial weight to government views. To minimize the damage, the Center and the *Wheeler* plaintiffs filed a joint response. Questioning the empirical basis for the government's position, the joint brief argued that individual rights cannot be abandoned simply because "mass justice" is more efficient. The recipients' lawyers asserted that the Constitution guarantees a minimum level of due process that a state cannot strip away, regardless of the expense.[28]

While the lawyers waited for the oral argument, a turf war that developed between MFY and the Center reflected the Center's growing separation from the grass-roots welfare rights movement. Several MFY lawyers felt that Albert was not the appropriate person to conduct the argument.[29] They were afraid that Albert would lose the justices with his complex syntax or put them off with his British accent. More profoundly, the lawyers at MFY felt increasingly estranged from the litigation they had started and wanted to reassert control by choosing their own representative before the Supreme Court.[30]

A series of tense meetings were convened to discuss who should argue

Goldberg v. Kelly. MFY proposed Archibald Cox. The former solicitor general had appeared before the Supreme Court to reargue *Shapiro v. Thompson* and, in the view of many, snatched an important victory from the talons of defeat.[31]

At first, Albert made an effort to compromise with MFY, offering to split the argument with Cox. But when Cox insisted on conducting the entire argument, Albert refused to step aside. Albert was, after all, a full-time federal legal services lawyer, albeit one whose connection to welfare recipients was attenuated. In addition, Albert recalled the disdain that some justices had shown for Cox during Albert's year as a clerk for Justice White. Though they seemed deferential during Cox's arguments, some of them found Cox pedantic. Albert refused to budge and, as the argument approached, opposition from MFY dissipated.[32]

Goldberg v. Kelly was Albert's first Supreme Court argument, though he had seen many of them during his year as a law clerk. To prepare he organized a moot court session with lawyers from MFY and the Center. Albert also met with the legal services attorneys from the *Wheeler* case. It was agreed that the *Wheeler* lawyers would set out the statutory and regulatory framework and that Albert would handle any remaining issues, reshaping his argument as the case went along to address particular concerns raised by the justices.

The Supreme Court called the case of *Wheeler v. Montgomery* at 10:25 A.M. on October 13, 1969. It was the first argument of the day. Because of Justice Fortas' recent resignation over questions about his financial interests, there were only eight justices on the bench: Chief Justice Burger and Justices Black, Douglas, Harlan, Brennan, Stewart, White, and Marshall. Fortas' chair had not been removed; it simply sat vacant and, according to Black's wife, Elizabeth, who attended the argument, "spoke eloquently of the man who wasn't there."[33]

Peter Sitkin of San Francisco Legal Services, representing the recipients in *Wheeler,* spoke first. "The basic issue presented by this case," he began, "is whether welfare recipients, after being found eligible, after full and vigorous investigation, are to have their benefits terminated without an opportunity for a full and fair adjudicative hearing." Under California regulations, Sitkin explained, "prior to termination of benefits, a welfare recipient is *not* afforded an adjudicative hearing to contest the reasons on which the department has based its decision to terminate. A welfare recipient is only provided with an opportunity to confer *informally,* usually with the very individual who has made the initial decision to terminate, at a conference which can take place at a minimum of three days before a check will be . . . withheld."[34]

Sitkin was suddenly interrupted by Black: "There is no trial-type hearing before he is found eligible, is there?"[35]

Sitkin conceded that there was no such hearing, then tried to lead the discussion back to the narrow issue before the Court—whether there should be a pretermination hearing.

But Black would not be led. "[A recipient] is declared eligible without any trial-type procedure, and your argument is that it is unconstitutional to cut him off without a trial-type procedure," Black challenged Sitkin.

"That is our position," Sitkin replied. "The one overwhelming and unique factor which is present in the welfare programs . . . is that maintenance of the welfare grant is the difference between . . . starvation and continuation of some kind of sustenance. It is this fundamental interest on the part of the individual that we assert must be protected."[36]

Again, Black confronted Sitkin. "Suppose a pension has been granted to a recipient," Black asked, "and the Congress or the Legislature wants to repeal it. . . . Would it be your position that a pension cannot be cut off where it has once been decided that a man gets a pension without giving him some kind of hearing before it is cut off?"[37]

Sitkin tried to maintain his focus on the issues before the Court. "Given the vital interest of the individuals who were involved here," he answered, "it is our position that due process requires the procedural protections which we assert are required in this case."[38]

Next, Elizabeth Palmer, representing the state of California, approached the lectern. The justices' questions to Palmer were informational. What exactly is the procedure given welfare recipients in California when their benefits are terminated, one justice asked. Palmer pointed out that notice of termination was preceded by a thorough investigation. If a recipient asked for more time, could he get it? Palmer thought that would vary from recipient to recipient. Has California had any success in recouping payment made to recipients who were later discovered to be ineligible? No, not really.

"I can't defend the welfare system," Palmer concluded. "I don't think anyone can. It is indefensible. No one is happy with it. Certainly the poor are not happy with it, and the taxpayer is less happy because of the enormous amount of money that goes into it. I am not defending the system. I am merely saying that the procedure that California has adopted does satisfy, at this stage of the proceeding, due process."[39]

Burger next called on John Loflin to present the city's position in *Goldberg v. Kelly*. Loflin's wife and two children who accompanied him to Washington leaned forward on the cushioned seats in the gallery to hear his first words to the Court. Loflin tried to control his excitement as he approached the lectern. "If you're a litigator," he later recalled, "you don't get too many shots at the Supreme Court. This was important. I worked very hard to get ready for it."[40]

Loflin's argument was skillful and persuasive. According to Albert, Loflin "was a sympathetic, feeling individual who well carried out the posture of the city in this case as a welfare administration with the most progressive leaders in the country but without the resources to create an ideal system. The message was 'We're doing the best we can,' and Loflin had the humanity to convey that position."[41]

Nevertheless, Loflin's position—that New York City should be allowed to terminate benefits after a paper review only—was less palatable than it had seemed before the lower court. A paper review in New York under the supervision of respected liberal social workers like Mitchell Ginsberg and Jack Goldberg was one thing. To allow such reviews on a national scale was another matter entirely.

Offering the liberal counterweight to Black, Marshall interrupted Loflin a dozen times.

"Do you see any difference between a government employee making $20,000 a year and a welfare recipient as to being able to live" while waiting for a hearing, asked Marshall rhetorically.

Feeling baited, Loflin replied, "obviously the impact on the individual is much worse if we make an error in the case of someone who is destitute than if we make an error in the case of someone who is well off." Marshall continued to press: "A personal conference is nothing close to a due process hearing, is it?"[42]

Now Loflin was angry. "I thought Justice Marshall was twisting my arguments out of shape," he later recalled. "I didn't want to play the role of the villain. I didn't feel villainous. But he kept putting a black hat on me."[43]

"Your honor," Loflin addressed Marshall, "I contend that [the personal conference] is part of a procedure which, when taken in its entirety, constitutes such basic fairness that it is due process of law."

Marshall shook his head in disbelief. "That is your idea of due process," he said and, after a dramatic pause, sat back in his leather chair.[44]

Loflin then explained that a full fair hearing would be held, whenever requested, as soon as possible after termination. The time elapsed before such a fair hearing "varies tremendously" but, he said, "we hope" to hold hearings within sixty days of termination.[45]

Albert followed Loflin. As with his argument before the three-judge court, Albert began shakily. "In discussing the procedures that have been added or the administrative changes since this case was before the District Court between January and June 1968, it is well, I think, to look at briefly the situation, the procedures used for the termination of the 20 appellees—not each one individually, of course—in this very case."

"Are those the ones we are going to be passing upon?" Justice White helpfully asked his former clerk.

"Those are certainly the people who, but for the lawsuit and the injunction below, are faced with the same kinds of termination problems that they already experienced," was Albert's reply.[46]

Albert's argument was nevertheless going well. He successfully focused on the plight of the welfare recipients, specifically mentioning John Kelly, Leroy Pavey, and Angelina Velez. To demonstrate the inadequacy of Option B's paper review Albert told the justices that when Antonio Soto's benefits were terminated Soto "received a notice informing him of his 'failure to attend rehabilitation COC.' "[47] Because "rehabilitation COC" meant nothing to him, Soto was unable to respond to the notice or to challenge the basis of the Welfare Department's decision.

Then, in a continuation of his earlier colloquy with Sitkin, Black began questioning Albert. "Are you arguing that it is arbitrary and capricious of the government to cut off a gift or gratuity?"

Albert started to answer, but Burger interrupted. It was noon, and the chief justice was eager to keep to a tight schedule. "Mr. Albert," Burger announced, "if you will bear the pending question in mind, we will recess at this time."[48]

During the lunch break, Albert gathered his thoughts. He knew that it was important to respond to Black's concern that if the plaintiffs won the case it would henceforth be impossible for Congress to repeal any government benefit program.[49] Ironically, that was the ultimate goal of the welfare rights litigation strategy: a guaranteed minimum income constitutionally secured by the right to live. But to win Black over to the plaintiffs' side Albert would have to disavow that goal.

Burger called the courtroom to order again at 12:35. (Later in his first term he would extend the traditional thirty-minute lunch period to a more civilized hour.)

Albert began with the statement he had prepared to address Black: "May it please the Court: We left off before the lunchtime recess on the threshold and fundamental question of whether the due process procedural guarantees apply to public assistance benefits at all. If one looks to the nature of the factors that the Court has traditionally deemed relevant, the nature of the individual interest, the nature of the government interest, the burden on the program or proceedings, one finds that all of those factors compel one answer."[50]

Albert told the Court of the 24 to 51 percent reversal rate of caseworker decisions. In an attempt to placate Justice Black, Albert made the narrowest claims possible for the plaintiffs' case, telling the justices that the principle established in *Goldberg* would apply only to welfare recipients, not to government employees who might argue that they are entitled to hearings before losing their jobs or suffering wage reductions.

The Court was engaged, even after two full hours of argument on this issue. When Albert's half-hour was over and Burger tried to cut off his argument, Harlan interrupted and asked yet another question, followed by Brennan and White. Burger scowled and, after a few minutes of additional questioning, he banged his gavel to signal the end of the argument. But Harlan had one more question, which he asked despite Burger's attempts to move on.[51]

Finally Burger called on Loflin for rebuttal. "There is room for innovation at the local level in state and local governments, and I feel that our innovation meets the standards that this Court has indicated are required for due process," said Loflin, summing up his position.

"Thank you, Mr. Loflin," said Burger as Loflin took his seat. "Are there any more questions?" he pointedly asked his brethren, implying that in future arguments he expected them to promptly cease their questioning at the bang of his gavel. Seeing none, he announced that "the case is submitted." The argument was over by 1:00 P.M.[52]

The postargument conference on *Wheeler v. Montgomery* and *Goldberg v. Kelly* was held that Friday. Sitting around a table without their usual accoutrements—robes and clerks—in order of seniority each justice stated his position on each case heard during the week. In addition, the justices discussed the progress of opinion-writing on previously decided cases.

Burger, sitting at the head of the table, went first. He voted to reverse Feinberg's decision and uphold the city's procedures.

As the senior associate justice on the Court, Justice Black sat opposite Burger at the conference table and spoke immediately after the chief justice. He also voted to reverse.

Douglas followed, expressing his view that welfare benefits were a "species of property" and voting to affirm the lower court.[53]

Harlan spoke next, also voting to affirm Feinberg. "This is not a gratuity," he told his colleagues. "It is an entitlement or right under the federal program and in state programs . . . a vested right as long as the state chooses to give it."[54] He emphasized, however, that the Court's approach must be flexible in determining what type of hearing might be required.[55] Brennan also voted to affirm, as did Marshall.

"I am more with John than with the two Bills," explained White when his turn came. "The impact here is so severe that the balance should be cast for a full hearing before termination."[56]

Finally, Stewart voted to reverse the three-court judge while specifically rejecting Black's view that welfare was not a form of property. "I don't think the distinction between a vested right and a gratuity is significant as to what requirements of due process obtain," he said. But "the totality of procedures here . . . satisfies due process."[57]

Burger spoke again. "We should let these cases alone," he advised. "It's like pulling up radishes to see how they are growing and ending up with no radishes."[58]

Because he was in the minority in the *Goldberg* and *Wheeler* cases, Burger indicated that Douglas, the senior member of the majority, should assign the opinions. Sensing a close vote, which might require some compromise to keep White and Harlan in the majority, Douglas gave the task of writing the opinions to Brennan.[59]

Justice Brennan's interest in due process issues dated back to his years on the New Jersey Supreme Court in the 1950s. According to Justice Brennan, "I had been looking for a 'new property' case. I knew of Charles Reich's work—I remembered him from his clerkship with Justice Black—but I was interested in the issue before that, back in New Jersey."[60] Not that Brennan had any particular connection to the welfare rights movement—he didn't. But perhaps, like Justice Black, he was held up in traffic around Resurrection City, the welfare recipients' encampment at the base of the Washington Monument during the Poor People's March in the summer of 1968.[61]

More than many of the justices, however, Brennan had a sense of what issues were being litigated in the lower courts: he was the only justice who examined all of the petitions for certiorari filed by parties seeking Supreme Court review of their cases. Other justices delegated a substantial portion of this mammoth task to their clerks. But the practice gave Brennan an overview of the lower courts' activity, and he could see that the scope of "property" under the due process clause was a considerable problem. "*Goldberg v. Kelly,*" Brennan later recalled, "seemed to be a good vehicle to present the issue. I wasn't concerned about it particularly in the welfare context, but more generally."[62]

Brennan's law clerks for the 1969 term were Richard Cooper, a Harvard Law School graduate, and Taylor Reveley, a Southerner from the University of Virginia Law School. Two other law clerks, Douglas Poe and Marshall Moriarty, were chosen by Burger and assigned to Brennan's staff.

Brennan typically prepared himself for oral arguments by reading the parties' briefs. After an argument, he might ask one of his clerks to help research a particular point of law prior to the Friday conference at which the justices reviewed the week's cases. Following the conference, Brennan returned to his chambers, preceded by a messenger drawing a large cart loaded with the books on which the justice had relied in reaching his decision. According to Reveley, "These books, along with his notes of the conference, would go to his clerks, and we would get to work."[63] It was the clerks' job to write the first draft of Brennan's opinions, which he would then review and edit. Because there was not a clear division of labor in Brennan's chambers—each clerk chipped in as he had the time—all of the clerks worked on various aspects of drafting the *Wheeler* and *Goldberg* opinions.

Brennan's two-page draft of the *Wheeler* opinion was printed and circulated within a week of the October 17 conference. It simply reversed the lower court's opinion on the ground that "procedural due process requires . . . a trial-type pre-termination hearing before welfare payments may be discontinued or suspended" and referred to the Court's opinion in *Goldberg,* yet unwritten.[64]

By the end of November the justices were drafting opinions and choosing sides. Burger circulated a memo indicating that he intended to dissent in both *Wheeler* and *Goldberg* and that he would await Black's opinion.[65] At the same time, Burger sent Black a copy of a draft dissent in which he worked out in more detail his "radish" theory.

"Hugo," the draft began, "here are some 'thoughts while shaving' " on the New York and California welfare cases. "The states and the federal agencies should be permitted to experiment rather than being forced into a mold which may or may not be suited either to expanding or contracting benefits. At least one generation of welfare recipients has grown up without the procedural safeguards now found to be imperative under the Constitution. . . . If the history of the cost and complexity of the administrative processes and judicial review, as we have seen it since the 1930s, is repeated and this new layer of procedural protection is subsidized, as it must be, by the public treasury, the zealous advocates for welfare claimants may be on the way to 'killing the golden goose.' "[66]

Brennan's first draft of the *Goldberg* opinion was circulated to the Court on November 24, 1969, with a second draft following on November 28. Although the initial outline of the opinion prepared by Reveley chronicled the story of each welfare recipient involved in the case, the circulated version focused on two representative plaintiffs, Altagrazia Guzman and Juan DeJesus. The clerk also wrote at length about the nature of poverty, calling it "largely a product of impersonal forces." Welfare, he wrote, was the "treatment of a disorder inherent in our society. Government has an overriding interest in providing welfare to the eligible, both to help maintain the dignity and well-being of a large segment of the population and to guard against the societal malaise that may flow from a widespread sense of unwarranted frustration and insecurity."[67]

The exposition was included in the first draft circulated to the Court, but after Harlan labeled the discussion "offensive" and White flatly refused to accept it, the passage was excised.[68] In its place, Brennan crafted a paragraph reflecting White's view that welfare is not a societal obligation but a benefit given to help the poor participate fully in society.[69]

The second draft also addressed the dissents Brennan anticipated. In an attempt to allay Black's fears, Brennan specifically stated that in *Goldberg v. Kelly* "we do not consider whether a recipient has a substantive due process right to receive welfare" but limit consideration to the requirements of procedural due process. Brennan then asserted, citing Charles Reich's work, that "it may be realistic today to regard welfare entitlements as more like 'property' than a 'gratuity.' "[70] Thus, wrote Brennan, welfare benefits could no longer be considered charity, and the requirements of the due process clause must apply to their administration. Brennan concluded that because the recipient lacks "the very means by which to live while he waits" for a hearing, the hearings must be held before termination. The government may have an interest in conserving its fiscal and administrative resources, but in light of the recipients' need, "governmental interests are not overriding in the welfare context."[71]

Finally, Brennan spelled out the meaning of a trial-type hearing: "timely and adequate notice detailing the reasons for a proposed termination . . . an effective opportunity to defend by confronting any adverse witnesses and by presenting his own arguments and evidence orally . . . and an impartial decisionmaker."[72]

Marshall and Douglas joined Brennan's opinions in *Wheeler* and *Goldberg* immediately.[73] White followed on December 2.[74]

Black, however, was stirred after reading the majority's preliminary opinion. His wife, Elizabeth, recorded in her diary for December 4, 1969, that "Hugo couldn't sleep. He was extremely exhilarated. He had a dissent rolling around in his mind (to Bill Brennan's opinion saying a hearing is due to anyone severed from Relief Roll as a constitutional right). Hugo was like other years when he would get on fire about an opinion."[75]

The next day, Black was still agitated. "He woke up at 3:00 A.M.," wrote Elizabeth Black, "and got up and talked. He said his mind was racing and he was 'writing' an opinion in his mind. It must be, said he, the Holmes-type opinion—short, classic, citing no authorities—about 'I am fearful that the Court goes farther and farther on the Due Process Clause,' in regard to a case whereby if anyone ever gets his name on the welfare rolls, he is entitled constitutionally to a hearing before he is removed. Hugo still couldn't sleep at 4:00, and so he got up and took a drink."[76]

By 1969 Black's dissents were different from those written during his early years on the Court. In his dissent in *Barsky v. Board of Regents*, for example, Black compared Barsky's medical license to "liberty," defended Barsky's freedom of association, and condemned the state's sidelong attempts to, in effect, coerce Barsky by threatening to revoke his license. Similarly, Black sided with individual lawyers in a series of cases challenging states' attempts to control freedom of speech by barring Communists from the practice of law. As the years passed, however, Black grew less willing to accommodate individual rights that were not squarely set out in the text of the Constitution. Black's former clerk, Charles Reich, wrote in a 1962 tribute to his mentor that constitutional principles must move "in the same direction and at the same rate as the rest of society."[77] Black responded to Reich in his dissent in *Griswold v. Connecticut* in 1965, in which the majority of the Court found that individuals have a constitutional privacy right to make personal decisions regarding contraception. Black wrote, "I realize that many good and able men have eloquently spoken and written, sometimes in rhapsodical strains, about the duty of this Court to keep the Constitution in tune with the times. The idea is that the Constitution must be changed from time to time and that this Court is charged with a duty to make those changes. For myself, I must with all deference reject that philosophy. The Constitution makers knew the need for change and provided for it. Amendments suggested by the people's elected representatives can be submitted. . . . That method of change was good for our Fathers, and being somewhat old-fashioned I must add it is good enough for me."[78] Later, while reading Charles Reich's 1970 book *The Greening of America*, Black announced that he was a "Consciousness I" man, described in Reich's book as one who "is unwilling or unable to comprehend the transformation of America" from the nineteenth to twentieth centuries.[79]

By 1969 Black viewed the Constitution as a document that definitively identified and limited potential government excesses. He was not open to arguments that the definition of property under the due process clause must be revised in light of contemporary government's dealings with its beneficiaries.

In the margins of Brennan's draft opinion, Black scribbled notes to himself. Where Brennan had written that "we do not say that counsel must be provided at the pretermination hearing, but only that the recipient must be allowed to retain an attorney if he so desires," Black scrawled, "But of course, the next thing is to provide counsel for the indigent."[80]

Black wrote his dissent during the next few weeks. It began with a review of the Constitutional Convention and the structure of government intended by the Constitution's framers. "The judicial department was to have no part whatsoever in making any laws," wrote Black. The majority of the Court, however, "says that failure of the government to pay a promised charitable installment to an individual deprives that individual of *his property*, and thus violates the due process clause of the Fourteenth Amendment." According to Black, the majority's opinion was tantamount to substantive due process: "This is another variant of the view often expressed by some members of the Court that the due process clause forbids any conduct that a majority of the Court believes is 'unfair,' 'indecent,' or 'shocking to the conscience.'

"Had the Constitution meant by the due process clause to leave judges such ambulatory power to declare laws unconstitutional," Black argued, "the chief value of a written constitution as the Founders saw would have been lost. In fact, if that view of due process is right, the due process clause would swallow up all other parts of the Constitution."

Black concluded with an approving nod to Burger's dissent. "The function of a welfare state," he wrote, "is a new experiment for our nation. For this reason, among others, I agree with the Chief Justice that new experiments in carrying on such a state should not be frozen into our Constitutional structure, but should be left as are other legislative determinations, to the Congress which the people elect to make our laws."[81] Black completed the draft dissent during his midwinter Florida vacation and mailed it from Miami.[82]

When Black's dissent arrived, Brennan was ready. During the weeks since he circulated his draft opinion, Brennan asked his clerk to study Black's previous decisions on the due process clause. The clerk concluded that, in Black's view, "welfare recipients . . . depend on affirmative state action; they have . . . no interests, expectations or rights with respect to welfare."[83] As one of Black's law clerks later explained his employer's vehement opposition to the majority opinion, "The Justice has become increasingly concerned that various members of the Court have let their views run wild. Thus he's eager to take an unusually strict constructionist—The Words—approach to attempt to pull the Court back into line. A part of his eagerness stems from an awareness that each year may be his last as an active Justice."[84]

On December 11, Brennan received a letter from Harlan concerning the draft majority opinion. The two justices had already talked about their points of disagreement, and the letter simply set them out formally. "There are some things in your opinion," Harlan wrote, "to which I would not wish to subscribe, and in order to avoid any separate writing on my part (which I would much prefer not to have to do) I thought I would put such matters to you for consideration."[85]

Harlan's objections were mostly minor. He questioned the term "trial-type hearing," which he believed was not sufficiently precise. Harlan suggested that "evidentiary hearing" be used instead.

Harlan also asserted that fair hearings should be limited to cases involving factual disputes—for example, whether the recipient was employed—as opposed to those involving such statutory interpretations as whether a state welfare regulation conformed to federal requirements. "In a case where a welfare recipient is simply attacking the validity of a statute or regulation on its face," wrote Harlan, "due process, in my view, does not require an opportunity for cross-examination or an oral argument.[86]

"If you can see your way clear to meeting my suggestions," he concluded, "I am prepared to join your opinion, which I think is a very good one, subject to further suggestions, or possibly some separate writing, after the dissent makes its appearance."[87]

Brennan asked his law clerk Richard Cooper to research the issues raised by Harlan. Cooper concluded that there was "no problem" regarding most of the suggestions.[88] But Harlan's assertion that there was no right to a full hearing when the termination of benefits involves a purely legal issue seemed to Cooper "to make bad law."[89]

Brennan replied to Harlan in a letter dated December 15. He agreed to revise his draft opinion based on Harlan's comments, asking Harlan to compromise only on his insistence that due process did not necessarily require a full hearing when purely legal issues were at stake. Brennan asked simply that Harlan agree to leave the issue open, to be resolved in a future case.[90]

On February 19, 1970, Harlan wrote to accept Brennan's compromise, adding that "I have decided to do no separate writing in either case myself." Harlan also asked that Brennan consider adding a final paragraph to his opinion, stating that "in reaching these conclusions, we wish to add that we, no less than the minority, recognize the importance of not imposing upon the states or the federal government in this developing field of the law any procedural requirements beyond those demanded by rudimentary due process." Harlan added that "I am content to leave this last suggestion in your hands, but for myself would consider it an appropriate thought to add."[91] Brennan added the sentence to the opinion following his discussion of the minimal procedural safeguards necessary to ensure due process.[92]

On February 17 Stewart circulated his one-sentence dissent from Brennan's opinion. "The question for me is a close one," he wrote, but "I do not believe that the procedures that New York and California now follow in terminating welfare payments are violative of the United States Constitution."[93]

The opinions were announced on March 23. As in his earlier drafts, the majority opinion by Brennan adopted Reich's functional view of property and noted, in consonance with Richard Cloward's "opportunity theory," that "welfare, by meeting the basic demands of subsistence, can help bring within the reach of the poor the same opportunities that are available to others to participate meaningfully in the life of the community."[94] The majority opinion expressly rejected the argument that the financial concerns of New York City outweighed the rights of recipients. Finally, the opinion spelled out the basic requirements of due process: a right to an appeal before an independent adjudicator, a right to present oral evidence, and a right to cross-examine witnesses.

Black, Stewart, and Burger wrote separate dissents, substantially the same as those they had circulated.

Though the Court had resolved *Goldberg v. Kelly,* two more welfare rights cases pending before the Court remained to be decided. These cases raised the central issue in the welfare rights movement: the inadequacy of benefits.

Chapter 9

The Impasse

I think that we have to face up to the fact that you cannot eat welfare rights, you cannot clothe your children with legal rights, you do not really take your place in society only by reason of having a remedy for injustice under the law. The concept of legal rights can only assure those who are covered in any particular way that they will be treated fairly under the constitution, that they will not be subject to discriminatory action, that they will have redress for mistreatment. But so far, at least, we have not found the way to make this instrument of law give people an adequate basis of existence.

—Elizabeth Wickenden, 1969

As poor people across the country joined the welfare rolls and organized to claim more benefits, the cost of operating welfare programs soared. Increased scrutiny by the federal courts ensured that states could no longer control the number of recipients by imposing arbitrary eligibility rules. The states looked to Congress to relieve the pressure, and in late 1967 Congress responded.

In August 1967 the Democrat-led House of Representatives passed, 415–3, a social security bill that would set up mandatory work training programs for AFDC recipients, provide day-care centers to help welfare mothers work, and allow recipients to keep a small portion of their earnings. The bill also sought to discourage expansion of AFDC by freezing the number of children covered by federal matching grants.[1]

Advocates opposed the bill's most punitive provisions—the mandatory work requirements and the AFDC freeze—on a number of grounds. According to the National Social Welfare Assembly (NSWA), which represented more than forty organizations and individuals active in welfare administration, poor mothers should not be "forced to leave their children and go out to work against their own best judgment." Instead, NSWA charged that the children's welfare should be the prime consideration.

Recipient activists felt that the bill failed to address the root causes of their poverty: the lack of good jobs at decent wages and the absence of a national policy of supporting families. Calling the proposed freeze and mandatory work requirements "a betrayal of the poor, a declaration of war upon our families, and a fraud on the future of our nation," NWRO responded with a massive, peaceful lobbying effort on Capitol Hill.[2] When no legislators reacted, NWRO members conducted a sit-in during the Senate Finance Committee hearings on the bill, refusing to leave the witness table until all members of the committee heard their testimony on the measure.[3]

Angered by the confrontation, Senator Russell Long, the powerful Louisiana Democrat who chaired the Finance Committee, announced that the welfare mothers were "brood mares." According to Long, "If they can find the time to march in the streets, picket, and sit all day in committee hearing rooms, they can find the time to do some useful work."[4]

On October 27 Senator Robert Kennedy introduced amendments to eliminate the most punitive of the bill's provisions. Although some of these amendments were passed by the Senate, the so-called antiwelfare provisions were restored by the House-Senate Conference Committee, chaired by Long and Representative Wilbur Mills, the Arkansas Democrat who was chairman of the House Ways and Means Committee. "The taxpayers want us to be rough," Mills explained. Under pressure from the measure's Congressional sponsors, President Johnson signed the bill into law on January 2, 1968.[5]

The leadership of the NWRO reacted with some dismay. Searching for new allies and new strategies, executive director George Wiley and the NWRO executive board scheduled a long-awaited meeting with Martin Luther King, Jr.[6]

The NWRO meeting with King signaled a conceptual turning point in the civil rights movement. Poverty had always been a distant second behind race on the civil rights movement's agenda. No one disputed that the two were linked: in the mid-1960s unemployment among nonwhites was more than twice that of whites; black children were seven times as likely to receive AFDC as their white counterparts; and in 1966, 41 percent of nonwhites fell below the federal poverty line of $207 per month while the rate of poverty among whites was only 12 percent.[7] But until the movement began to fracture in the late 1960s most civil rights leaders shied away from the negative images that might be projected if they focused directly on welfare rights. As Whitney Young, director of the Urban League, told Richard Cloward and Frances Fox Piven, "It is more important to get one black woman into a job as an airline stewardess than it is to get fifty poor families onto welfare."[8]

By 1968, however, having failed in his most recent campaign for open housing in Chicago, King was ready to heed the longstanding contention of his associate, Bayard Rustin, that economics, rather than race, must be at the center of a civil rights movement.[9] King was expanding the Poor People's Campaign planned by the Southern Christian Leadership Conference—a recent effort by the civil rights movement to move from discrimination into class and economic issues—and he wanted the cooperation of NWRO.

During the meeting between King and NWRO representatives, welfare recipients explained that their 1968 strategy was to lobby for repeal of the restrictive 1967 social security law. King agreed to incorporate NWRO concerns into the Poor People's Campaign and, in exchange, asked for NWRO assistance in organizing the Poor People's March on Washington, scheduled for April 22. Wiley agreed to give token support to King's march, but he continued to focus NWRO efforts on grass-roots organizing of the poor.[10]

Both the NWRO's lobbying strategy in Washington and the Poor People's March were failures. After King's assassination on April 4, the Poor People's Campaign's momentum was gone, and Resurrection City, built by protesters on the Washington Mall, was figuratively and literally mired in the mud during two rainy months in Washington.[11] With legislators focusing on the Vietnam War and the 1968 presidential election, the attempts of NWRO to repeal the antiwelfare law were also fruitless.

After the election, however, the incoming Nixon administration presented an occasion for NWRO to revise old strategies and devise new ones. Carl Rachlin, general counsel at NWRO, began rethinking the organization's approach to mandatory work requirements. Writing to Wiley, Rachlin urged that in light of shrinking funds for welfare NWRO "propose a program which would be of help to the recipients . . . and at the same time might interest the new Administration." In Rachlin's view, the organization's opposition to the work provision of the 1967 law rested not on "the possibility of jobs" but on the "punitive" way in which recipients were required to accept jobs. Rachlin suggested that NWRO sponsor a voluntary work program to demonstrate that employable recipients are, with proper training and support, eager to work. The key factors, wrote Rachlin, were offering inducements to enter the program, such as guaranteed work and wage levels; training people based on a real investigation of job opportunities paying minimum wage or more; and providing quality child care to parents participating in the program.[12]

Wiley pursued this new direction for NWRO by seeking funding, notably from the federal government, to establish a demonstration work-training project for welfare recipients. In December 1968 NWRO was awarded a federal grant of $434,930 to explore means of involving welfare recipients in leadership roles in federal work programs.[13]

At the same time, NWRO, working with welfare rights lawyers from the Center and MFY, continued to push the new administration for enforcement of existing welfare laws. The leaders of NWRO were pleasantly surprised when Nixon's chief adviser on domestic affairs, Daniel Patrick Moynihan, invited Wiley to meet with him, and they were even more pleased when the new HEW secretary, Robert Finch, agreed to meet with NWRO leaders.[14]

At each of these meetings NWRO called for strict application of one of the few provisions in the 1967 act favorable to recipients: the requirement that, by July 1, 1969, each state reassess and adjust its "standard of need" under AFDC to reflect changes in the cost of living. The standard of need was intended to reflect the minimal income necessary to live in the state and to be used as "a yardstick for measuring who [was] eligible for public assistance."[15] Under the 1967 Social Security Act, states were required to "provide that by July 1, 1969, the amounts used by the State to determine the needs of individuals will have been adjusted to reflect fully changes in living costs since such amounts were established, and any maximums that the State imposes on the amount of aid paid to families will have been proportionately adjusted."[16]

Representatives of HEW took the position that the 1967 law addressed only the standard of need and nothing more. According to HEW regulations, states remained free to disregard the standard in setting actual benefit levels.[17]

Welfare rights advocates, on the other hand, asserted that the intent of the law was that benefit levels—the "standard of payment"—be increased to the readjusted standard of need or, at the very least, to a reasonable percentage of the standard of need. Advocates knew that if their interpretation prevailed some states would be required to double or triple their benefit levels. In Alabama, for instance, benefits were set at only 32 percent of the state's standard of need. Only a few states, including New Jersey and Wisconsin, set benefits at 100 percent of their minimal standard of need, and even those benefit levels were still below the federal poverty line.[18]

It soon became clear that few states intended to raise their benefit levels in response to the law. New York, for instance, abolished special needs grants and replaced them with a so-called demonstration project of flat grants of $100 per year. Welfare rights advocates argued that the new procedures not only reduced benefits and ignored the individual needs of recipients, they also violated the 1967 law.

In late 1968 lawyers and activists held a series of meetings, chaired by Hulbert James of the City-Wide Coordinating Committee of Welfare Groups, to plan litigation attacking the flat grant system.[19] Within a few months, the complaint—prepared by Lee Albert and Rachlin in tense collaboration—was ready to be filed on behalf of eight welfare recipients. The complaint sought to enjoin the flat grant "experiment," claiming that because the grants were unrelated to need, the program violated the equal protection rights of recipients as well as their rights under Section 402 of the 1967 act. Further, the complaint claimed that the experiment violated plaintiffs' First Amendment rights. The state was well aware of the importance of special grants to recipient organizing efforts, plaintiffs claimed, and its motivation in abolishing the special grant system was primarily to curtail recipients' demonstrations.[20]

Shortly after the flat grant case was filed, however, the plaintiffs' claims were superseded by even greater changes in the New York welfare program. In January 1969 Governor Nelson Rockefeller disclosed plans to cut back drastically on public assistance benefits in the state. Rockefeller's proposals, announced only a few days after the new federal administration unveiled plans to ease rules on establishing welfare eligibility, included making eligibility standards more stringent, reducing home relief grants, and eliminating the remaining vestiges of the special grant system.[21] Under the new plan, a family of four in New York City would receive $208 a month while a family of four outside of the city would receive $183 a month; amounts were to cover all expenses except rent and fuel. Under the prior plan, payments for a family of four in the state averaged $222 a month in addition to grants for transportation, special diets, or other individual needs. In all, benefits to 173,900 families in New York City were to be decreased by a total of $5.95 million per month.[22]

Reactions in New York City, which would be hardest hit by the cuts, were uniformly negative. According to Mitchell Ginsberg, commissioner of the Human Resources Administration, the "indefensible" plan was a "repeat of the mistakes that have been made for the last 30 years."[23] Welfare chief Jack Goldberg added that "the poor are being sacrificed for the petty politics of selfish, misguided men. What looks like savings now is simply a political mirage. In the months and years ahead it will cost a hell of a lot more." Within a few weeks, Ginsberg himself was openly raising questions about the legality of the plan under the 1967 act.[24]

Despite the protests in New York City, Rockefeller's budget cuts were approved by the state legislature on March 31, 1969. Little more than a week later the Center and NWRO legal teams were in court with a case, *Rosado v. Wyman*, charging that, once again, an attempt to reduce New York welfare payments in a manner unrelated to need violated not only the 1967 welfare law but also recipients' equal protection rights to a minimum level of benefits.[25]

As the July 1 deadline for adjusting standards of need approached, Rachlin of NWRO and Henry Freedman and Paul Dodyk of the Center worked to initiate similar lawsuits in a dozen states. Lawyers from both offices were excited about making headway toward addressing the "key 'political issue' " for welfare rights groups: the adequacy of the grant. As Freedman wrote to Rachlin as they planned litigation in Ohio, "The Center hopes to see some victories in narrow, clear-cut cases like the maximum grant and percentage reduction cases so that the WROs can then successfully move into broader economic questions. . . . You will recall our discussion at your apartment about development of new common law doctrine to serve the poor rather than established interests. That is exactly what is at stake in the attempts of poverty lawyers throughout the country to attack inadequacy through the Equal Protection Clause."

Working for such a clear, fundamental principle was exhilarating. "This should be a very exciting case," Freedman wrote. "A victory will create a significant advance not only in Ohio but throughout the country." With a nod to the tension between Rachlin and Albert, Freedman added that "it will be fun to work together with you and your office on this."[26]

In Ohio the state paid AFDC recipients only a fraction of the standard of need while recipients of such federal benefits as Old Age Assistance received the entire amount. Recipients of AFDC filed suit in late 1968, alleging that the differential between AFDC and other federal benefits was racially motivated "since AFDC is considered the 'black' category of public assistance, and others, 'white.' " Similar suits, coordinated by Freedman, were filed in Texas and Florida.[27]

Plaintiffs in Mississippi also challenged the differential between AFDC and other aid categories: recipients of Aid to the Blind received 100 percent of the standard of need, but AFDC payments were set at 26 percent of the standard. In addition, Mississippi enforced a maximum grant, denying AFDC recipients any increase in public assistance grants for children beyond a certain number. Because the Center believed that the Mississippi case was a particularly egregious example of discrimination against AFDC recipients and might ultimately reach the Supreme Court, Paul Dodyk, the Center's faculty director, argued the case with the assistance of the Lawyers' Committee for Civil Rights Under Law.[28]

The NWRO aimed to initiate as many cases as possible challenging the welfare grant level. In some states, however, legal services lawyers initiated their own lawsuits without assistance from the Center or NWRO. As Freedman later noted, "In 1966, it was possible to know what was going on in the poverty litigation field. By 1968–69, too much was happening."[29] In addition to the first round of lawsuits, by early August 1969 suits were also in progress in West Virginia, Alabama, California, South Carolina, Indiana, and Utah. By mid-August lawsuits had been initiated in eight more states: Virginia, Idaho, Colorado, Wyoming, Rhode Island, Nevada, New Mexico, and Nebraska. According to NWRO, "The federal laws regulating the treatment of welfare recipients and the operation of welfare programs are being flagrantly violated in every state in this country."[30]

The lawsuits fell into several categories. In states such as New York and Louisiana, which did not implemented the 1967 law, NWRO claimed that the failure to raise the standard of need and level of benefits violated both the statute and the equal protection clause of the Constitution.

In states like Maryland and Mississippi that set upper limits on benefit levels recipients claimed that the maximum itself violated the equal protection clause by discriminating against children in large families.

And NWRO claimed that states such as Ohio and Mississippi that funded 100 percent of the standard of need for individuals in non-AFDC programs—like those for the disabled or elderly—while providing only a fraction of the standard of need for AFDC recipients, violated the equal protection rights of AFDC recipients.

In each of these cases, welfare rights lawyers asserted that a state's motives in reducing or limiting benefits should be strictly scrutinized by the courts. The state would have to show a "compelling interest" in limiting or reducing benefits; mere financial savings would not be enough. The Iowa Supreme Court had adopted this construction of the equal protection clause as early as 1957 to strike down an offensive welfare law.[31] According to Dodyk, the Center intended to move from cases challenging, in Jacobus tenBroek's words, "dual systems" like family and individual maximums and differential benefits to "the destruction of the AFDC structure."[32]

By and large, federal courts agreed with NWRO and the Center. In Arizona, Maine, Maryland, California, and Washington, recipients won their cases.[33] The Texas case was also decided in the recipients' favor.[34] A New

York federal district court ruled in the recipients' favor on the statutory issue. In Louisiana, however, the case was dismissed as not ripe, and in Dodyk's case in Mississippi the judge simply withheld decision, waiting to see what other courts might do.[35]

As lead counsel in the New York case, *Rosado v. Wyman*, Albert and the Center joined the race to present the equal protection clause argument to the Supreme Court. Emboldened by their victories in the district courts and by Supreme Court pronouncements in *Shapiro*, welfare rights advocates were cautiously optimistic about their chances of success in a case challenging grant levels. According to his colleague Henry Freedman, "Lee pushed *Rosado* very hard to get it to the Supreme Court. Not only was there a lot of money at stake for recipients, but Lee wanted to be the one up there arguing this issue before the Court."[36]

Steering *Rosado* to the Supreme Court, however, was easier said than done. After initiating the case on an emergency basis, the plaintiffs were lucky enough to draw Jack Weinstein—a judge who was well-respected as a legal scholar and notoriously efficient in his disposition of cases.

In *Rosado* the plaintiffs initially claimed that the benefit differentials between New York City and other areas in the state violated the equal protection clause. In light of this constitutional claim, Weinstein agreed to convene a three-judge "constitutional" court.[37] Before the three-judge court heard arguments on the case, however, the New York State Legislature amended the benefits law to allow the state commissioner of social services to equalize benefits among areas of the state. The three-judge court concluded that the amendment rendered the constitutional issues moot, at least until the commissioner acted.[38] Since the remaining issues in the case were statutory rather than constitutional, the court remanded the case to Weinstein for resolution. Within a few days Weinstein issued a preliminary injunction prohibiting the state from reducing or discontinuing payments of special grants payable under the prior law.[39] Because the initial decision was rendered by an individual judge rather than the three-judge court, there was no appeal directly to the Supreme Court, and the defendants appealed the decision to the Second Circuit Court of Appeals. On June 11, 1969, in an interim order and without reaching the merits of the case, the Court of Appeals granted the state's request for a stay of Weinstein's opinion, thereby permitting the welfare cuts to go into effect on July 1, 1969, as originally planned.

In an aggressive attempt to block implementation of the legislation and let the Supreme Court know that the case was on its way through the system, Albert employed a tactic reminiscent of his amicus brief in *Wheeler v. Montgomery.* The Center filed a highly unusual "petition for certiorari before the judgment of the Court of Appeals" and a motion for expedited review with Supreme Court Justice Harlan, who had jurisdiction over matters arising in the Second Circuit. Because Harlan was on his way out of town, he asked Justice Brennan to review the matter.[40]

Brennan reviewed the papers provided by the parties. Although he concluded that the Supreme Court could not take the case before the Court of Appeals ruled on the merits, he informed the members of the Supreme Court that "I have . . . decided to grant the motion to vacate the Court of Appeals' stay, for I believe that the case clearly presents certworthy issues and that the status quo should be retained until they are decided by this Court." As a prudential matter, however, Brennan resolved to withhold the announcement of his decision until after the Friday conference of the justices.[41] And following that discussion, which was conducted without Douglas and Harlan, the justices voted to deny the Center's motion and dismiss the appeal for lack of jurisdiction.[42]

On July 16, 1969, a divided Court of Appeals issued three separate opinions in the case. Chief Judge J. Edward Lumbard and Judge Paul R. Hays agreed that Weinstein had overstepped his bounds in ruling on the case without waiting for HEW to review, and possibly reject, the New York state AFDC plan. Hays further suggested that New York had complied with Section 402 of the 1967 Act when, in May 1968, it revised its standard of need; once it had completed that revision, he concluded, the state was free to abolish any increases, whether before or after July 1, 1969.

The third member of the court, Judge Feinberg, had been exposed to welfare litigation during his consideration of *Goldberg v. Kelly.* Vigorously disagreeing with his colleagues, Feinberg voted to uphold Weinstein's opinion. According to Feinberg, Hays' construction of Section 402 made "a mockery of congressional purpose" and would allow "New York to receive millions of federally granted dollars and then proceed to ignore federal law."[43]

The Center quickly began work on an appeal of the circuit court's decision to the Supreme Court. But before the Center completed the petition, Ed Sparer, Carl Rachlin, and several others convened a series of meetings to discuss whether *Rosado* should be appealed at all. Sparer believed that the Texas case challenging that state's implementation of the 1967 Act—which was pending on a writ of certiorari before the Supreme Court—was a more effective vehicle for recipients' claims.[44] Because benefits were much lower in Texas than in New York, the Court might respond more sympathetically. In addition, the Texas case contained a strong claim of racial discrimination that had never been part of *Rosado*.

Sparer's attempts to direct the cases put some of his old colleagues on edge. According to one former MFY attorney, "Ed began to think of himself as a statesman, which is a danger. He was a good teacher and an inspiring figure. But it's not like he was Einstein. He had some good ideas, but it was too early to make him a deity."[45]

The resentment against Sparer gave the Center room to maneuver. Albert and Sylvia Law argued ardently in favor of appealing *Rosado*. Few were swayed, but no one had a convincing argument against the appeal either. The choice was simply between Sparer's plea to hold *Rosado* in abeyance and the Center's legal assessment that there was no reason to do so. In the end, Albert made a decision to ignore Sparer and proceed with the *Rosado* appeal.[46]

By the time the petition for certiorari was filed, *Rosado* was a cause célèbre. Nearly every public interest lawyer in New York wanted to have the name of his or her organization listed on the papers of a case that might lead to significant benefit increases for welfare recipients. The papers filed with the Court listed the lawyers from the Center; the NWRO legal team; Martin Garbus of the ACLU; Burt Neuborne of the New York Civil Liberties Union; David Gilman representing the City-Wide Coordinating Committee of Welfare Groups; Cesar Perales of Williamsburg Legal Services; Virginia Schuler of Brownsville Legal Services; Sparer; three MFY lawyers— Harold Rothwax, David Diamond, and Marianne Rosenfield; Mort Cohen of South Brooklyn Legal Services; and Morton Friedman of St. Albans, New York.

As Brennan had predicted, certiorari was granted, and the Supreme Court scheduled oral argument in *Rosado* for November 19, 1969, less than five weeks after the argument in *Goldberg v. Kelly*. On the same day the Court also accepted *Dandridge v. Williams*, the case brought by a group of local legal services lawyers who were challenging Maryland's practice of setting maximum public assistance grants. The argument was scheduled for December 9, 1969. While *Rosado* concerned states' obligations under the 1967 Act, *Dandridge* required that the Supreme Court squarely address the extent of recipients' rights under the equal protection clause. According to the *New York Times*, the appeals set the stage for a broad ruling on states' welfare authority while "in the background is a growing chorus of complaints from state and local officials that the Federal courts are encroaching upon [their] authority . . . to set their own welfare policies in light of their available resources."[47]

In briefing *Rosado* the Center focused on the consequences to individual recipients of the elimination of special grants. "The cost of living rose in New York 10.1% from the time of the last adjustment of AFDC need standards in May 1968, to July 1, 1969," wrote the Center. But "rather than increasing grants to keep pace with inflationary living costs, the New York legislature, in March, 1969, repealed a long-standing authorization to [the state] to make yearly increases for rising living costs and to set grant levels 'in accordance with standards of health and decency in the community.'" These budget cuts were accomplished, petitioners wrote, by slashing the "amounts afforded to meet the needs of families with older children, particularly teenage children, and abolishing entirely amounts to meet such basic needs as clothing and home furnishings . . . and such urgent or special needs as diets for diabetics and cardiacs and medically-dictated telephones."[48]

In addition, the Center submitted to the Court excerpts from testimony given before the district court by HRA head Mitchell Ginsberg and City Welfare Commissioner Jack Goldberg. Under direct examination by Albert, Ginsberg's testimony authoritatively explained the effects of the cutbacks on welfare recipients.

> ALBERT: To what extent do present grants provide for a nutritional, adequate diet for a family of four?
> GINSBERG: There is no question, certainly based on experience of those of us who are in the business, that the diets of people on welfare are, if adequate, are minimally adequate.
> ALBERT: With regard to those items [formerly] available through special needs grants, recipients would be expected to use whatever they will get under the new system for those needs?
> GINSBERG: There will be no alternative. . . . You are going to inevitably be faced by a choice by a client of having less food for himself or herself and the family, or doing without some of these items. Some of which they cannot do without. So I think the inevitable result will be less food and therefore, it's very clear to me in cases of some of these people that there are bound to be medical effects.

At the same time, Center attorneys worked frantically to prepare an amicus brief in *Dandridge v. Williams*. That case, which had been handled from the outset by Maryland legal services attorneys with minimal Center involvement, directly raised the issue of whether regulations setting a family maximum, in place in more than twenty states, violated the equal protection clause.[49]

Under Maryland's maximum grant regulation a family of seven or more members could receive no more than $250 per month in AFDC benefits. Smaller families received graduated amounts depending on size.

The Maryland plaintiffs had initiated the lawsuit as a class action, claiming that "the maximum grant regulation has the effect of treating needy children differently based on an arbitrary standard not related to the purpose of AFDC—the size of the family," in violation of the equal protection clause. The plaintiffs included Linda Williams, a single mother of eight children, ages four and sixteen, who could not work because of a serious medical condition. Junius and Jeanette Gary sued on behalf of themselves and their eight children, ages four to eleven. Like Linda Williams, health conditions precluded the Garys from working; their only income was the maximum grant of $250 per month.[50] Because of the family maximum, each person in the Gary family received public assistance at a rate of $25 per person, even though the state standard of need indicated that they should receive assistance at the rate of $33.15 per person.

The state of Maryland defended the family maximum on five grounds: as a work incentive; as a family stabilizer; as a disincentive to childbearing; as a means to maintain public confidence in and support for the fairness of the welfare program among the lower middle class and working poor; and as the best means of allocating limited funds.[51] According to the state, enforcement of the mandatory work provisions of the 1967 act was enhanced by keeping benefits low. Similarly, the state argued that low benefits would discourage desertion by wage-earners. Finally, the state argued that it had broad discretion to allocate welfare benefits and that the family maximum was well within the bounds of that discretion.

In their amicus brief, the Center, joined again by dozens of affiliated attorneys, explained the equal protection claim. The family maximum divides public assistance recipients into two classes, they asserted, those with small families ("deserving" poor) and those with large families ("undeserving" poor), and it deprives children in larger families of equal benefits. Invoking the right to live, the Center argued that because the regulation "affects the availability of the fundamental rudiments of human existence," the court's scrutiny of the regulation must be searching and strict. According to the Center, the maximum "reaches a class characterized by political powerlessness; it undermines the integrity of the basic family unit, and it creates a class of children based on a status over which they have no control."[52]

As scheduled, the *Rosado* oral argument was conducted on November 19, followed by the *Dandridge* argument on December 9.[53] The *Dandridge* argument, in particular, was eagerly awaited by welfare rights advocates who hoped that it would yield an important expansion of recipients' rights. When the day came, however, it was less encouraging than advocates had hoped. Perhaps the most sobering note was an exchange between Justice Marshall, who was expected to support the recipients' equal protection claims, and Joseph Matera, the recipients' attorney.

In their briefs, the plaintiffs had attempted to frame the case as a complete denial of benefits to individual children in a large family rather than an incremental limit on the family's benefits as a whole.

Marshall began by asking Matera to explain the equal protection claims. Matera answered, "The equal protection argument refers, your honor, to the fact that children of large families are not having their needs recognized once they become, unfortunately, the fifth or sixth child in the family."

> MARSHALL: They'll eat right along with the rest; it just means that everybody would eat less.
>
> MATERA: That's, in effect, what would happen, yes. Because the mother would not sit there and allow—other than that, she would simply send the child out [to foster care], as she can do, as I pointed out, under the Act.
>
> MARSHALL: I have a great problem with the equal protection argument without the first argument. . . . I think that you have to establish that this is basic subsistence and nothing else will do. Otherwise, I have trouble with the equal protection argument.[54]

The plaintiffs' advocates were naturally disturbed by this dialogue. If their characterization of the family maximum as a complete denial of benefits to certain children did not even convince Marshall, one of their staunchest supporters on the Court, would any of the justices accept the argument that life and death subsistence issues were at stake?

The answer came four months later—on April 6—when the opinions in both *Rosado* and *Dandridge* were issued.[55] In a 6–2 decision written by Harlan, the Court ruled that the New York Legislature acted illegally when it haphazardly eliminated special grants. The *Rosado* decision was only a partial, Pyrrhic victory for recipients, however, since the Court made clear that under the 1967 act the state may, "after recomputing its standard of need, pare down payments to accommodate budgetary realities by reducing the percent of benefits paid."[56]

Dandridge, on the other hand, was an unmitigated loss. The vote to uphold Maryland's practice of setting family maximums was 5–3. Brennan, Marshall, and Douglas dissented, not on the equal protection claim but on the ground that a family maximum was inconsistent with the Social Security Act.

The majority decision by Stewart was a direct and unequivocal statement both to recipients and to the lower courts. Rejecting strict scrutiny of states' welfare procedures, Stewart went out of his way to repudiate the Court's statements in *Shapiro* that had fueled hopes that the Court would eventually uphold a fundamental right to live. He squarely denied recipients' claims that bare subsistence was at issue: "Although the appellees argue that the younger and more recently arrived children in such families are totally deprived of aid, a more realistic view is that the lot of the entire family is diminished because of the presence of additional children without any increase in payments. . . . It is no more accurate to say that the last child's grant is wholly taken away than to say that the grant of the first child is totally rescinded. In fact, it is the *family* grant that is affected."[57]

It was for the state of Maryland to decide how to distribute its scarce resources, Stewart concluded: "The intractable economic, social, and even philosophical problems presented by public welfare assistance programs are not the business of this Court."[58]

Chapter 10

A Different America

I am writing to express our extreme sense of frustration with the current course of the meetings between NWRO and HEW. NWRO is desirous of meeting with HEW and is prepared to work with HEW in a positive manner. We feel, however, that you might give your urgent, personal attention to the serious degeneration of these meetings, a degeneration which threatens to turn the meetings into a mere charade. . . . The recent conduct of HEW people at these meetings unmistakably demonstrates that your people do not take meeting with poor people seriously.

—Letter from Margaret Hayes, NWRO Legal Committee, to John Twiname, HEW, 1971

Even from the distance of his office at University of Pennsylvania Law School, Ed Sparer was perhaps more shaken by the collapse of his litigation strategy after *Dandridge* than were his colleagues on the front lines. As he wrote a year after the decision,

> A contrary result in *Dandridge* would have permitted wholesale challenges to the barriers created by state legislatures and Congress to deny welfare assistance to groups of needy people. Distinctions between grant levels of individuals in equal need, whether because of differences in categories or their state of residence, might have been brought down. Traditional divisions between state and federal authority, and between the three branches of government, would doubtless have been altered. The equal protection clause would have become the main vehicle for establishing a constitutional guarantee of human life. In these and other ways, affirmative judicial scrutiny to guarantee equal protection could have led to a different America.[1]

Sylvia Law believed that the Center should have pushed harder to handle *Dandridge* rather than allowing neighborhood legal services lawyers to take the lead in the litigation. "If we'd done it," she later reflected, "I think we would have won."[2]

There was no indication from the Supreme Court, however, that its decision in *Dandridge* was anything but inevitable. During the next term, welfare recipients' losses of constitutional claims before the Court continued.

Wyman v. James concerned the issue, identified by Sparer for litigation in 1965, of whether a welfare recipient had the right to prohibit a caseworker from searching her home without forfeiting welfare benefits.[3] According to David Gilman, who worked on the case with the Center, "The client, Barbara James, just walked into my office and presented herself. She said that she had read an article in the NWRO newsletter, that she understood that she didn't have to let her caseworker into her home, that she'd refused her caseworker access, and that now she was ready to litigate the issue."[4]

James's case was filed in June 1969 before the federal district court in New York City. With one dissent, the three-judge district court found that the mandatory inspection rule—which permitted inspections without a warrant—violated recipients' rights to privacy and to be free of unreasonable searches under the Fourth and Fourteenth Amendments.[5]

On appeal, the Supreme Court reversed the lower court.

Writing his first opinion on the Court, Justice Harry Blackmun made every effort to repudiate prior decisions suggesting that public assistance was a right. According to Blackmun, caseworkers did not require a warrant because "one who dispenses purely private charity naturally has an interest in and expects to know how his charitable funds are utilized and put to work. The public, when it is the provider, rightly expects the same."[6]

The following year, 1972, whatever was left of the Center's grand strategy was shattered when *Jefferson v. Hackney*, appealed for a second time by Texas legal services lawyers, was decided by the Supreme Court. Adhering to the implications of *Rosado* and *Dandridge*, the Court upheld the state practice of paying differential percentages of the standard of need for various benefits categories: 100 percent for the predominantly white recipients of Aid to the Aged and less than 70 percent for the predominantly black and Latino recipients of AFDC. According to the Court, these statistical disparities were not enough to prove that the differences were attributable to "invidious discrimination" warranting strict scrutiny.[7]

The devastating loss of *Jefferson* revived feelings that, had the Center followed Sparer's advice and positioned *Jefferson* as the first "equal protection" case to reach the Supreme Court, things might have been different. It seemed clear that the overall strategy—if not the New York recipients who benefited from the partial victory in *Rosado*—would have been better served if both the statutory argument under the 1967 law and the equal protection argument had been presented together in the context of the more dramatic and egregious facts of *Jefferson v. Hackney*.

By the time that *Jefferson* was decided, however, many of the mainstays of the Center had scattered. Lee Albert was teaching at Yale Law School;

Sylvia Law was teaching at the London School of Economics; and Dodyk was in private practice.

At MFY Legal Services, David Diamond left to teach at Syracuse Law School; Harold Rothwax went first to teach at Columbia Law School and then to the state court bench; David Gilman left to work on a study of juvenile rights.

At NWRO, Carl Rachlin departed to serve as general counsel of Hunter College in New York. After a few months out of touch, George Wiley dropped a quick note to Rachlin, whose response hinted at his level of melancholy: "I was glad to hear from you. . . . I hadn't heard from any one at NWRO, so I thought it was merely the end of an era."[8]

One former Reggie who left MFY in mid-1971 explained the feeling that was shared by many of those who had, for a few years, devoted so much energy to the welfare rights movement: "I felt that I was making no progress. The special grant system was dead. The Burger Court was in. I felt that legal services had become a backwater. No one noticed what we were doing. I felt that I wasn't making any difference."[9]

Those of the original group who continued their work in poverty law— Ron Pollack and Henry Freedman (succeeding Albert as director) at the Center, Wiley at NWRO—were joined by a steady influx of new colleagues such as Adele Blong, who had served twelve years in the HEW office of the general counsel, and Richard Greenberg, a transplant from Ohio legal services.[10] After Rachlin's departure Sparer assumed the mantle of general counsel at NWRO while continuing to teach at Penn.

The Center took the occasion of Albert's departure to reassess its goals, resolving "to increase and improve our back-up service to assure that neighborhood offices are kept fully informed of welfare law developments." In addition, the Center planned "to reestablish good working relations with NWRO and other recipient groups to plug our efforts into the needs and desires of recipients."[11]

While this reemphasis on direct services coincided with the demise of the test case litigation strategy, the focus was also demanded by the Center's major funder, the federal government. During his tenure as director, Albert had exchanged several letters with Hugh Duffy at the OEO offices in Washington, defending the Center's test case activities as necessary if the Center were to replicate the successes of the NAACP Legal Defense and Educational Fund.[12] Albert's arguments, however, were no match for the political pressure of an increasingly conservative Congress. "Law reform" activities—including test case litigation and lobbying—were an explicit priority for legal services offices until at least 1967. But after a steady stream of successful cases against state and city governments, pressure on Congress to cut back on legal services appropriations increased. A number of restrictive amendments were passed, barring legal services' representation of criminal clients, limiting participation in class actions, and restricting partisan political activities. Finally, in 1971, the federal appropriations for legal services were frozen, the first step in a decades-long conservative effort to eliminate the program entirely.[13]

Responding to this financial threat, as well as to the exigencies of recent case law, the Center focused on shoring up prior victories and enforcing existing statutes. In 1971, for example, the Center embarked on a comprehensive and successful effort to enforce the Supreme Court's decision in *Goldberg v. Kelly*. According to the Center, "As was expected, many welfare departments are denying recipients the right to a hearing before public assistance is terminated. . . . [A] number [of states] have resisted openly and others fail to comply in practice." To enforce the *Goldberg* decision, the Center sued the local welfare authority in the case of *Almenares v. Wyman* in New York and assisted with similar cases in Delaware, Ohio, Tennessee, New Jersey, and California.[14]

In addition, the Center initiated litigation to enforce Medicaid statutes, to eliminate discriminatory procedures from school lunch programs, and to challenge restrictive food stamp regulations.[15] Several of these campaigns utilized local NWRO members as advocates and plaintiffs. None, however, represented a comprehensive organizing strategy.

The effect on NWRO of recent losses in the courts was more attenuated. It had been several years since lawsuits had directly strengthened their organizing efforts and membership drives, as in the case of the special needs campaign. Rather, welfare rights litigation had contributed to the perception of NWRO power, both political and moral; the Supreme Court losses of the early 1970s betrayed the limits of that power.

Throughout 1970 and 1971 NWRO continued to press HEW to enforce existing welfare laws. A report published by HEW in 1970 revealed that thirty-nine states had failed to meet federal standards.[16] Eight states had yet to abolish residency requirements in compliance with *Shapiro v. Thompson*. Fifteen states still enforced man-in-the-house rules, despite the Supreme Court's decision in *King v. Smith*. The NWRO pressured HEW to call a series of "conformity hearings" to assess whether these states should be penalized through cuts in their federal AFDC grants. Though ultimately successful in forcing compliance, the hearings were by no means expeditious. The state of California, which was challenged over its failure to raise maximum grants as required by the 1967 law, used opposition and lobbying to hold up HEW's decision for several months. California finally raised its grants nearly eleven months after the hearing.[17]

The NWRO took enforcement into its own hands in Nevada. In December 1970 the administrator of the state welfare department announced a major campaign against "welfare cheaters." On January 1, 1971, without further warning, 3,000 Nevada mothers and children did not receive their benefit checks. Checks to 4,200 more individuals were abruptly reduced. Altogether, 51 percent of Nevada's welfare recipients were affected by the so-called audit of the welfare rolls.

Responding to pleas from local welfare rights organizers, NWRO, with Sparer in the lead, organized "Operation Nevada." According to Sylvia Law, who participated in the effort, "by the second week of February dozens of welfare recipient leaders from around the country, some 40 lawyers, more than 70 law students, and organizers from the NWRO staff began to work for periods ranging from a few days to a few weeks."[18] Their hope was to provide a "model of resistance" in Nevada to deter the consideration of antiwelfare measures in a number of states.

The lawyers and organizers who descended on Nevada located people whose benefits had been terminated and were afraid to come forward, held seminars on recipients' rights, staged demonstrations, and represented individuals in fair hearings. They also initiated a federal lawsuit seeking to vacate all of the terminations and reductions on the ground that the notice and hearing mandated under *Goldberg v. Kelly* had not been provided. On March 20, the federal district court issued an order reinstating everyone whose benefits had been terminated or reduced in the audit. According to the Court, "the Administrator and his staff ran roughshod over the constitutional rights of eligible and ineligible recipients alike."[19]

The effort in Nevada was an unequivocal success. Yet NWRO remained uncertain about the prospects for defeating similar efforts in other states. Sparer and Freedman worried that "organizers and lawyers elsewhere— especially in New York and California—have not yet absorbed the point underlying the Operation Nevada tactics. . . . Little mass administrative work has been organized in these states. And the immediate future is, to say the least, uncertain."[20]

The NWRO focused its remaining energy—and the bulk of its shrinking budget—on opposing President Nixon's proposal for a $1,600-a-year guaranteed minimum income for a family of four.[21] Many of the fundamental elements of the Family Assistance Plan (FAP), announced in late 1969, were liberal, and the scheme to replace AFDC with a federal minimum income would relieve states of some of the fiscal burden of the rising welfare rolls. But the plan would have brought *higher* benefits only to the handful of states paying less than $1,600 a year; most states would have been forced to continue supplementing the federal payment to meet recipients' minimal needs—a state of affairs resembling that under AFDC. In addition, NWRO objected to the FAP requirement that "employable" recipients take jobs at less than minimum wage.

Initial reactions to Nixon's plan were mixed. HRA commissioner Mitchell Ginsberg supported it as a first step toward federalization of all income maintenance programs, "allowing the local community to concentrate on services." Roy Wilkins of the NAACP also supported the plan. Sparer, in contrast, viewed it as "a step backwards." According to Sparer, "Our single greatest need in welfare today is to define and guarantee an adequate money grant to the poor. . . . This Nixon plan does not help, and may hurt, that issue."[22]

After some debate and an initial false step in supporting the plan, NWRO finally rejected the proposal and instead called for a guaranteed income of $6,500 a year. One popular NWRO poster showed a picture of Nixon's three dogs posed in front of the White House with the caption: "This family of three has a yearly budget of $2,700. Their master, who lives in that white mansion, believes that a family of three *people* can live on $1,300 a year ($1,600 for a family of four) . . . for food, clothing, housing . . . everything!"

The NWRO had some political allies. Senator Eugene McCarthy introduced the NWRO-drafted Adequate Income Act of 1970, and thirty members of the House of Representatives called for a guaranteed annual income of $6,500 a year for a family of four. Even among those who believed that $6,500 a year was unreasonably high, the principle of a guaranteed annual income was accepted as sound public policy. Representative John Conyers from Michigan, for example, proposed that the level be set at $3,200 a year.[23]

But welfare rights advocates opposing the FAP found themselves in an uncomfortable coalition with conservatives who wanted no guaranteed income at all. The lukewarm support of its sponsors and opposition from both sides of the political aisle finally signaled the plan's demise. By 1971 the plan was dead; Nixon formally abandoned it in 1972.[24] It was the last time for almost a decade that the nation would seriously debate welfare reform. The NWRO no longer had the power to keep the issue on the national agenda.

Following a series of embarrassingly ill-attended demonstrations and tactical errors for which NWRO members held Wiley responsible, George Wiley came to loggerheads with the NWRO executive board over the question of whether the organization should initiate efforts to organize the working poor. The recipient leadership of the NWRO, all women on AFDC, felt that such a broad agenda would diminish the attention given their special problems. Wiley believed that forming coalitions was the only solution to the organization's malaise, particularly because the executive board members no longer had a strong following among NWRO members.[25]

Wiley's debate with his executive board mirrored the turmoil among lawyers in the movement seeking a post-*Dandridge* strategy. As the extent of the antiwelfare backlash sank in, activists began to offer opinions on how the movement should respond.

Elizabeth Wickenden circulated a memorandum advocating a focus on welfare legislation pending in Congress. "The wave of regressive reaction to liberal welfare policy has now surfaced and is inescapably clear to everyone," she observed. "Every day there is more and more talk of welfare "cheaters," "free loaders," and "greed." . . . Recent Supreme Court opinions are also not encouraging. The tone of the Blackmun opinion in the *James* case on right of entry with its emphasis on "charity" and Chief Justice Burger's appeal for less reliance on federal courts in cases involving state laws do not auger well for the future of the courts as a recourse."[26]

Some lawyers still had hopes of devising a viable litigation strategy. Rachlin, for example, suggested that "while we may not be able to move temporarily, to get more welfare money, perhaps . . . health rights and rehabilitation, job rights, etc., are open for grabs."[27] Like Wiley, Sparer envisioned a coordinated effort to recruit both new lawyers and new recipients, expanding the movement's political base while providing increased legal services to the poor.[28] Standing in the way of this strategy for expansion, Sparer believed, were organizational interests—such as the City-Wide Coordinating Committee of Welfare Groups, the Center, and MFY—that were afraid of losing their power.

On April 27, 1971, the Center convened a meeting of movement lawyers to discuss the "lawyers welfare strategy" in the wake of *Dandridge* and *Wyman*. In an emotional letter to Wiley afterward, Sparer labeled the meeting "a disaster" for which he accepted "personal responsibility." "As I see it," wrote Sparer,

> the most important question—was whether the hold of the small 'strategy' or 'organizing' group on the campaign could be either broken or at least broadened. . . . It was necessary, among other reasons, simply to bring in the large new lawyer and law constituencies that had to [be] brought in if any large-scale campaign was to happen. I made what I thought was a detailed proposal on how to go about getting various local [legal services] offices to take responsibility for various [neighborhood] centers, the [National Lawyers] Guild for various other centers, the NYCLU for some, the Law Associates Volunteers Committee for some, the Black Lawyers Conference for some, a materials preparation group, a coordinating committee, etc., etc. . . . It lost—and it lost the minute during the mid-afternoon when Hulbert [James] wrote Gilman's name, address and phone on the board and said that lawyers interested in helping the Center activity should call Gilman.[29]

In short, the Center and the City-Wide Coordinating Committee (represented by Hulbert James) used the meeting to consolidate their role as movement leaders. Those in attendance agreed to create a "litigation task force" headed by Freedman, but there was little serious discussion of—or apparent will to address—the political work necessary to sustain the movement.

Speculating that the meeting might have gone better if he had tried to resolve these turf issues with Gilman and James beforehand, Sparer concluded that it was "all in all, a very bad day—and I [am] sick at the lost possibilities. I am also sick at (of) myself and this half-assed position I have been in of trying to influence things while remaining at Penn. . . . One has to be ready to commit oneself, and live and fight in the areas where the fight is being waged (or not too many will listen). If I really respected myself—if I really loved my country, I would cut these lines."[30] Nevertheless, Sparer stayed at Penn.

Similarly, Wiley was unable to refocus the NWRO along the broader lines that he envisioned, and by 1972 he had lost the support and confidence of the NWRO staff and members. During the years of combating the FAP his office had consistently failed to provide adequate financial assistance to the grass-roots branches of the organization struggling to maintain their membership. Only a handful of NWRO affiliates remained active. Not only had the NWRO lost its membership base, it also had lost the allegiance of many of its senior field organizers.[31]

Amid accusations on all sides, Wiley resigned from the NWRO effective January 31, 1973. He was killed in a boating accident nine months later while on a brief vacation from his effort to organize a new Movement for Economic Justice, which he envisioned as a coalition of welfare recipients and the working poor.[32]

With the Supreme Court's decision in *Jefferson v. Hackney* in 1972, the demise of the guaranteed income plan later that year, and Wiley's death, the welfare rights movement represented by the NWRO and the first wave of welfare rights lawyers was effectively over. Sparer continued to teach at Penn until 1985, when he suffered a fatal heart attack at age fifty-five. Sparer died at his family's country house in Woodstock, New York, a retreat that he had often made available to members of the movement—recipients, lawyers, and organizers—for weekend strategy sessions away from the distractions of the city.

Chapter 11

Open Questions

Too many persons, including a large percentage of welfare lawyers, do not understand that large forward movements are possible only as the expectations of people increase as a result of numerous small struggles, reforms, and increased understanding.

—Edward V. Sparer, 1971

During the 1960s poor people's organizations first established a sustained collaboration with lawyers in pursuit of social change through litigation and legislation. Such a joint effort had been impossible so long as legal aid to the poor was limited to routine services designed simply to reduce public opposition to the legal monopoly held by the bar. But once the political coalition to establish federally funded legal services was in place, the new poverty lawyers worked with their clients to redefine poverty law. Drawing on settlement house models, storefront law offices were situated in poor communities, accessible to clients. Looking to the civil rights movement, lawyers developed a systematic, affirmative legal strategy. And joining with social workers and other activists in the community, many poverty lawyers considered it their job to organize welfare recipients, educate recipients about the welfare system, litigate routine as well as impact cases, and develop and analyze policy initiatives on the city, state, and federal levels.[1]

This collaboration between lawyers and recipient activists was hugely successful in many respects. Baseline rights of procedural and substantive fairness were established in such cases as *Goldberg v. Kelly, Shapiro v. Thompson,* and *King v. Smith.* As a direct result of efforts to enforce recipients' statutory and constitutional rights, many needy individuals received greater benefits than they would otherwise have received. Fair hearing campaigns and, later, rights-oriented lawsuits often formed the locus for recipient organizing and education concerning their rights; legal victories made participation in the movement empowering, worthwhile, and attractive. Finally, lawyers' skill at translating recipients needs into legal or quasi-legal claims—as in the right to live—gave those claims a grounding and legitimacy that facilitated the movement's political and educational work.

Analyses of the ultimate failure of the litigation strategy proposed by Ed Sparer has, unfortunately, tended to overshadow the positive aspects of the lawyer-activist-recipient collaboration. Such analyses are worthwhile, however, as a basis for understanding the limits of litigation, if not the role of the lawyers, in such a social movement.

One factor in the failure of the litigation strategy was likely the short duration of the organized welfare rights movement. Whereas the NAACP Legal Defense and Educational Fund labored for more than twenty-five years to reach the result in *Brown v. Board of Education,* welfare rights lawyers tried to achieve perhaps even more revolutionary victories between 1965 and 1970. This short time frame was the result, in part, of government-imposed restrictions that made it difficult for legal services lawyers to pursue their course while the Congress, courts, and federal administration shifted to the right. According to political scientist Samuel Krislov, "There was not enough time for the necessary analysis, criticism and refinement of the 'right to life' doctrine. There was not enough time to permit a judicial acceptance of a new constitutional doctrine nor was there time to obscure the fine line between judicial and legislative rulemaking authority."[2] Even within this short time frame, though, a number of federal district and courts of appeals judges accepted the right to live theory, suggesting that a more measured approach—including law review articles and simultaneous litigation based on state constitutions—might indeed have been more successful.[3]

Similarly, there was not time to develop a legal strategy tailored to the dynamics of poverty advocacy. The Center tried, with varying degrees of success, to model its test case litigation strategy on that of the NAACP Legal Defense Fund to eliminate the doctrine of separate but equal. Such a strategy may be ill suited to the poverty law context because it puts lawyers— whose knowledge of issues facing poor clients is at best second-hand—at the center of power and decision making in the movement. It tends, in the long term, to undermine the often fragile organizing power of the grass-roots movement.[4] The dozens of food stamp cases developed by Ron Pollack, in contrast, retained a local focus and used the pressure of numbers as well as legal arguments to achieve change. As a tactic on behalf of clients, the food stamp campaign arguably came closer than the vertical test case strategy to utilizing legal services' particular strength: the ability to provide clients with a combination of direct service and strategic legal work.[5]

More profoundly, the social isolation and stigmatization of the poor may frustrate broad reform through litigation. Comparing the NAACP campaign against segregation with the welfare rights campaign, civil libertarian Aryeh Neier concludes that the public's perception of the poor as "undeserving" was the key difference: "The Supreme Court could take on the enormous task of ending legal segregation of the races because of the apparent morality of the cause. . . . But the Court would not and could not take on the even larger task of establishing for the poor a right to live . . . [because] the claim by the poor that they had a right to assistance appeared to most Americans to lack morality."[6] Notably, in those instances where welfare rights litigants were successful—such as *Goldberg* and *Shapiro*—courts stressed the "brutal need" of recipients as a fundamental moral factor in their decisions.

The result in *Goldberg*, which provided fair procedures to evaluate the claims of individuals in brutal need, may indeed mark the limit of the willingness to squarely engage in redistributive justice.[7] As the wave of activism in the 1960s demonstrated, however, public perceptions of morality and need are changeable. The attempt to expand the pool of deserving poor through appeals to individual equality rights did not end with *Dandridge* or *Jefferson v. Hackney*. Writing in 1972, for example, welfare recipient leader Johnnie Tillmon compellingly posed AFDC eligibility restrictions in feminist terms: "People still believe that old lie that AFDC mothers keep on having kids just to get a bigger welfare check. On the average, another baby means another $35 a month—barely enough for food and clothing. Having babies for profit is a lie that only men could make up, and only men could believe. . . . There are a lot of other lies that male society tells about welfare mothers; that AFDC mothers are immoral, that AFDC mothers are lazy, misuse their welfare checks, spend it all on booze, and are stupid and incompetent. If people are willing to believe these lies, it's partly because they're just special versions of the lies that society tells about *all* women."[8]

Sparer also recognized the need to define the issue of poverty in a way that had wider resonance, taking a cue from the Great Depression, a time when the interests of the welfare poor, the working poor, and lower middle class coincided to create the political impetus for the reforms of the Social Security Act. Sparer concluded that "law reform *and* adequate service for the poor, in the final analysis, had to fail so long as it was cast within the war against poverty context. This context was (and remains) to a very large degree, income redistribution from the not so well off to the very poor. The not-so-well-off folks will not put up with such a redistribution. . . . [T]he content of [Legal Services'] work should help bridge the gap (rather than increase the gap) that divides the very poor from the working and lower middle classes."[9]

Whether these notions could ever sustain a litigation strategy or, for that matter, a social movement, remains an unanswered question. Certainly the failure of Sparer's welfare rights litigation strategy mitigates against reliance on litigation as the sole focus of a broad effort to promote change in the welfare system. At the same time, the history of lawyers' collaboration with recipient activists demonstrates that poverty law can involve more than simply access to justice and that both legal strategies and lawyers themselves can play an important role in a social movement of poor people.

Individuals Interviewed

Lee Albert
Gary Bellow
Richard Blaskovich
Robert Borsody
George Brager
William J. Brennan, Jr.
Martin Burdick
Richard Carburry
Richard Cloward
Richard Cooper
Peter Darrow
David Diamond
Matthew Diller
Paul Dodyk
Wilfred Feinberg
Henry Freedman
Louise Gans
Martin Garbus
David Gilman
Brian Glick

Jack Greenberg
Mary Handler
Eric Hirschhorn
Sylvia Law
John Loflin
Frances Fox Piven
Carl Rachlin
Charles Reich
Taylor Reveley
Marianne Rosenfield
Harold Rothwax
Barbara Sard
Michael Sparer
Tanya Sparer
Peter Strauss
Johnny Weiss
Elizabeth Wickenden
Stephen Wizner
Melvyn Wulf
Max Zimny

Note on Archival Sources

There is no central repository of documents relating to lawyers and the welfare rights movement in the 1960s. Neither the papers of Mobilization for Youth (MFY) nor those of the Center on Social Welfare Policy and Law are collected in any archive. A Freedom of Information Act request seeking Office of Economic Opportunity records relating to MFY was unrevealing; most of the government's records have apparently been destroyed or ceded to private collections. Much of the most interesting material on this period remains in the personal collections of the participants. Plans are, however, currently under way to establish a National Equal Justice Library at the Washington College of Law of the American University in Washington, D.C. The library, scheduled to open in 1995, will be a research facility housing a broad range of original source materials on legal representation of the poor.

The Center and MFY Legal Services, both in New York City, maintain slim records of their activities in the 1960s and 1970s. A number of documents relating to the activities of the Center and Edward Sparer are available in the George Wiley Papers and the records of the Scholarship, Education, and Defense Fund for Racial Equality, 1944–1976 (SEDFRE), housed in the Social Action Collection, Archives Division, State Historical Society of Wisconsin in Madison. These records provide a broader picture of lawyers' work on welfare rights issues during those years. The American Civil Liberties Union Archives at the Seeley G. Mudd Manuscript Library at Princeton University are also helpful in this regard. In addition, the ACLU and SEDFRE papers and the Mark DeWolfe Howe Papers provide useful background on the creation and activities of the Lawyers Constitutional Defense Committee, which laid the groundwork for welfare rights work in the South. The Howe papers are at the Special Collections Department, Manuscript Division, Harvard Law School Library.

The Ford Foundation Archives has an extensive grant file on Mobilization for Youth—No. 62–369—a portion of which is devoted to the creation and first two years of operation of the MFY Legal Unit. The library of the Columbia University School of Social Work has perhaps the most extensive collection of publications and records pertaining to the other activities of MFY. This collection, in bound volumes in the library's open stacks, contains some information about the work of the MFY Legal Unit as well. In addition, Whitney M. Young, Jr., who was a member of the MFY board of directors until the late 1960s, received a number of mailings, newsletters, board minutes, and other MFY-related information, which can be found in his papers at the Rare Book and Manuscript Library, Columbia University.

Case files of litigation are public records. Records of the New York area federal cases discussed here have been transferred from the courthouse files to the Federal

Records Center in Bayonne, New Jersey, operated by the National Archives and Records Administration. Many law schools maintain complete microfiche records of U.S. Supreme Court cases, including all filings in the case and written transcripts of oral arguments. Tape recordings of oral arguments before the Supreme Court can be heard at the Motion Picture, Sound, and Video Recording Branch of the National Archives in Washington, D.C.

The papers of Supreme Court Justices William J. Brennan, Jr., Hugo L. Black, and William O. Douglas are housed at the Library of Congress, Manuscript Division, in Washington, D.C. Access to the collections of Brennan and Black may be restricted; researchers should contact the Library of Congress for information concerning permission to view the records. Justice John M. Harlan's papers are available at the Seeley G. Mudd Manuscript Library at Princeton University.

Abbreviations

The following abbreviations are used in these notes. Where possible, citations include box and file numbers.

ACLU	American Civil Liberties Union Papers, Seeley G. Mudd Manuscript Library, Princeton University
CSSW	Whitney M. Young, Jr., Library, Columbia University School of Social Work
CSWPL	Center on Social Welfare Policy and Law
CW	Charles E. Wyzanski, Jr., Papers, Special Collections, Manuscript Division, Harvard Law School Library
EVS	Edward V. Sparer Papers, International Ladies Garment Workers Union
EW	Elizabeth Wickenden Papers, personal collection
Ford	Mobilization for Youth Grant File No. 62–369, Ford Foundation Archives
GB	George Brager Papers, personal collection
GW	George Wiley Papers, Social Action Collection, Archives Division, State Historical Society of Wisconsin
HLB	Justice Hugo L. Black Papers, Manuscript Division, Library of Congress
HSSH	Henry Street Settlement House
JMH	Justice John M. Harlan Papers, Seeley G. Mudd Manuscript Library, Princeton University
LW	Lillian Wald Papers, New York Public Library
MDH	Mark DeWolfe Howe Papers, Special Collections, Manuscript Division, Harvard Law School Library
MFY	MFY Legal Services
ND	Norman Dorsen Papers, New York University Law School Library
SED	Scholarship, Education, and Defense Fund for Racial Equality Records, 1944–1976, Social Action Collection, Archives Division, State Historical Society of Wisconsin

W J B	Justice William J. Brennan, Jr., Papers, Manuscript Division, Library of Congress
W L H U	Widener Library, Harvard University
W O D	Justice William O. Douglas Papers, Manuscript Division, Library of Congress

Notes

Introduction

1. *See generally* Alan Matusow, *The Unraveling of America* (New York: Harper & Row, 1984), pp. 217–40.

2. *See, e.g.,* Larry Jackson and William A. Johnson, *Protest by the Poor* (Lexington, Mass.: Lexington Books, 1984); Guida West, *The National Welfare Rights Movement: The Social Protest of Poor Women* (New York: Praeger, 1981); Susan Handley Hertz, *The Welfare Mothers Movement: A Decade of Change for Poor Women?* (Lanham, Md.: University Press of America, 1981); and Lawrence Bailis, *Bread or Justice: Grassroots Organizing in the Welfare Rights Movement* (Lexington, Mass.: Lexington Books, 1972).

3. Michael Katz, *In the Shadow of the Poorhouse* (New York: Basic Books, 1986), pp. 251–73; James T. Patterson, *America's Struggle Against Poverty, 1900–1985* (Cambridge: Harvard University Press, 1986), pp. 99–198; Mark V. Tushnet, *The NAACP's Legal Strategy Against Segregated Education, 1925–1950* (Chapel Hill: University of North Carolina Press, 1987); and Richard Kluger, *Simple Justice* (New York: Knopf, 1976).

4. Michael Harrington, *The Other America: Poverty in the United States* (New York: Macmillan, 1962), pp. 8–10; and Richard A. Cloward and Lloyd E. Ohlin, *Delinquency and Opportunity: A Theory of Delinquent Gangs* (Glencoe, Ill.: Free Press, 1960).

5. Author interview with Sylvia Law, Oct. 4, 1988.

Chapter 1: Welfare and "The Man"

1. Michael Katz, *In the Shadow of the Poorhouse* (New York: Basic Books, 1986), pp. 208–10.

2. Walter I. Trattner, *From Poor Law to Welfare State: A History of Social Welfare in America* (New York: Free Press, 1989, 4th ed.), pp. 249–50.

3. M. Katz, pp. 210, 213.

4. Trattner, p. 252.

5. M. Katz, pp. 219–20, 224–25. *See also* Trattner, pp. 259–61; and James T. Patterson, *America's Struggle Against Poverty, 1900–1985* (Cambridge: Harvard University Press, 1986), p. 57.

6. *Ibid.* at p. 226.

7. J. Patterson, pp. 61–62.

8. *Ibid.* at p. 60.

9. M. Katz, p. 239. *See, e.g., Schechter Poultry Corp. v. United States*, 295 U.S. 495 (1935).

10. The Social Security Act of 1935 was upheld by the Supreme Court in two decisions, *Steward Machine Co. v. Davis*, 301 U.S. 548 (1937), and *Helvering v. Davis*, 301 U.S. 619 (1937), in what many believe were a series of politically influenced opinions expanding the regulatory power of the federal government. Following the Supreme Court's decisions affirming the constitutionality of federal labor regulations—e.g., NLRB v. *Jones & Laughlin Steel Corp.*, 301 U.S. 1 (1937)—Professor Felix Frankfurter of Harvard Law School wrote to Charles Wyzanski, Jr., an attorney on the U.S. Solicitor General's litigation team, that "the lawyer who won these cases is the lawyer who never argued them—Franklin D. Roosevelt. To me it is all painful beyond words—the poignant grief of one whose life has been dedicated to faith in the disinterestedness of a tribunal and its freedom from responsiveness to the most obvious immediacies of politics. And to envelop it all with the appearance of devotion to the disinterested response to the requirements of law gives one the sickening feeling which is aroused when moral standards are adulterated in a convent." Letter from Felix Frankfurter to Charles Wyzanski, Jr., April 13, 1937 [CW, B1 F11].

11. Mimi Abramovitz, *Regulating the Lives of Women: Social Welfare Policy from Colonial Times to the Present* (Boston: South End Press, 1988), pp. 190–95. Aid to Dependent Children was extended to mothers in 1950 and renamed Aid to Families with Dependent Children in 1962. To avoid confusion, the program is here referred to as AFDC.

12. *Ibid.* at pp. 315, 321.

13. *Ibid.* at pp. 323–26. *See also* M. Katz, p. 253; and J. Patterson, pp. 87–88.

14. The lack of strict federal supervision of states' practices may be attributable to Congress' sympathy with moralistic and punitive welfare practices. Martha Derthick, *The Influence of Federal Grants: Public Assistance in Massachusetts* (Cambridge: Harvard University Press, 1970), pp. 74–75.

15. M. Katz, p. 247.

16. Winifred Bell, *Aid to Dependent Children* (New York: Columbia University Press, 1965), pp. 137–42.

17. *See generally* Rickie Solinger, *Wake Up Little Susie: Single Pregnancy and Race Before Roe v. Wade* (New York: Routledge, 1992), pp. 22–23.

Chapter 2: Poor Law and Poverty Lawyers

1. Susan E. Lawrence, *The Poor in Court: The Legal Services Program and Supreme Court Decision Making* (Princeton: Princeton University Press, 1990), p. 22.

2. Lawrence, pp. 28–29; and Earl Johnson, Jr., *Justice and Reform: The Formative Years of the American Legal Services Program* (New Brunswick, N.J.: Transaction Books, 1978), p. 188.

3. Johnson, p. 189.

4. Lawrence, pp. 9–10, n.25.

5. John M. Maguire, *The Lance of Justice: A Semi-Centennial History of the Legal Aid Society, 1876–1926* (Cambridge: Harvard University Press, 1928), p. 19.

Early legal aid societies were also established in Chicago by members of the Chicago Women's Club and Chicago Ethical Cultural Society. Johnson, pp. 4–5. *See also* Emery A. Brownell, *Legal Aid in the United States* (Rochester, N.Y.: Lawyers Cooperative Publishing, 1951), pp. 170–71 (table 19). Many of the legal aid societies later established were patterned on the New York society. Arthur Von Briesen, "The Legal Aid Society," 11 *University Settlement Studies* (July 1906), p. 55 [WLHU].

  6. Von Briesen, p. 53.

  7. Ronald Sanders, *The Lower East Side* (New York: Dover, 1979), p. 5.

  8. Von Briesen, p. 56.

  9. *Ibid.* at p. 52.

  10. Maguire, pp. 253–60.

  11. University Settlement, Annual Report (1902), p. 9 [WLHU].

  12. Von Briesen, pp. 52, 56.

  13. Maguire, pp. 61, 74–75.

  14. Robert P. Patterson, "A Brief History of the Legal Aid Society," 65 *The Legal Aid Review* (1968–69), p. 27. In 1899 the Legal Aid Society also established a Seamen's Branch and a Women's Branch, which was staffed by women lawyers.

  15. Roy Lubove, *The Progressives and the Slums* (Pittsburgh: University of Pittsburgh Press, 1962), pp. 28–32.

  16. Susan E. Lyman, *The Story of New York* (New York: Crown, 1975, rev. ed.), p. 206.

  17. *Year Book of the University Settlement Society of New York* (1899), pp. 50–51 [WLHU].

  18. *Ibid.* at p. 51.

  19. University Settlement, Annual Report (1900), pp. 49–50 [WLHU].

  20. *Year Book of the University Settlement Society,* p. 52.

  21. Maguire, p. 162.

  22. *Ibid.*

  23. Jack Katz, *Poor People's Lawyers in Transition* (New Brunswick, N.J.: Rutgers University Press, 1982), pp. 58–59.

  24. Maguire, p. 162.

  25. *See generally* Jacob Riis, *How the Other Half Lives* (New York: Charles Scribner's Sons, 1890; New York: Dover, 1971); Judith Trolander, *Professionalism and Social Change* (New York: Columbia University Press, 1987); and Harry P. Kraus, *The Settlement House Movement in New York City, 1886–1914* (New York: Arno, 1980).

  26. "Settlements and Community Centers," *Encyclopedia of Social Work,* vol. 2 (Silver Spring, Md.: National Association of Social Workers, 1987, 18th ed.), pp. 556–61.

  27. Sanders, p. 39.

  28. Trolander, pp. 12–13.

  29. Jerold S. Auerbach, *Unequal Justice* (Oxford: Oxford University Press, 1976), p. 58.

  30. Letter from Louis Marshall to Lillian Wald, April 5, 1906 [LW]. *See generally*

Charles Reznikoff, ed., *Louis Marshall, Champion of Liberty: Selected Papers and Addresses* (New York: Jewish Publication Society of America, 1957), pp. xiv–xv.

31. *Muller v. Oregon*, 208 U.S. 412 (1908). *See generally* Lewis J. Paper, *Brandeis* (Englewood Cliffs, N.J.: Prentice-Hall, 1983), pp. 163–65.

32. Auerbach, pp. 57–58.

33. Judith Trolander, *Settlement Houses and the Great Depression* (Detroit: Wayne State University Press, 1975), pp. 20–21.

34. Trolander, *Professionalism*, pp. 2, 23.

35. Walter I. Trattner, *From Poor Law to Welfare State: A History of Social Welfare in America* (New York: Free Press, 1989, 4th ed.), pp. 231–45.

36. Von Briesen, p. 58. This rule, and the rule that Legal Aid would handle only civil cases, may have been initiated to conserve the Legal Aid Society's resources, but it also ensured that private practitioners would not be threatened by the organization.

37. Auerbach, p. 59.

38. Maguire, p. 201.

39. Lawrence, p. 19.

40. Johnson, p. 5.

41. Reginald Heber Smith, *Justice and the Poor* (New York: Charles Scribner's Sons, 1919), p. 8.

42. Brownell, pp. 6–7.

43. Smith, p. ix.

44. Johnson, p. 9.

45. *Ibid.* at p. 8; and Brownell, pp. 167–68 (table 18).

46. Auerbach, p. 160.

47. *Ibid.* at p. 161.

48. Harlan F. Stone, "The Public Influence of the Bar," 48 *Harv. L. Rev.* (1934), p. 7.

49. Auerbach, pp. 161–66.

50. Ronald Dworkin, *Taking Rights Seriously* (London: Duckworth, 1977), pp. 3–4.

51. Karl Llewellyn, Book Review, 31 *Colum. L. Rev.* (1931), p. 1217.

52. Auerbach, p. 166. *See also* Alan Hunt, *The Sociological Movement in Law* (London: Macmillan, 1978), p. 48; and William Twining, *Karl Llewellyn and the Realist Movement* (Norman: University of Oklahoma Press, 1985), pp. 57–58.

53. Hunt, p. 39.

54. Brownell, p. 173.

55. Auerbach, pp. 207–9. *See also* "Proposal for a Legal Service Bureau for the Metropolitan Area of Chicago," 1 *National Lawyers Guild Quarterly* (March 1938), pp. 149–54.

56. Mark V. Tushnet, *The NAACP's Legal Strategy Against Segregated Education, 1925–1950* (Chapel Hill: University of North Carolina Press, 1987), pp. 118–19.

57. Johnson, p. 9. *See also* Sar Levitan, *The Great Society's Poor Law* (Baltimore: Johns Hopkins University Press, 1969), p. 183.

58. Auerbach, p. 236.

59. Johnson, p. 9.

60. Auerbach, p. 238.

61. Brownell, p. xiii.

62. "Prof. Jacobus TenBroek is Dead; President of Federation of Blind," *New York Times*, March 28, 1968, p. 47, col. 4.

63. Joel Handler, ed., *Family Law and the Poor: Essays by Jacobus TenBroek* (Westport, Conn.: Greenwood Press, 1971 ed.), pp. ix–xix. Daniel R. Mandelker also contributed early influential writing on the constitutionality of welfare laws. *See generally* Daniel R. Mandelker, "Exclusion and Removal Legislation," 1956 *Wis. L. Rev.*, p. 57.

64. *Korematsu v. United States*, 323 U.S. 214 (1944).

65. *Ibid.* at p. 216.

66. *Brown v. Board of Education*, 347 U.S. 483 (1954).

67. Joseph Tussman and Jacobus tenBroek, "The Equal Protection of the Laws," 37 *Cal. L. Rev.* (1949), p. 341.

68. Handler, pp. xiv–xv, quoting *Edwards v. California*, 314 U.S. 160, 184 (1941) (Jackson, J.).

69. Jacobus tenBroek, *The Constitution and the Right of Free Movement* (National Travelers Aid Association, 1955), p. 15.

70. Jacobus tenBroek, "California's Dual System of Family Law: Its Origin, Development, and Present Status," 16 *Stan. L. Rev.* (1964), pp. 257, 900 (pts. 1–2) and 17 *Stan. L. Rev.* (1965), p. 614 (pt. 3).

71. *Gideon v. Wainwright*, 372 U.S. 335 (1963).

72. Handler, pp. xv–xvi, 145–213.

Chapter 3: The Welfare Law Guru

1. *See, e.g.*, Aryeh Neier, *Only Judgment* (Middletown, Conn.: Wesleyan University Press, 1982), p. 130.

2. Edward V. Sparer, "Fundamental Human Rights, Legal Entitlements, and the Social Struggle," 36 *Stan. L. Rev.* (1984), pp. 540–41.

3. *Ibid.*

4. " 'Sit-Down' Staged at City College Over Exoneration of Professor," *New York Times*, Sept. 30, 1948, p. 24, col. 4.

5. Sparer, "Fundamental Human Rights," p. 541.

6. "City College Students Clash With Police in 'Bias' Strike," *New York Times*, April 12, 1949, p. 1, col. 2.

7. Author interview with Tanya Sparer, Feb. 28, 1989.

8. *Ibid.*

9. *Ibid.*

10. Sparer, "Fundamental Human Rights," p. 543.

11. Author interview with Tanya Sparer, Feb. 28, 1989.

12. Sparer, "Fundamental Human Rights," p. 543.

13. *Ibid.*

14. David G. Trager, "Are Lawyers Professionals or Do They Only Profess to Be?" *New York Law Journal*, Sept. 2, 1983, p. 1, col. 1 (quoting letter from Edward V. Sparer to Dean Prince, Brooklyn Law School).

15. Author interviews with Tanya Sparer, Feb. 28, 1989; and Michael Sparer, February 1989.

16. Author interview with Tanya Sparer, Feb. 28, 1989.

17. Trager, p. 1, col. 1.

18. Author interview with Tanya Sparer, Feb. 28, 1989.

19. Stanley Aronowitz, *Working Class Hero: A New Strategy for Labor* (New York: Adama Books, 1983), p. 44.

20. Memorandum from Morris Glushien to the file, April 21, 1959 [EVS].

21. Author interview with Max Zimny, January 1989.

22. Aronowitz, p. 42.

23. Author interviews with Max Zimny, January 1989; Tanya Sparer, Feb. 28, 1989; and Michael Sparer, February 1989.

24. Monthly Progress Reports from Edward V. Sparer to Morris Glushien, Sept. 30, 1959; Oct. 30, 1959; April 19, 1960; May 31, 1960 [EVS].

25. Author interview with Tanya Sparer, Feb. 28, 1989.

26. *Ibid.*

27. *Ibid.*

28. Harry P. Kraus, *The Settlement House Movement in New York City, 1886–1914* (New York: Arno, 1980), pp. 78–83. *See generally* Lillian Wald, *The House on Henry Street* (New York: Holt, 1915; New York: Dover, 1972); and R. L. Duffus, *Lillian Wald: Neighbor and Crusader* (New York: Macmillan, 1938).

29. Frances Piven, "Conceptual Themes in the Evolution of MFY" (Prepared for the Columbia University School of Social Work–Mobilization for Youth Training Institute on Urban Community Development Projects: Selected Aspects of the Mobilization for Youth Experience, April 27–May 1, 1964), p. 1, in Mobilization for Youth Training Department Publications, vol. 4 [CSSW].

30. Joseph H. Helfgot, *Professional Reforming* (Lexington, Mass.: Lexington Books, 1981), p. 39; and Helen Hall, *Unfinished Business* (New York: Macmillan, 1971), pp. 269–76.

31. Minutes of the Meeting of the Board of Directors of the Henry Street Settlement House, Oct. 9, 1958, pp. 2–3 [HSSH]. For an extensive discussion of efforts to raise funds for MFY, *see* Helfgot, pp. 19–41.

32. Richard A. Cloward and Lloyd E. Ohlin, *Delinquency and Opportunity: A Theory of Delinquent Gangs* (Glencoe, Ill.: Free Press, 1960).

33. Mobilization for Youth, "A Proposal for the Prevention and Control of Delinquency by Expanding Opportunities, A Summary," Jan. 10, 1962, p. 3 (emphasis in original) [Ford].

---

34. Allen J. Matusow, *The Unraveling of America* (New York: Harper & Row, 1984), pp. 109–11; and Helfgot, pp. 29–31. Not coincidentally, Lloyd Ohlin left his position at Columbia in 1962 to serve as director of the Office for Juvenile Delinquency, the funding arm of the President's Committee on Juvenile Delinquency.

35. Jack Newfield, *New York Post*, Aug. 30, 1964, cited in Daniel P. Moynihan, *Maximum Feasible Misunderstanding* (New York: Free Press, 1969), p. 106 & n.1.

36. MFY Neighborhood Service Center proposal, adopted by the Board of Directors, Dec. 9, 1961 (describing discussions with Legal Aid Society for provision of legal services) [WY, Box 33]. *See also* Memorandum from George Brager to James McCarthy and Richard Cloward, May 17, 1962, re. Individual Services and Legal Program [GB] (hereinafter Brager Mem., May 17, 1962).

37. Brager Mem., May 17, 1962.

38. "Draft Summary of the Proposal for the Establishment of a Legal Services Program Under the Neighborhood Service Center," n.d., p. 1 [GB].

39. *Ibid.* at p. 2.

40. Vera Foundation, "A Proposal to Set Up a Legal Unit for Mobilization for Youth," May 1963, p. 3 [MFY].

41. Memorandum from Edward V. Sparer to Monrad G. Paulsen, chairman, supervisory committee of the Legal Services Unit, MFY, Nov. 29, 1963, pp. 10–11 [MFY].

42. Memorandum from George Brager to Charles Grosser, cc. Edward Sparer, Jan. 20, 1964, p. 1 [GB].

43. Memorandum from Ed Sparer to members of the Policy Committee, MFY Legal Services Unit, March 4, 1964, p. 5 [GB] (hereinafter Sparer Mem., March 4, 1964).

44. *Ibid.* at p. 8.

45. *Ibid.* at p. 7.

46. *Ibid.* at p. 17.

47. Mobilization for Youth Legal Unit Report, November 1965, p. 3 [MFY].

48. Charles F. Grosser and Edward V. Sparer, "Social Welfare and Social Justice," in George A. Brager and Francis P. Purcell, eds., *Community Action Against Poverty: Readings from the Mobilization Experience* (New Haven: College & University Press, 1967), p. 299.

49. Edward V. Sparer, "Education Regarding Common Legal Difficulties Faced by the Low Income Community: Methods Employed in New York's Lower East Side by the Mobilization for Youth Legal Services Unit" (Paper presented at the Conference on the Extension of Legal Services to the Poor, Department of Health, Education, and Welfare, Washington, D.C., Nov. 12, 1964) [CSSW].

50. *See* Memorandum from Christopher F. Edley to the file, March 2, 1965, re. report on examination of Legal Services Unit, p. 2 [Ford] (hereinafter Edley Mem., March 2, 1965).

51. *Ibid.* at pp. 1–2.

52. Author interview with Marianne Rosenfield, Nov. 18, 1988.

53. Sparer Mem., March 4, 1964, p. 1.

54. *Ibid.* at p. 18.

55. Johnson, pp. 24–25.

56. Murray Kempton, "The Heart of the Matter," *New York World Telegram and Sun*, Nov. 24, 1964; Susan Brownmiller, "Out of the Trenches: Mobilization for Youth—One Year Later," *Village Voice*, Oct. 28, 1965, p. 13 (compiled in *Mobilization for Youth, the Crisis: A Documentary Record*, prepared by Research Center, Columbia University School of Social Work) [CSSW].

57. 42 U.S.C. § 2782(a)(3). *See generally* Note, "Participation of the Poor: Section 202(a)(3) Organizations Under the Economic Opportunity Act of 1964," 75 *Yale L.J.* (1966), p. 599; and William F. Haddad, "Mr. Shriver and the Savage Politics of Poverty," *Harper's*, December 1965, p. 44.

58. Johnson, pp. 39–70; and Edgar S. Cahn and Jean C. Cahn, "The War on Poverty: A Civilian Perspective," 73 *Yale L.J.* (1964), p. 1317. *See also* Ellen Hollingsworth, "Ten Years of Legal Services for the Poor," in Robert H. Haveman, ed., *A Decade of Federal Antipoverty Programs* (New York: Academic Press, 1977), pp. 294–95.

59. Johnson, pp. 22–23. Jean Cahn, then an attorney at the New Haven office, had accepted representation of a black man indicted for raping a white woman. Because of the controversy over the case, the office closed only seven weeks after it opened.

60. *Ibid.* at p. 26.

61. *Ibid.* at pp. 30–31; and Letter from Edward V. Sparer to Robert Chandler, Ford Foundation, May, 28, 1965 [Ford].

62. *See* Johnson, p. 32.

63. Johnson, p. 57; and Note, "Neighborhood Law Offices: The New Wave in Legal Services for the Poor," 80 *Harv. L. Rev.* (1967), p. 839.

64. Despite ABA support on the national level, many state and local bar associations vehemently opposed federally funded legal services. The president of the Tennessee Bar Association, for example, described the program as "the greatest threat that has ever faced the legal profession," designed to encourage "the fomenting of social unrest in this country." "Bar Aide Scores Poverty Lawyers," *New York Times*, Feb. 20, 1966, p. 38, col. 3.

65. Johnson, p. 71.

66. Sar Levitan, *The Great Society's Poor Law* (Baltimore: Johns Hopkins University Press, 1969), p. 180.

67. Author interview with Gary Bellow, April 1989; and Levitan, p. 180 (noting National Legal Aid and Defender's Association opposition to OEO's emphasis on law reform).

68. Edley Mem., March 2, 1965, p. 2.

69. Memorandum from Christopher F. Edley to Bob Chandler, May 17, 1965, re. MFY Legal Services Unit [Ford].

70. *See generally* Dorothy J. Samuels, "Expanding Justice: A Review of the Ford Foundation's Legal Services Program" (Manuscript, January 1984) [MFY].

71. Author interview with Harold Rothwax, Sept. 9, 1988.

---

72. Remarks of Harold Rothwax in the Proceedings of the Harvard Conference on Law and Poverty, Harvard Law School (Cambridge, Mass., March 17–19, 1967), pp. 63–64.

73. Edward V. Sparer, "The New Legal Aid as an Instrument of Social Change," *U. Ill. L.F.* (1965), pp. 59–60 (emphasis in original).

74. Edward V. Sparer, "The Role of the Welfare Client's Lawyer," 12 *UCLA L. Rev.* (1965), pp. 366–67.

75. Edward V. Sparer, "Social Welfare Law Testing," 12 *Prac. Law.* (April 1966), pp. 14–15.

76. Elizabeth Wickenden, "Poverty and the Law: The Constitutional Rights of Assistance Recipients," Feb. 25, 1963 [EW].

77. Sparer, "Social Welfare Law Testing," pp. 16–17; and Sparer Mem., March 4, 1964, p. 11, n.9.

78. Author interview with Tanya Sparer, Feb. 29, 1989.

79. Brief for Appellant, *In re Minnie Lee Nixon* (State of New York, Department of Social Welfare, 1964), Mobilization for Youth Publications, vol. 12, pp. i–ii [CSSW].

80. Edward V. Sparer, "The Right to Welfare," in Norman Dorsen, ed., *The Rights of Americans* (New York: Pantheon, 1971), p. 82.

81. A. Delafield Smith, *The Right to Life* (Chapel Hill: University of North Carolina Press, 1955), p. 7.

82. *Ibid.* at pp. 103–21.

83. *Ibid.* at pp. 5–6.

84. "Guarantee of 'Right to Live' is Urged," *New York Times*, Sept. 28, 1969, p. 40, col. 4.

85. *Ibid.*

86. *Ibid.*

87. *Lochner v. New York*, 198 U.S. 45 (1905).

Chapter 4: The Movement

1. Lawrence Bailis, *Bread or Justice: Grassroots Organizing in the Welfare Rights Movement* (Lexington, Mass.: Lexington Books, 1972), p. 11; and "Alliance of Poor Sought on Jersey," *New York Times*, Aug. 30, 1965, sec. B, p. 13, col. 3; and Susan Handley Hertz, *The Welfare Mothers Movement: A Decade of Change for Poor Women?* (Lanham, Md.: University Press of America, 1981), pp. 32–37. *See also* Nick Kotz and Mary Kotz, *A Passion for Equality* (New York: Norton, 1977), pp. 221; and Edward V. Sparer, Howard Thorkelson, and Jonathan Weiss, "The Lay Advocate," 43 *U. Det. L.J.* (1966), pp. 506–7.

2. Richard A. Cloward and Richard M. Elman, "The Storefront on Stanton Street," in George A. Brager and Francis P. Purcell, eds., *Community Action Against Poverty* (New Haven: College & University Press, 1967), pp. 267–68, 270; and Charles R. Morris, *The Cost of Good Intentions: New York City and the Liberal Experiment, 1960–1975* (New York: Norton, 1980), pp. 68–69.

3. Charles Grosser, "Neighborhood Legal Service: A Strategy to Meet Human Need" (Paper presented at the Conference on the Extension of Legal Services to the Poor, Department of Health, Education, and Welfare, Washington, D.C., Nov. 12, 1964), p. 4 & n.2 [CSSW].

4. *See* Morris, p. 69.

5. Larry R. Jackson and William A. Johnson, *Protest by the Poor* (Lexington, Mass.: Lexington Books, 1974), pp. 75–81; and "The Welfare Battlefield," 5 *MFY News Bulletin* (Spring 1966), p. 3 [WY, Box 55].

6. Morris, pp. 68–69; "U.S. Ruling Asked on Welfare Raids," *New York Times,* Aug. 23, 1964, p. 66, col. 1; and "Welfare Chief Gets Fast Start," *New York Times,* Feb. 15, 1966, p. 27, col. 1.

7. "Relief Test Here Will Be Dropped," *New York Times,* March 10, 1966, p. 1, col. 6; and Morris, p. 70.

8. Author interviews with Richard Carburry and Richard Blaskovich, April 14, 1989.

9. Author interviews with Richard Carburry and Richard Blaskovich, April 14, 1989; Martin Burdick, June 24, 1989; and David Gilman, Oct. 5, 1988.

10. Memorandum from Ed Sparer to members of the Policy Committee, MFY Legal Services Unit, March 4, 1964, p. 11 [GB].

11. Clayborne Carson, *In Struggle: SNCC and the Black Awakening of the 1960s* (Cambridge: Harvard University Press, 1981), pp. 186, 229–43; and Kotz and Kotz, pp. 153–54.

12. "Brooklyn CORE Plans a Change in Its Tactics," *New York Times,* Nov. 8, 1967, p. 42, col. 5.

13. Kotz and Kotz, p. 182; and Richard Cloward and Frances Fox Piven, "A Strategy to End Poverty," *The Nation,* May 2, 1966.

14. Kotz and Kotz, p. 183.

15. *Ibid.* at pp. 184–87.

16. Jackson and Johnson, p. 33.

17. *Ibid.* at p. 34; Frances Fox Piven and Richard Cloward, *Poor People's Movements* (New York: Vintage, 1979), p. 294.

18. Jackson and Johnson, p. 37.

19. Author interviews with Richard Cloward and Frances Fox Piven, March 30, 1989.

20. Author interview with David Gilman, Oct. 5, 1988. These meetings also led to an attempt in 1968 by Gabe Kaimowitz, a lawyer with the Center on Social Welfare Policy and Law, to create a Poverty Bar Association. *See* Letter from Gabe Kaimowitz to Stephen Nagler, May 7, 1968 [SED B30 F52].

21. "Welfare Agency Faces 2 Revolts," *New York Times,* Sept. 19, 1966, p. 45, col. 1; "Work Load Spurs Welfare Protest," *New York Times,* Sept. 20, 1966, p. 1, col. 1; and "Relief Caseloads Reduced By City," *New York Times,* Sept. 21, 1966, p. 49, col. 1.

22. *See* Jackson and Johnson, p. 141 (table 14–1). *See also* "Life on Welfare: A Daily Struggle for Existence," *New York Times,* Dec. 19, 1966, p. 1, col. 4.

---

23. Theodore Caplow, "Still With Us," *New York Times*, Feb. 5, 1967, p. 36 (book review); "The Welfare Labyrinth," *Newsweek*, Aug. 28, 1967, pp. 22–25.

24. "Welfare Protest Made at City Hall," *New York Times*, July 1, 1966, p. 44, col. 1.

25. The state adopted regulations in 1968 that allowed home relief recipients to request fair hearings under similar circumstances.

26. Affidavit of David Gilman in Opposition to Defendants' Motion for Summary Judgment, sworn to June 22, 1968, *Kelly v. Wyman*, 68 Civ. 394 (S.D.N.Y.), ¶ 5.

27. Author interview with David Gilman, Oct. 5, 1988.

28. Author interview with Richard Carburry, April 14, 1989.

29. Jackson and Johnson, pp. 109–10.

30. Author interview with Richard Cloward, March 30, 1989. For a discussion of the role of religious leaders in organizing Brooklyn welfare recipients, *see* Jackie Pope, "Women in the Welfare Rights Struggle: The Brooklyn Welfare Action Council," in Guida West and Rhoda Blumberg, eds., *Women and Social Protest* (New York: Oxford University Press, 1990), p. 57.

31. The Massachusetts special grants campaign was particularly successful. *See generally* Bailis, pp. 11–13.

32. Letter from Elizabeth Wickenden to Richard Cloward, June 27, 1966 [SED B30 F3].

33. Author interview with David Gilman, Oct. 5, 1988.

34. Allen J. Matusow, *The Unraveling of America* (New York: Harper & Row, 1984), p. 363.

35. *Ibid.* at pp. 362–63; and James Miller, *Democracy Is in the Streets* (New York: Simon & Schuster, 1987), pp. 273–74.

36. Jackson and Johnson, pp. 112, 114 (table 10-2); and "City's Welfare Roll Outpacing Forecast," *New York Times*, Nov. 23, 1967, p. 1, col. 3.

37. Morris, pp. 46–47; "New Poverty Chief," *New York Times*, Aug. 18, 1967, p. 20, col. 6; and "New Welfare Chief," *New York Times*, Dec. 2, 1967, p. 50, col. 3.

38. Jackson and Johnson, p. 114.

39. "Welfare Clients Press to Collect Thousands Owed Them by City," *New York Times*, Oct. 3, 1967, p. 1, col. 5; Author interview with David Gilman, Oct. 5, 1988; and Harold Rothwax, speech delivered at 25th anniversary celebration of MFY, New York, Oct. 28, 1988.

40. Author interview with David Gilman, Oct. 5, 1988.

41. Memorandum from Stephen M. Nagler to Carl Rachlin, n.d., re. minimum standards welfare cases [SED B9 F4].

42. *Ibid.*

43. Jackson and Johnson, p. 119.

44. "Welfare Clients Press to Collect Thousands Owed Them By City," p. 1, col. 5.

45. Columbia University School of Social Work, "Report on the 1966 Activities and Future Perspective of the Center on Social Welfare Policy and Law," pp. 29–30

[CSWPL]; and Author interviews with Carl Rachlin, March 1, 1989, Mel Wulf, May 30, 1969, and Martin Garbus, Oct. 28, 1988. *See generally* Samuel Walker, *In Defense of American Liberties* (New York: Oxford University Press, 1990), pp. 313–14.

46. "Lawyers Begin Drive Against Poverty," *New York Times*, Nov. 20, 1966, p. 83, col. 2.

47. Memorandum from George Wiley to Tim Sampson, John Lewis, Ed Day, and Calvin Hicks, n.d., re. San Francisco office and staff, p.2 [GW B24 F13].

48. Jackson and Johnson, pp. 120–21.

49. "The Deepening Welfare Crisis," *New York Times*, Aug. 1, 1968, p. 23, col. 4; and "Welfare Sit-ins Netting Millions," *New York Times*, May 30, 1968, p. 22, col. 3.

50. "Welfare Clients Continue Sit-In at Goldberg's Office," *New York Times*, June 30, 1968, p. 39, col. 1; "38 Are Arrested in Relief Protest," *New York Times*, July 2, 1968, p. 18, col. 1; and "Welfare Protest Group Warns Mayor That Drive Will Continue," *New York Times*, July 4, 1968, p. 7, col. 2.

51. "More Relief Aid Is Sought Here," *New York Times*, Nov. 3, 1968, p. 38, col. 1; "The Deepening Welfare Crisis," p. 23, col. 4; and "Book Tells Ways to Get on Relief," *New York Times*, July 7, 1968, p. 44, col. 3.

52. Jackson and Johnson, p. 122; "Welfare Protest Enters 2d Week," Sept. 4, 1968, p. 96, col. 1; and "State and City Study Standard Welfare Payments," *New York Times*, June 26, 1968, p. 27, col. 26.

53. "Relief Recipients and Police Clash," *New York Times*, Aug. 28, 1968, p. 1, col. 5.

54. "Welfare System Due for Changes," *New York Times*, Sept. 2, 1968, p. 14, col. 1. In fact, the New York Civil Liberties Union supported the flat grant proposal as fundamentally fair, provided the grant levels were high enough. "Fixed Sum Backed for Poor in City," *New York Times*, July 28, 1968, p. 51, col. 4.

55. "Relief Recipients and Police Clash," p. 1, col. 5; "Protests Disrupt Welfare Centers," *New York Times*, Aug. 30, 1968, p. 31, col. 4; and "Welfare Protest Enters 2d Week," p. 96, col. 1.

56. "City Hall," *New Yorker*, Sept. 7, 1968, p. 24; "18 Arrested Here in 2d Day of Relief Recipient-Police Clashes," Aug. 29, 1968, p. 30, col. 2; and Memorandum from Carl Rachlin to SEDFRE Board of Directors, Jan. 15, 1969, p. 2 [SED B30 F1].

57. "Welfare Reaches Record 1.5 Million," *New York Times*, March 7, 1968, p. 58, col. 4; "75 Welfare Recipients Go on Rampage, Closing 3 Brooklyn Centers," *New York Times*, Sept. 18, 1968, p. 1, col. 4; and "Welfare Clients Renew Protests," *New York Times*, Dec. 6, 1968, p. 43, col. 1.

58. *See* Richard A. Cloward and Frances Fox Piven, "Finessing the Poor," *The Nation*, Oct. 7, 1968, p. 332.

59. "An Action Proposal: New Organizing Techniques in Flat Grant States," NWRO Action Conference, Aug. 22–25, 1968, p. 1 [SED B39 F6].

60. *Ibid.*

61. *Ibid.* at pp. 1–2.

62. Steiner, pp. 300–301; and Kotz and Kotz, pp. 236–37.

Chapter 5: Southern Strategy

1. Author interview with Henry Freedman, May 17, 1989. *See generally* Mark V. Tushnet, *The NAACP's Legal Strategy Against Segregated Education, 1925–1950* (Chapel Hill: University of North Carolina Press, 1987); Richard Kluger, *Simple Justice* (New York: Knopf, 1976).

2. *See, e.g.,* Jack Greenberg, "Litigation for Social Change: Methods, Limits and Role in Democracy" 29 *The Record of the Association of the Bar of the City of New York* (April 1974), p. 338.

3. Columbia University School of Social Work, "Report on the 1966 Activities and Future Perspective of the Center on Social Welfare Policy and Law," pp. 22, 24 [CSWPL].

4. Memorandum from Carl Rachlin to Marvin Rich, Oct. 14, 1966, p. 2 [SED B29 F23].

5. "Report on the 1966 Activities and Future Perspective of the Center on Social Welfare Policy and Law," p. 30, footnote.

6. Carl Rachlin, Annual Report, Legal Department, p. 1 [SED B9 F6]; Author interview with Carl Rachlin, March 1, 1989; and August Meier and Elliott Rudwick, *CORE: A Study in the Civil Rights Movement* (Urbana: University of Illinois Press, 1975), pp. 411–12.

7. Minutes of Meeting, April 2, 1964, re. Lawyers Constitutional Defense Committee (describing formation of LCDC) [MDH, B14 F7]; Memorandum from Carl Rachlin to James Farmer, May 11, 1964, re. status of efforts to organize lawyers for Freedom Summer [SED B29 F15]; Memorandum from Carl Rachlin to James Farmer et al., July 20, 1964, re. activities of LCDC and other lawyers during Freedom Summer [SED B29 F16]; and Jerry DeMuth, "Summer in Mississippi," *The Nation,* Sept. 14, 1964, p. 107.

8. "Robert Kennedy Bids the Bar Join Fight Against Social Ills," *New York Times,* May 2, 1964, p. 22, col. 4.

9. Author interview with Stephen Wizner, Oct. 11, 1988.

10. Earl Johnson, Jr., *Justice and Reform: The Formative Years of the American Legal Services Program* (New Brunswick, N.J.: Transaction Books, 1978), pp. 178–80.

11. *Ibid.* at p. 179.

12. Author interview with Henry Freedman, May 17, 1989.

13. Barbara Black and Stephen Wizner et al., "Tributes to Robert M. Cover," 96 *Yale L.J.* (1987), pp. 1704–5, 1708, 1719.

14. *Ibid.* at p. 1704.

15. *Ibid.* at pp. 1707–8.

16. Robert Cover, Note, "Federal Judicial Review of State Welfare Practices," 67 *Colum. L. Rev.* (1967), p. 91; Brief for Appellees, *King v. Smith,* No. 949 (U.S., Oct. Term 1967), pp. 18–20; and Elizabeth Wickenden, "A Decade of Poverty Rights Efforts" (Paper presented at the Third Annual Forum of Welfare Rights Organiza-

tion of Arizona, Phoenix, Dec. 5, 1969), pp. 1–3 (describing Louisiana's nonconformity hearing) [EW].

17. Cover, pp. 92–94.

18. *Ibid.* at pp. 94–95.

19. Author interview with Stephen Wizner, Oct. 11, 1988.

20. *King v. Smith,* 392 U.S. 309 (1968).

21. *Smith v. King,* 277 F. Supp. 31, 35 (M.D. Ala. 1967); and Complaint, *Smith v. King,* Civil Action No. 2495-N (N.D. Ala., Dec. 2, 1966), ¶ 9(c).

22. Complaint, *Smith v. King,* Civil Action No. 2495-N (N.D. Ala., Dec. 2, 1966), ¶ 4.

23. Martin Garbus, *Ready for the Defense* (New York: Farrar, Straus & Giroux, 1971), p. 164.

24. *King v. Smith,* 392 U.S. at 314, n.9; Complaint, *Smith v. King,* Civil Action No. 2495-N (N.D. Ala., Dec. 2, 1966), p. 1, ¶ E.

25. Author interviews with Carl Rachlin, March 1, 1989; and Mel Wulf, May 30, 1989.

26. When he left the LCDC in 1967, Jelinek became the director of the Southern Rural Research Project. "Alabama Negroes Lose Food Pleas," *New York Times,* March 26, 1968, p. 15, col. 1.

27. "Suit Today Will Seek to Force Freeman to Feed the Starving," *New York Times,* March 25, 1968, p. 47, col. 6; and Garbus, p. 146.

28. Author interview with Martin Garbus, Oct. 28, 1988.

29. *Ibid.*

30. *Anderson v. Schaefer,* Civil Action No. 10443 (N.D. Ga. 1966); and "Report on the 1966 Activities and Future Perspective of the Center on Social Welfare Policy and Law," pp. 4–5.

31. "Report on the 1966 Activities and Future Perspective of the Center on Social Welfare Policy and Law," p. 5.

32. Complaint, *Smith v. King,* Civil Action No. 2495-N (N.D. Ala., Dec. 2, 1966), p. 5, ¶ 5; p. 11, ¶ D. The case was a class action brought by AFDC recipients against the District's Board of Commissioners and other local welfare department officials.

33. Garbus, p. 153.

34. *Smith v. Board of Commissioners,* 259 F. Supp. 423, 424 (D.C.D.C. 1966).

35. Garbus, p. 154.

36. *Ibid.* at pp. 155–56. *See generally* Tinsley Yarborough, *Judge Frank Johnson and Human Rights in Alabama* (University: University of Alabama Press, 1981).

37. Garbus, p. 157.

38. The first Brandeis brief, prepared by Brandeis, Josephine Goldmark, and Florence Kelley, a nonpracticing lawyer associated with the Henry Street Settlement House, was filed in *Muller v. Oregon,* 208 U.S. 412 (1908), in support of laws regulating work hours for women. *See* Lewis J. Paper, *Brandeis* (Englewood Cliffs, N.J.: Prentice-Hall, 1983), pp. 163–65; and Leonard Baker, *Brandeis and Frankfurter* (New York: Harper & Row, 1984), pp. 13–16.

39. Garbus, pp. 159–61.

40. *Ibid.* at pp. 164–65; and Brief for Appellees, No. 949 (U.S. Oct. Term, 1967), pp. 51–52 & n.39.

41. 380 F.2d 632 (D.C. Cir. 1967).

42. *Smith v. King,* 277 F. Supp. 31 (M.D. Ala. 1967).

43. *Ibid.* at p. 37, n.7.

44. *King v. Smith,* 20 L.Ed.2d 1710 (1968) (briefs of counsel); and "Alabama Warns of Welfare Cut," *New York Times,* Nov. 22, 1967, p. 60, col. 3. The Social Security Act of 1967 was enacted while *King v. Smith* was pending before the Supreme Court. Under the law, federal funding was frozen at current levels as of July 1, 1978. If Alabama had been permitted to drop children affected by the state's substitute father regulation from the welfare rolls pending the appeal of *King,* the AFDC freeze might have effectively barred these children from later rejoining the rolls even if their appeal was successful. Martin Garbus persuaded the Supreme Court to instead order Alabama to maintain the children on the welfare rolls pending the Supreme Court's decision. Garbus, pp. 175–79.

45. Brief for Appellees, *King v. Smith,* No. 949 (U.S., Oct. Term, 1967), pp. 66–76.

46. *Ibid.* at p. 34, n.23 (emphasis in original).

47. *Ibid.* at pp. 24–25 & n.12.

48. Garbus, p. 175.

49. Motion for Leave to File Brief *Amici Curiae* and Brief *Amici Curiae* of the NAACP Legal Defense and Educational Fund, Inc., the National Office for the Rights of the Indigent, and the Center on Social Welfare Policy and Law, *King. v. Smith,* No. 949 (U.S., Oct. Term, 1967).

50. "Rights Legal Fund Says Gardner Lags on Aid Complaints," *New York Times,* Jan. 14, 1967, p. 28, col. 1.

51. Garbus, pp. 196–99.

52. Abe Fortas, "Equal Rights for Whom?" address at New York University Law School, March 29, 1966 [ND].

53. Letter from Roger Baldwin to Gil Jonas, March 6, 1968 [ACLU vol. 13]. *See also* Samuel Walker, *In Defense of American Liberties* (New York: Oxford University Press, 1990), p. 315.

54. Letter from Roger Baldwin to Gil Jonas, March 6, 1968.

55. *King v. Smith,* 392 U.S. at 320.

56. "Alabama Loses Welfare Appeal," *New York Times,* June 18, 1968, p. 33, col. 5; and "Foundation Fights Welfare Law Allowing Recipients' Assets to Be Seized," *New York Times,* Jan. 16, 1968, p. 21, col. 2.

57. Center Materials Prepared Since May 1, 1967, Tentative List, Oct. 18, 1967, p. 1 (discussing *Williams v. Gandy,* Civ. No. GC 6728 [N.D. Miss. 1967]) [CSWPL].

58. Edward V. Sparer, "The Right to Welfare," in Norman Dorsen, ed., *The Rights of Americans* (New York: Pantheon, 1971), p. 86.

59. Craig W. Christensen, "Of Prior Hearings and Welfare as 'New Property,' " 3 *Clearinghouse Rev.* (April 1970), p. 336.

Chapter 6: The Middle Years

Epigraph: Poverty/Rights Action Center, "Goals for a National Welfare Rights Movement" (Report of Workshop 2, National Welfare Rights Meeting, Chicago, Aug. 6–7, 1966), p. 2 [GW B7 F6].

1. "President Is Firm on Poverty Drive," *New York Times,* May 9, 1967, p. 1, col. 2.

2. Tom Wicker, "In the Nation: The Real Questions About Welfare," *New York Times,* May 11, 1967, p. 46, col. 3. *See also* "Kennedy Charges Welfare Has Failed to Help the Poor," *New York Times,* May 9, 1967, p. 1, col. 2.

3. *See, e.g.,* "Poverty: The Welfare Labyrinth," *Newsweek,* Aug. 28, 1967, pp. 22–25; and "How Much Is Enough in Helping the Poor?" *Business Week,* July 29, 1967, pp. 24–25.

4. Letter from Susan S. O'Connor, attorney at Newark Legal Services Program, to Shirley Lacy, director, Welfare Program, Welfare Rights Project, Newark, March 8, 1968 [SED B12 F3].

5. "A Pledged Income Will Be Tried Out," *New York Times,* Nov. 2, 1967, p. 53, col. 1.

6. "Poverty: The Welfare Labyrinth," p. 25. *See also* "The Case for a Family Allowance," *New York Times Magazine,* Feb. 5, 1967, p. 13.

7. Nick Kotz and Mary Kotz, *A Passion for Equality* (New York: Norton, 1977), p. 260.

8. Letter from Henry Freedman to Carl Rachlin, Sept. 26, 1968, p. 2 [SED B44 F24].

9. *Ibid.* at p. 1.

10. Author interview with Gary Bellow, April 1989. Bellow also served as general counsel to both the California Rural Legal Assistance Program and the Black Panther Party.

11. Author interview with Henry Freedman, May 17, 1989.

12. Author interview with Stephen Wizner, Oct. 11, 1988.

13. Author interview with Martin Garbus, Oct. 28, 1988.

14. Author interview with David Gilman, Oct. 4, 1988.

15. Letter from Edward V. Sparer to Carl Rachlin, July 26, 1968, p. 1 [SED B43 F4].

16. Author interviews with Brian Glick, April 29, 1989; and Johnny Weiss, Dec. 17, 1988.

17. Author interviews with Paul Dodyk, June 23, 1989; and Lee Albert, Oct. 19, 1988.

18. Author interview with Lee Albert, Oct. 19, 1988.

19. *See* Note, "Beyond the Neighborhood Office—OEO's Special Grants in Legal Services," 56 *Geo. L.J.* (1969), p. 759.

20. Letter from Frederic S. LeClercq, assistant professor at Emory University Law School, to Hugh G. Duffy, chief of planning and research, OEO Legal Services Program, Aug. 4, 1968, pp. 2–3 [CSWPL].

———

21. Proposal, Center on Social Welfare Policy and Law, June 1968, pp. 12–13 [CSWPL].

22. *See, e.g.,* Letter from Ronald Pollack to George Wiley, Dec. 29, 1969 [GW B14 F10].

23. Author interview with Lee Albert, Oct. 19, 1988.

24. *Ibid.*

25. Gabe Kaimowitz, "The Legal Services Corporation Has Forgotten Its Mission," 17 *Human Rights* (Summer 1990), p. 43; Center Docket, Feb. 11, 1969, pp. 19–23 [CSWPL]; Center on Social Welfare Policy and Law, "Can Starvation Be Outlawed in the United States?" (press release), Nov. 19, 1968 [GW B14 F10].

26. *See* Kaimowitz, p. 43; and Earl Johnson, Jr., *Justice and Reform: The Formative Years of the American Legal Services Program* (New Brunswick, N.J.: Transaction Books, 1978), pp. 204–5 & nn.113–17.

27. Letter from Henry Freedman to Carl Rachlin, p. 2.

28. Complaint, *Thompson v. Shapiro,* Civil Action No. 11821 (D. Conn., Feb. 14, 1967), ¶ 7.

29. 42 U.S.C. § 602(b) (1959). *See also Thompson v. Shapiro,* 270 F. Supp. 331, 333 (D. Conn. 1967).

30. Center Materials Prepared Since May 1, 1967, Draft, p. 1, ¶ I.A.2 [CSWPL]; and Brief for Appellees, *Washington v. Harrell,* No. 33 (U.S., Oct. Term, 1968), pp. 31–33 [SED B42 F26].

31. Author interview with Elizabeth Wickenden, Feb. 1, 1989.

32. Bernard Schwartz, *The Unpublished Opinions of the Warren Court* (Oxford: Oxford University Press, 1985), pp. 305–6.

33. *Ibid.* at pp. 306–7.

34. Author interviews with Tanya Sparer, Feb. 28, 1989; and Archibald Cox, June 6, 1989.

35. Philip B. Kurland and Gerhard Casper, eds., *Landmark Briefs and Arguments of the Supreme Court of the United States* (University Publications of America, 1975), vol. 68, pp. 378 *et seq.*

36. Schwartz, *Warren Court,* p. 387.

37. *Shapiro v. Thompson,* 394 U.S. at 633.

38. *Shapiro v. Thompson,* 394 U.S. at 661 (Harlan, J., dissenting).

39. Interoffice correspondence from Henry Freedman to Lee Albert, May 23, 1969, p. 1 [CSWPL].

40. Edward V. Sparer, "The Right to Welfare," in Norman Dorsen, ed., *The Rights of Americans* (New York: Pantheon, 1971), p. 81.

41. Interoffice correspondence from Henry Freedman to Lee Albert, p. 1.

Chapter 7: Life, Liberty, Property, and Welfare

1. *See* William Van Alstyne, "Cracks in 'The New Property,' " 62 *Cornell L. Rev.* (1977), p. 445.

2. Edward Hudson, "Justine Wise Polier Is Dead; A Judge and Child Advocate," *New York Times*, Aug. 2, 1987, p. 36, col. 2; and "Shad Polier, Lawyer, Dead; Active in Civil Rights Cases," *New York Times*, July 1, 1976, p. 32, col. 4.

3. Author interview with Charles Reich, Jan. 21, 1989.

4. *Barsky v. Board of Regents*, 347 U.S. 442 (1954).

5. Author interview with Charles Reich, Jan. 21, 1989.

6. *Barsky v. Board of Regents*, 347 U.S. at 459.

7. *See, e.g., Konigsberg v. State Bar*, 353 U.S. 252 (1957), *on appeal*, 366 U.S. 36 (1961) (Black, J., dissenting); *In re Anastaplo*, 366 U.S. 82 (1961) (Black, J., dissenting); and *Cohen v. Hurley*, 366 U.S. 117 (1961) (Black, J., dissenting).

8. Edwin Seligman, ed., *Encyclopaedia of the Social Sciences*, s.v. "property" (New York: Macmillan, 1951 ed.); and Author interview with Charles Reich, Jan. 29, 1989.

9. *See, e.g.*, Bulletin of Yale University Law School for the Academic Year 1960–61, 56th ser., no. 16 (Aug. 15, 1960), p. 46.

10. Bruce Allen Murphy, *Fortas: The Rise and Ruin of a Supreme Court Justice* (New York: Morrow, 1988), p. 47.

11. Elizabeth Wickenden, "Poverty and the Law: The Constitutional Rights of Assistance Recipients," Feb. 25, 1963 [EW]; and Author interview with Elizabeth Wickenden, Feb. 1, 1989. *See also* Elizabeth Wickenden, "A Decade of Poverty Rights Efforts" (Paper presented at the Third Annual Forum of Welfare Rights Organization of Arizona, Phoenix, Dec. 5, 1969), pp. 3–4 [EW].

12. Charles A. Reich, "Midnight Welfare Searches and the Social Security Act," 72 *Yale L.J.* (1963), pp. 1355, 1359–60.

13. Author interview with Charles Reich, Jan. 21, 1989.

14. Author interview with Peter Strauss, Dec. 19, 1988.

15. Charles A. Reich, "The New Property," 73 *Yale L.J.* (1964), p. 768.

16. *Ibid.* at p. 779.

17. *Ibid.* at p. 787.

18. *See, e.g.*, Edward V. Sparer, "The New Public Law: The Relationship of State Administration to the Legal Problems of the Poor" (Paper presented at the Conference on the Extension of Legal Services to the Poor, Department of Health, Education, and Welfare, Washington, D.C., Nov. 12, 1964), reprinted in 23 *Legal Aid Briefcase* (February 1965), p. 133; and Edward V. Sparer, "Social Welfare Law Testing," 12 *Prac. Law.* (April 1966), p. 30.

19. Author interview with David Diamond, Oct. 5, 1988.

20. Affidavit of Neal I. Rosenthal in Opposition to Defendants' Motions for Summary Judgment, sworn to June 21, 1968, ¶ 3A; affidavit of Harold Weinberger in Opposition to Defendants' Motions for Summary Judgment, sworn to June 21, 1968, ¶ 4–5; and affidavit of David Gilman in Opposition to Defendants' Motions for Summary Judgment, sworn to June 22, 1968, ¶ 9 ("The average time from initial request to the receipt of a hearing is from four to five months"), in *Kelly v. Wyman*, 68 Civil Action No. 394 (S.D.N.Y.).

21. This account of Peter Darrow's interview with John Kelly is based on an interview with Darrow, the complaint in *Kelly v. Wyman*, 68 Civ. 394 (S.D.N.Y.), and the appendix submitted to the U.S. Supreme Court in *Goldberg v. Kelly*, No. 62 (U.S., Oct. Term, 1969), setting out the basis for Kelly's claim.

22. Author interview with Peter Darrow, Nov. 15, 1988.

23. *Roe v. Wade*, 410 U.S. 113 (1973).

24. Author interview with Louise Gans, Sept. 16, 1988.

25. Fed. R. Civ. P. 8.

26. *See generally* Opinion No. 34801 of Bryan, D.J., *Kelly v. Wyman*, 68 Civ. 394 (S.D.N.Y., May 17, 1968), p. 2, n.2.

27. "Welfare Clients Get Appeal Right," *New York Times*, Jan. 17, 1968, p. 95, col. 2.

28. Author interview with David Diamond, Sept. 18, 1988.

29. *Ibid.*

30. *Ibid.*

31. Author interview with David Gilman, Oct. 5, 1988.

32. *Wheeler v. Montgomery*, 397 U.S. 254 (1970).

33. Affidavit of Edward V. Sparer in Support of Foregoing Complaint, sworn to January 28, 1968, *Kelly v. Wyman*, 68 Civ. 394 (S.D.N.Y.), ¶ 3.

34. *Ibid.*, ¶ 4(b) (emphasis in original).

35. Affidavit of Peter Darrow in Support of Foregoing Complaint, sworn to January 29, 1968, *Kelly v. Wyman*, 68 Civ. 394 (S.D.N.Y.), ¶ 7.

36. Affidavit of Merrill Charlton in Opposition to Plaintiffs' Motion and in Support of Cross-Motion, sworn to February 29, 1968, *Kelly v. Wyman*, 68 Civ. 394 (S.D.N.Y.).

37. *Ibid.*

38. Author interview with Lee Albert, Oct. 19, 1988.

39. Author interview with John Loflin, Sept. 9, 1988.

40. Defendant Jack R. Goldberg's Memorandum of Law in Support of His Motion for a Summary Judgment, *Kelly v. Wyman*, 68 Civ. 394 (S.D.N.Y., June 17, 1968), pp. 6, 9–10.

41. Affidavit of Joel H. Sachs in Support of Defendants' Motion, sworn to February 21, 1968, *Kelly v. Wyman*, 68 Civ. 394 (S.D.N.Y.).

42. New York City Record, June 30, 1966, p. 52, and June 29, 1967, p. 75.

43. Opinion No. 34801 of Bryan, D.J., *Kelly v. Wyman*, 68 Civ. 394 (S.D.N.Y., May 17, 1968).

44. Author interview with Wilfred Feinberg, March 17, 1989.

45. Author interview with David Diamond, Sept. 18, 1988.

46. Transcript of oral argument, *Kelly v. Wyman*, 68 Civ. 394 (S.D.N.Y., June 26, 1968), pp. 16–17.

47. *Ibid.* at pp. 24–28.

48. Author interview with Johnny Weiss, Dec. 19, 1988.

49. Transcript of oral argument, *Kelly v. Wyman*, 68 Civ. 394, (S.D.N.Y., June 26, 1968), pp. 47–48.

50. *Ibid.* at p. 92.

51. *Ibid.* at pp. 105–6.

52. *Ibid.* at p. 114.

53. *Ibid.* at p. 118.

54. *Kelly v. Wyman,* 294 F. Supp. 893, 901, n.17 (S.D.N.Y. 1968).

55. Transcript of conference, *Kelly v. Wyman,* 68 Civ. 394 (S.D.N.Y., July 8, 1968).

56. Brief of the United States Amicus Curiae, *Kelly v. Wyman,* 68 Civ. 394 (S.D.N.Y., Oct. 1968), p. 1.

57. *Kelly v. Wyman,* 294 F. Supp. 893, 904–5 (S.D.N.Y. 1968).

58. *Ibid.* at p. 901.

59. *Ibid.* at p. 900.

60. Christopher May, "Withdrawal of Public Welfare: The Right to a Prior Hearing," 76 *Yale L.J.* (1967), p. 1244.

61. Author interview with Wilfred Feinberg, March 17, 1989.

62. *Ibid.*

Chapter 8: The Road to Washington

1. Edgar S. Cahn and Jean C. Cahn, "The War on Poverty: A Civilian Perspective," 73 *Yale L.J.* (1964), p. 1317.

2. Note, "Beyond Neighborhood Offices—OEO's Special Grants in Legal Services," 56 *Geo. L.J.* (1968), pp. 756–60; and Author interview with Lee Albert, Oct. 19, 1988.

3. Author interviews with Martin Garbus, Oct. 28, 1988; and Lee Albert, Oct. 19, 1988.

4. National Welfare Rights Organization, Proposal for Reshaping the Legal Operation in the National Office, n.d. [GW B7 F5].

5. Letter from Lee Albert to Carl Rachlin, Jan. 3, 1969 [SED B38 F4].

6. Letter from Carl Rachlin to Lee Albert, Jan. 9, 1969 [SED B38 F4].

7. Memorandum from Hulbert James to NWRO Executive Committee, Aug. 28, 1969, re. reorganization of national staff [GW B9 F2]; and Letter from George A. Wiley to David Filvaroff, director, Reginald Heber Smith Community Lawyer Fellowship Program, Jan. 22, 1969 [GW B33 F3].

8. Author interview with Lee Albert, Oct. 19, 1988.

9. Brief Amici Curiae of the Columbia Center on Social Welfare Policy and Law, Roger Baldwin Foundation of the American Civil Liberties Union, Mobilization for Youth, Williamsburg Neighborhood Legal Services, Morrisania Neighborhood Legal Services, and Legal Aid Society of New York, *Wheeler v. Montgomery,* No. 634 (U.S., Oct. Term, 1968).

10. *Ibid.* at pp. 4–5; and Author interview with Lee Albert, Oct. 19, 1988.

11. Memorandum from Mel Wulf to Martin Garbus, Dec. 19, 1968 (emphasis in original) [ACLU, vol. 13].

12. Denial of Stay by Justice Harlan, *Goldberg v. Kelly* (U.S., Jan. 10, 1969).

13. Author interview with John Loflin, Sept. 9, 1988.

14. Author interview with Sylvia Law, Oct. 4, 1988.

15. *Ibid.*

16. Sylvia Law, remarks delivered at symposium, "The Legacy of *Goldberg v. Kelly:* A Twenty-Year Perspective," Brooklyn Law School, May 4, 1990.

17. Author interviews with Johnny Weiss, Dec. 19, 1988, and Lee Albert, Oct. 19, 1988; and Brief for Appellees (Aug. 30, 1969), *Goldberg v. Kelly,* No. 62 (U.S., Oct. Term, 1969), pp. 12–18.

18. Author interview with Lee Albert, Oct. 19, 1988.

19. Brief for Appellees (Aug. 30, 1969), *Goldberg v. Kelly,* No. 62 (U.S., Oct. Term 1969), p. 27.

20. Author interview with Lee Albert, Oct. 19, 1988.

21. *Rothstein v. Wyman,* 303 F. Supp. 339 (S.D.N.Y. 1969). *See* "Guarantee of 'Right to Live' Is Urged," *New York Times,* Sept. 28, 1969, p. 40, col. 4.

22. *Rothstein v. Wyman,* 303 F. Supp. at 346–47.

23. Brief for Appellees (Aug. 30, 1969), *Goldberg v. Kelly,* No. 62 (U.S., Oct. Term 1969), p. 39.

24. *Ibid.* at pp. 25, nn.25, 37 & 44.

25. *Ibid.* at pp. 43–44.

26. *Ibid.* at p. 71.

27. Brief for the United States as Amicus Curiae, *Goldberg v. Kelly,* No. 62 (Sept. 2, 1969) (U.S., Oct. Term, 1969), pp. 27–28, 34–35. The National Institute for Education in Law and Poverty, a legal services backup center based at Northwestern University Law School, also filed an amicus brief. Brief of Amicus Curiae on Behalf of Appellees, filed by National Institute for Education in Law and Poverty, *Goldberg v. Kelly,* No. 62 (Sept. 2, 1969) (U.S., Oct. Term, 1969).

28. Brief in Reply to the United States as Amicus Curiae, *Goldberg v. Kelly,* No. 62 (Oct. 8, 1969) (U.S., Oct. Term, 1969), p. 5.

29. Author interview with Stephen Wizner, Oct. 11, 1988.

30. Author interview with Lee Albert, Oct. 19, 1988.

31. Author interviews with Johnny Weiss, Dec. 19, 1988; Martin Garbus, Oct. 28, 1988; and Archibald Cox, June 6, 1989.

32. Author interview with Lee Albert, Oct. 19, 1988.

33. Hugo L. Black and Elizabeth Black, *Mr. Justice and Mrs. Black* (New York: Random House, 1986), p. 232.

34. Transcript of oral argument, *Wheeler v. Montgomery,* No. 14 (U.S., Oct. 13, 1969), pp. 2–3 [National Archives, Record Group No. 267, Tape No. 748].

35. *Ibid.* at p. 4.

36. *Ibid.* at pp. 7–8.

37. *Ibid.* at pp. 12–13.

38. *Ibid.* at p. 20.

39. *Ibid.* at p. 31.

40. Author interview with John Loflin, Sept. 9, 1988.

41. Author interview with Lee Albert, Oct. 19, 1988.

42. Transcript of oral argument, *Goldberg v. Kelly,* No. 62 (U.S., Oct. 13, 1969), pp. 8–9 [National Archives, Record Group No. 267, Tape No. 748].

43. Author interview with John Loflin, Sept. 9, 1988.

44. Transcript of oral argument, *Goldberg v. Kelly,* No. 62 (U.S., Oct. 13, 1969), p. 10.

45. *Ibid.* at pp. 12–13.

46. *Ibid.* at pp. 20–21.

47. *Ibid.* at p. 23.

48. *Ibid.* at pp. 29–30.

49. Author interview with Lee Albert, Oct. 19, 1988.

50. Transcript of oral argument, *Goldberg v. Kelly,* No. 62 (U.S., Oct. 13, 1969), p. 31.

51. Author interview with Lee Albert, Oct. 19, 1988; Transcript of oral argument, *Goldberg v. Kelly,* No. 62 (U.S., October 13, 1969), p. 47.

52. Transcript of oral argument, *Goldberg v. Kelly,* No. 62 (U.S., October 13, 1969), p. 50.

53. William J. Brennan, Jr., Conference notes, n.d. [WJB].

54. *Ibid.*

55. Bernard Schwartz, *The Unpublished Opinions of the Burger Court* (Oxford: Oxford University Press, 1988), p. 376.

56. *Ibid.;* and Brennan, Conference notes.

57. Brennan, Conference notes.

58. William O. Douglas, Conference notes, Oct. 17, 1969 [WOD].

59. Letter from William O. Douglas to Warren E. Burger, Oct. 17, 1969 [WOD].

60. Author interview with William J. Brennan, Jr., March 14, 1989.

61. Black and Black, p. 197.

62. Author interview with William J. Brennan, Jr., March 14, 1989. Nevertheless, when the *Goldberg* appeal was first filed, Brennan voted to simply affirm Feinberg's opinion without oral argument before the Supreme Court, a vote that was outweighed by four of Brennan's brethren.

63. Author interview with Taylor Reveley, Dec. 1, 1988.

64. William J. Brennan, Jr., Draft of *Wheeler v. Montgomery,* Oct. 24, 1969 [HLB].

65. Memorandum from Warren E. Burger for the Conference, Nov. 25, 1969 [HLB].

66. Tentative dissent in #62 and #14, Warren E. Burger [HLB].

67. Clerk's draft, *Goldberg v. Kelly,* p. 6 [WJB].

68. Draft letter from John M. Harlan to William J. Brennan, Jr. [JMH, B378 F62]; and Schwartz, *Burger Court,* p. 378.

69. *Goldberg v. Kelly,* 397 U.S. 254, 265 (1970). *See* Schwartz, *Burger Court,* p. 378.

70. Draft, Opinion of the Court, *Goldberg v. Kelly,* Nov. 28, 1969, pp. 6–7, nn.7–8 [HLB].

71. *Ibid.* at pp. 10–11. By the time the Court's opinion was drafted, HEW had promulgated regulations to require pretermination fair hearings in AFDC beginning

in July 1970. Brennan's final opinion noted these regulations and, without ruling on their constitutionality, observed that the *Goldberg* case concerned solely the validity of New York state's regulations. At any rate, the federal regulations—applying only to AFDC—did not resolve the question of whether home relief recipients, such as DeJesus, had a right to a pretermination hearing. *Goldberg v. Kelly*, 397 U.S. 254, 257 n.3 (1970).

72. Draft, Opinion of the Court, *Goldberg v. Kelly*, Nov. 28, 1969, pp. 13–16 [HLB].

73. Letter from Thurgood Marshall to William J. Brennan, Jr., Nov. 25, 1969 [WJB]; and Letter from William O. Douglas to William J. Brennan, Jr., Nov. 24, 1969 [WJB].

74. Letter from Byron R. White to William J. Brennan, Jr., Dec. 2, 1969 [WJB].

75. Black and Black, p. 234.

76. *Ibid.*

77. Charles A. Reich, "Mr. Justice Black and the Living Constitution," 76 *Harv. L. Rev.* (1963), p. 730.

78. *Griswold v. Connecticut*, 381 U.S. 479, 522 (1965) (Black, J., dissenting).

79. Daniel J. Meador, *Mr. Justice Black and His Books* (Charlottesville: University Press of Virginia, 1974), p. 12; and Charles A. Reich, *The Greening of America* (New York: Random House, 1970), pp. 35–36.

80. William J. Brennan, Jr., Draft of majority opinion, with Hugo L. Black's margin notes, Nov. 28, 1969 [HLB]. Interestingly, Black was the author of *Gideon v. Wainwright*, 372 U.S. 335 (1963), which upheld the constitutional right of indigent criminal defendants to court-appointed counsel at trial.

81. Hugo L. Black, Draft dissent (handwritten), *Goldberg v. Kelly* [HLB].

82. Black and Black, p. 237.

83. Memorandum to the file, "Justice Black on Right to a Hearing," n.d., p. 3 [WJB].

84. Memorandum to the file, n.d., re. Feb. 20, 1970, Conference [WJB].

85. Letter from John M. Harlan to William J. Brennan, Jr., Dec. 11, 1969, p. 1 [JMH, B378 F62].

86. *Ibid.* at p. 2.

87. *Ibid.* at p. 3.

88. Memorandum from Richard Cooper, n.d., re. Justice Harlan's five suggestions in his letter of Dec. 11 [WJB].

89. Memorandum from Richard Cooper to the file, n.d., re. right to oral argument as a matter of due process, p. 2 [WJB].

90. Letter from William J. Brennan, Jr., to John M. Harlan, Dec. 15, 1969 [JMH, B378 F62].

91. Letter from John M. Harlan to William J. Brennan, Jr., Feb. 19, 1970 [JMH, B372 F14].

92. *Goldberg v. Kelly*, 397 U.S. at 267 (1970).

93. Potter Stewart, Draft dissent, *Goldberg v. Kelly*, Feb. 17, 1970 [JMH, B372 F14].

94. *Goldberg v. Kelly,* 397 U.S. at 265 (1970).

Chapter 9: The Impasse

1. "Poverty: The Welfare Labyrinth," *Newsweek,* Aug. 28, 1967, p. 25.
2. "1,000 on Welfare Lobby at Capitol," *New York Times,* Aug. 29, 1967, p. 22, col. 2.
3. "Negroes in Protest at Welfare Hearing," *New York Times,* Sept. 20, 1967, p. 23, col. 3; and Nick Kotz and Mary Kotz, *A Passion for Equality* (New York: Norton, 1977), pp. 250–51.
4. Kotz and Kotz, p. 251.
5. Kotz and Kotz, p. 251; and "Provisions of New Law," *New York Times,* Jan. 3, 1968, p. 29, col. 2.
6. Kotz and Kotz, pp. 248–49. As early as March 1966, Richard Cloward had contacted "King's people" and suggested that the SCLC work with Wiley. Notes on telephone conversation with Richard Cloward, March 27, 1966 [GW B3 F1].
7. Department of Labor, *The Negro Family: The Case for National Action* (Washington, D.C.: Department of Labor, 1965), pp. 12, 20–21; and James T. Patterson, *America's Struggle Against Poverty, 1900–1985* (Cambridge: Harvard University Press, 1986), p. 158.
8. Kotz and Kotz, p. 183.
9. Bayard Rustin, "From Protest to Politics: The Future of the Civil Rights Movement," *Commentary* (February 1965), pp. 25–31.
10. Kotz and Kotz, pp. 252, 255.
11. *Ibid.,* pp. 257–58.
12. Letter from Carl Rachlin to George Wiley, Jan. 10, 1969 [GW B33 F3].
13. Kotz and Kotz, p. 246; and Gilbert Y. Steiner, *The State of Welfare* (Washington, D.C.: Brookings Institution, 1971), pp. 293–94. *See also* Lawrence Bailis, *Bread or Justice: Grassroots Organizing in the Welfare Rights Movement* (Lexington, Mass.: Lexington Books, 1974), p. 145.
14. Kotz and Kotz, p. 260; Memorandum from Glenn Olds to Robert Finch, Jan. 17, 1969; and Letter from Robert Finch to George A. Wiley, Jan. 25, 1969 [both documents at GW B23 F3].
15. *Rosado v. Wyman,* 397 U.S. 397, 408 (1970).
16. Social Security Act of 1967, § 402.
17. Letter from Carl Rachlin to Lee Albert, Paul Dodyk, Norman Dorsen, David Gilman, John Gregory, and Nancy LeBlanc, Jan. 23, 1969, re. meeting with general counsel of HEW concerning implementation of Section 402(a)(23) of Social Security Act [GW B14 F10].
18. "New Poor Swell the Ranks," *Business Week,* Nov. 11, 1967, p. 77.
19. Notes taken on meeting at New York Theological Seminary concerning the proposed complaint, n.d., unsigned [SED B39 F6].
20. Center on Social Welfare Policy and Law, Center Docket, Feb. 11, 1969, pp. 11–12 (describing *Lowman v. Goldberg*) [CSWPL].

21. "U.S. Eases Rules on Welfare Test Used by States," *New York Times,* Jan. 19, 1969, p. 1, col. 1; and "Governor's Bid to Cut Welfare Is Denounced by Leaders Here," *New York Times,* Jan. 23, 1969, p. 16, col. 3.

22. "Ginsberg Fears Relief Cutbacks May Stop U.S. Aid," *New York Times,* March 31, 1969, p. 1, col. 1; and *Rosado v. Wyman,* 304 F. Supp. 1356, 1382 (E.D.N.Y. 1969).

23. "Governor's Bid to Cut Welfare Is Denounced," p. 16, col. 3.

24. "Ginsberg Fears Relief Cutbacks May Stop U.S. Aid," p. 1, col. 1.

25. Complaint, *Rosado v. Wyman,* 69 Civ. 355 (E.D.N.Y., April 10, 1969); and "2 Welfare Groups Sue Over State Aid," *New York Times,* April 11, 1969, p. 33, col. 1.

26. Letter from Henry Freedman to Carl Rachlin, Sept. 26, 1968 [SED B44 F24].

27. Center Docket, pp. 14–15 (describing *Young v. White* [D. Ohio]; *Simpson v. Roberts* [D. Fla.]; *Hodge v. Roberts* [D. Fla.]; and *Robinson v. Hackney* [D. Texas]).

28. Center Docket, p. 13 (describing *Ward v. Winstead* [D. Miss.]).

29. Author interview with Henry Freedman, May 17, 1989.

30. National Welfare Rights Organization, Statement, *NOW! News,* Aug. 7, 1969, p. 1 [GW B23 F3].

31. *Collins v. State Board of Social Welfare,* 248 Iowa 369, 81 N.W.2d 4 (1957).

32. Author interview with Paul Dodyk, June 23, 1989.

33. *Dews v. Henry,* 297 F. Supp. 587 (D. Ariz. 1969); *Williams v. Dandridge,* 297 F. Supp. 450 (D. Md. 1968); *Westberry v. Fisher,* 297 F. Supp. 1109 (D. Me. 1969); *Kaiser v. Montgomery,* 319 F. Supp. 329 (N.D. Cal. 1969); *Lindsey v. Smith,* 303 F. Supp. 1203 (W.D. Wash. 1969).

34. *Jefferson v. Hackney,* 304 F. Supp. 1332 (N.D. Texas 1969).

35. The Mississippi judge's decision was finally issued on July 1, 1970, after the Supreme Court decision in *Dandridge. See Ward v. Winstead,* 314 F. Supp. 1225 (N.D. Miss. 1970).

36. Author interview with Henry Freedman, May 17, 1989.

37. "U.S. Judge Blocks State Relief Cuts," *New York Times,* April 25, 1969, p. 1, col. 5.

38. *Rosado,* 397 U.S. at 399–400. The amended law was subsequently challenged by the Center, Nassau County Legal Services, and the Legal Aid Society of Westchester County in *Rothstein v. Wyman,* 303 F. Supp. 339 (S.D.N.Y.), *vacated and remanded,* 398 U.S. 275 (1970). The favorable district court decision in *Rothstein* was vacated by the Supreme Court in light of its decision in *Rosado. See also* "U.S. Court Backs Welfare Protest," *New York Times,* Aug. 5, 1969, p. 25, col. 1.

39. *Rosado v. Wyman,* 304 F. Supp. 1356 (E.D.N.Y. 1969); and "Court Bars Cuts in State Welfare," *New York Times,* May 17, 1969, p. 39, col. 1.

40. Memorandum from William J. Brennan, Jr., for the Conference, June 18, 1969, re. Nos. 1539 and 1540, *Rosado v. Wyman* (U.S., Oct. Term, 1968) [WOD].

41. *Ibid.*

42. *Rosado v. Wyman,* 395 U.S. 826 (1969) (per curiam); and "Supreme Court Won't Block State Relief Cutback," *New York Times,* June 24, 1969, p. 26, col. 3.

43. *Rosado v. Wyman*, 414 F.2d 170, 181, 188 (2d Cir. 1969).

44. Author interview with Sylvia Law, Oct. 4, 1988.

45. Author interview with Harold Rothwax, Sept. 9, 1988.

46. Author interview with Lee Albert, Oct. 19, 1988. The initial judgment in the Texas case, *Jefferson v. Hackney*, was vacated and remanded to the district court following the Supreme Court's opinion in *Rosado* (397 U.S. 821 [1970]). *Jefferson v. Hackney* was again appealed to the Supreme Court on the question of whether differential awards formulas for different types of public assistance violate the equal protection clause (406 U.S. 535 [1972]).

47. "High Court To Get Relief Cuts Case," *New York Times*, Oct. 14, 1969, p. 1, col. 1. Initially, *Dandridge* and *Rosado* were consolidated for argument, but at the Conference of Oct. 17, 1969, the Court ruled to rescind that order. William J. Brennan, Jr., Conference notes, Oct. 17, 1969 [WJB].

48. Petition for a Writ of Certiorari to the United States Court of Appeals for the Second Circuit and Motion to Advance, *Rosado v. Wyman*, No. 540 (U.S., Oct. Term, 1969), pp. 11–12.

49. Author interview with Sylvia Law, Oct. 4, 1968.

50. Complaint, *Williams v. Dandridge*, Civ. Action 19250 (D. Md.).

51. State's petition for a Writ of Certiorari, *Dandridge v. Williams*, (May 16, 1969), p. 3.

52. Brief of Amici Curiae: The Center on Social Welfare Policy and Law, National Welfare Rights Organization, Associated Catholic Charities, and Seven Neighborhood Legal Services Offices Now Prosecuting Similar Cases, *Dandridge v. Williams*, No. 131 (U.S., Oct. Term 1969).

53. Transcript of oral argument, *Rosado v. Wyman*, No. 540 (U.S. Nov. 19, 1969) [National Archives, Record Group No. 267, Tape No. 761]; and Transcript of oral argument, *Dandridge v. Williams*, No. 131 (U.S. Dec. 9, 1969) [National Archives, Record Group No. 267, Tape No. 764].

54. Transcript of oral argument, *Dandridge v. Williams*, No. 131 (U.S., Dec. 9, 1969), p. 34 [National Archives, Record Group No. 267, Tape No. 764].

55. "High Court Backs A Family Ceiling for Welfare Aid," *New York Times*, April 7, 1970, p. 1, col. 5.

56. *Rosado v. Wyman*, 397 U.S. at 413.

57. *Dandridge*, 397 U.S. 471, 477–78 (emphasis in original).

58. *Ibid.* at p. 487.

Chapter 10: A Different America

1. Edward V. Sparer, "The Right to Welfare," in Norman Dorsen, ed., *The Rights of Americans* (New York: Pantheon, 1971), p. 82.

2. Author interview with Sylvia Law, Oct. 4, 1988.

3. *Wyman v. James*, 400 U.S. 309 (1971)

4. Author interview with David Gilman, Oct. 5, 1988.

5. "Right of Relief Recipients To Bar Home Visits Upheld," *New York Times*, Aug. 19, 1969, p. 1, col. 2.

6. *Wyman v. James*, 400 U.S. 309 (1971).

7. *Jefferson v. Hackney*, 406 U.S. 535 (1972).

8. Letter from Carl Rachlin to George Wiley, Jan. 19, 1971 [GW B33 F3].

9. Author interview with Eric Hirschhorn, Nov. 7, 1988.

10. Center on Social Welfare Policy and Law, Report on Activities for Quarter, Aug. 1, 1971–Oct. 31, 1971, pp. 15–16 [CSWPL].

11. Center on Social Welfare Policy and Law, Plans and Priorities for 1970, Feb. 24, 1970, p. 1 [CSWPL].

12. Letter to Hugh Duffy from Lee Albert, Nov. 6, 1968 [CSWPL].

13. Susan E. Lawrence, *The Poor in Court: The Legal Services Programs and Supreme Court Decision Making* (Princeton: Princeton University Press, 1990), pp. 30, 36; Ellen Hollingsworth, "Ten Years of Legal Services for the Poor," in Robert H. Haveman, ed., *A Decade of Federal Antipoverty Programs* (New York: Academic Press, 1977), pp. 298, 311–12; and Marie A. Failinger and Larry May, "Litigating Against Poverty: Legal Services and Group Representation," 45 *Ohio St. L.J.* (1984), p. 1.

14. Report on Activities for Quarter, p. 3. *See also* Memorandum from Richard I. Greenberg, Center on Social Welfare Policy and Law, to New York state legal services programs and welfare rights organizations, Dec. 15, 1971, re. *Almenares v. Wyman* [GW B14 F11].

15. Report on Activities for Quarter.

16. "39 States Fail to Comply With Federal Welfare Requirements," *New York Times*, April 5, 1970, p. 60, col. 2.

17. Letter from Carl Rachlin to John Twiname, Department of Health, Education, and Welfare, July 9, 1970 (requesting that NWRO and affiliated chapters be permitted to appear as parties at the hearings) [GW B23 F3]; and Joel F. Handler, *Social Movements and the Legal System* (New York: Academic Press, 1978), pp. 158–59.

18. Sylvia Law, "Operation Nevada: Crisis in Welfare," *Welfare Law News* (September 1971), p. 4 [GW B18 F15].

19. *Ibid.*

20. Edward V. Sparer and Henry A. Freedman, "A Comment," *Welfare Law News* (September 1971), pp. 5–6 [GW B18 F15].

21. Frances Fox Piven and Richard A. Cloward, *Poor People's Movements* (Vintage Books: New York, 1979), pp. 343–49.

22. "Experts and the Average Citizen View Welfare Plans," *New York Times*, Aug. 16, 1969, p. 13, col. 1; and Letter from Roy Wilkins to George Wiley, Aug. 10, 1971 (expressing support for the plan) [GW B20 F23].

23. Lawrence Bailis, *Bread or Justice: Grassroots Organizing in the Welfare Rights Movement* (Lexington, Mass.: Lexington Books, 1974), p. 147; and NWRO, Comparison of the Welfare Plans [GW B17 F6].

24. Aryeh Neier, *Only Judgment: The Limits of Litigation in Social Change* (Middletown, Conn.: Wesleyan University Press, 1982), p. 139; Piven and Cloward, *Poor People's Movements*, pp. 341–43; and "Senate Reaction to Family Assistance

Plan Unclear After Nixon Speech," *Welfare Law News* (September 1971), p. 1 [GW B18 F15].

25. Guida West, *The National Welfare Rights Movement: The Social Protest of Poor Women* (New York: Praeger, 1981), p. 3; and Nick Kotz and Mary Kotz, *A Passion for Equality* (New York: Norton, 1977), pp. 288–89.

26. Memorandum from Elizabeth Wickenden to George Wiley, Jan. 21, 1971, re. notes on recent activities [GW B34 F13].

27. Letter from Carl Rachlin to George Wiley, Jan. 19, 1971 [GW B33 F3].

28. Kotz and Kotz, pp. 288–89.

29. Letter from Ed Sparer to George Wiley, April 28, 1971 [GW B14 F11].

30. *Ibid.*

31. Bailis, p. 2; and Piven and Cloward, *Poor People's Movements*, pp. 351–52.

32. Kotz and Kotz, pp. 290–306.

Chapter 11: Open Questions

1. *See, e.g.,* Susan E. Lawrence, *The Poor in Court: The Legal Services Programs and Supreme Court Decision Making* (Princeton: Princeton University Press, 1990), p. 14.

2. Samuel Krislov, "The OEO Lawyers Fail to Constitutionalize a Right to Welfare: A Study in the Uses and Limits of the Judicial Process," 58 *Minn. L. Rev.* (1973), p. 245.

3. For a discussion of litigation using state constitutions and state statutes to claim a right to basic needs, *see* Barbara Sard, "The Role of the Courts in Welfare Reform," *Clearinghouse Rev.* (August–September 1988), p. 367.

4. Sard, p. 387.

5. *See, e.g.,* Lawrence, pp. 40–46 (discussing legal services litigation strategies).

6. Aryeh Neier, *Only Judgment: The Limits of Litigation in Social Change* (Middletown, Conn.: Wesleyan University Press, 1982), p. 140.

7. *Ibid.* at p. 130.

8. Johnnie Tillmon, "Welfare Is a Women's Issue," in Rosalyn Baxandall, Linda Gordon, and Susan Reverby, eds., *America's Working Women* (New York: Vintage, 1976), p. 357 (emphasis in original).

9. Edward V. Sparer, discussant for Ellen Hollingsworth, "Ten Years of Legal Services for the Poor," in Robert H. Haveman, ed., *A Decade of Federal Antipoverty Programs* (New York: Academic Press, 1977), p. 326–27.

Index